The Complete
Book of
YOGURT

SHAUN NELSON-HENRICK

MACMILLAN PUBLISHING CO., INC.   New York

COLLIER MACMILLAN PUBLISHERS   London

The Complete
Book of
YOGURT

Macmillan Publishing Co., Inc.
866 Third Avenue, New York, N.Y. 10022
Collier Macmillan Canada, Ltd.

Library of Congress Cataloging in Publication Data

Nelson-Henrick, Shaun.
The complete book of yogurt.

Includes indexes.
1. Yogurt. 2. Cookery (Yogurt)   I. Title.
TX380.N44   1980   637'.146   80-12393
ISBN 0-02-551020-7

First Printing 1980

Designed by Jack Meserole

Printed in the United States of America

This one is for Peter

Contents

ALL ABOUT YOGURT

RECIPES

Preface

A FEW BRIEF THOUGHTS

Why a book about yogurt? Well, to begin with, I believe in heeding that old adage, generally given to fledgling writers, that says, "write about what you know." And, having been a yogurt lover for the past ten years, I was of the opinion—erroneous, I might add—that I knew a fair amount about yogurt. As I progressed in my research, I found that the subject was much deeper, and broader, than I'd ever imagined.

And, though it may be presumptuous of me, I believe this yogurt book-and-cookbook offers "something for everyone." For example, if you don't give a hoot about weight watching, I suggest you skip the chapter on calories and turn to the one on sourdough breads instead. Or, if you'd rather drink yogurt than eat it, check out the chapter on kefir (not yogurt, but tastes similar). Whatever your interest—from frozen desserts to unusual yogurt flavors—you'll find it here.

Finally, I'd like to add that my aim has been to present a *balanced* view of the world of yogurt. I have tried to avoid the dogmatic approach: the ironclad conclusions that I have seen in many nutrition and health food books. And I have attempted to winnow out "yogurt fantasy and myth." A lot of nonsense has been written about yogurt; I don't intend to add to it.

You'll notice that most of my comments about foods, products, prices, and stores apply to New York City. The reason? New York is where I live and work.

S.N.-H.

New York
February 1980

Acknowledgments

Acknowledgment is gratefully extended to the following companies and individuals for their cooperation and assistance: Alta-Dena Dairy, City of Industry, CA; Colombo Inc., Methuen, MA; Contempra Industries, Inc., Tinton Falls, NJ, Gerald D. Baker, Executive Vice President and General Manager; Continental Culture Specialists, Inc., Glendale, CA, Vasa Cubaleski, President; Dannon Milk Products, Long Island City, NY; Hamilton Beach Division, Scovill, Waterbury, CT; H.P. Hood, Inc., Boston, MA; National Dairy Council, Rosemont, IL; Proctor-Silex, SCM Corp., Philadelphia, PA; Richmond Cedar Works Manufacturing Corp., Danville, VA, G. Webster DeHoff, President; Rosell Institute, Montreal, Quebec; Salton, Inc., Bronx, NY; Sears, Roebuck and Company, Chicago, IL; The International Yogurt Company, Los Angeles, CA, Wayne P. Barnette and Reny Tille; The West Bend Company, West Bend, WI; Waring Products Division, Dynamics Corporation of America, New Hartford, CT; White Mountain Freezer Co., Winchendon, MA, William Potter, President.

I am also deeply grateful to the following people who graciously consented to be interviewed for this book: Mrs. Hilda Attarian; Edouard Brochu, President, Rosell Institute; Daniel Gates, The Gates Homestead Farms; Juan E. Metzger, Chairman, Dannon Milk Products; Mrs. William Wagner, Pure Goat Products, Inc.

A special appreciation to the following for permission to quote from their letters to me and to reprint from their works: Dr. John A. Alford, Laboratory Chief, Dairy Foods Nutrition Laboratory, Nutrition Institute, U.S. Department of Agriculture; Jane E. Brody, "Study Hints That Yogurt May Reduce Cholesterol," *New York Times*, June 23, 1974; Dr. Robert A. Buchanan, Director, Clinical Research, Warner-Lambert/Parke-Davis; Mr. Robert C. Finnie, Executive Vice President, Venture Foods, Inc.; Prof. Frances W.

James, Department of Sociology and Anthropology, College of Liberal Arts, The University of Mississippi; Mr. Alan E. Kligerman, Senior Partner, SugarLo Company; Dr. Albert M. Kligman, Dermatology Department, Monell Chemical Senses Center, Philadelphia; Dr. George V. Mann, Department of Biochemistry, School of Medicine, Vanderbilt University; Claudia Roden, *A Book of Middle Eastern Food*, New York: Alfred A. Knopf, 1968; Dr. James J. Vavra, The Upjohn Company; Dr. Ruth Beeler White, Director, Office of Consumer Inquiries, Department of Health, Education and Welfare, Public Health Service, Food and Drug Administration.

My deepest thanks to my editor, Elisabeth Scharlatt, and her staff for their help and support.

I wish to extend my thanks to the following for their recipe contributions: American Dairy Association, Rosemont, IL; Angostura International Ltd., U.S.A. Division, Elizabeth, NJ; Colombo Inc., Methuen, MA; Contempra Industries, Inc., Tinton Falls, NJ; Continental Culture Research Center, Continental Culture Specialists, Inc., Glendale, CA; Dannon Yogurt, Long Island City, NY; Gaylord (India) Restaurant, New York, NY; Hamilton Beach Division, Scovill, Waterbury, CT; Hickory Farms of Ohio, Inc., Maumee, Ohio; Proctor-Silex, SCM Corp., Philadelphia, PA; Rosell Institute, Montreal, Quebec; Salton, Inc., makers of Salton Yogurt Maker and Salton Ice Cream Machine, Bronx, NY; The International Yogurt Company, Los Angeles, CA; The West Bend Company, West Bend, WI; Waring Products Division, Dynamics Corporation of America, New Hartford, CT. Recipes developed for the Waring Ice Cream Parlor. Reprinted by permission.

From *A Taste of India* by Mary S. Atwood. Copyright © 1969 by Mary S. Atwood. Reprinted by permission of Houghton Mifflin Company, Boston, MA.

Borani from the *New York Times Cookbook* by Craig Claiborne. Copyright © 1961 by Craig Claiborne. Harper & Row, Publishers, Inc., New York.

The Blue Danube Cookbook by Maria Kozslik Donovan, 1967. Doubleday & Company, Inc., New York. Reprinted by permission of the author.

From *The World's 100 Best Recipes* by Roland Gööck, Culinary Arts Institute, Chicago, IL. Reprinted by permission of the publisher, Consolidated Book Publishers.

The New York Times Natural Foods Cookbook by Jean Hewitt, 1972. Quadrangle, The New York Times Book Company, Inc., New York.

The Natural Foods Cookbook by Beatrice Trum Hunter. Simon and Schuster, New York.

ALL ABOUT YOGURT

Background

I have read several versions of the history of yogurt (when it was discovered and in what country) and I've come to the conclusion that the early beginnings of yogurt are extremely difficult to pinpoint. We *do* know one thing for sure, however—yogurt has been around a long, long time. In a short publicity sheet entitled "Yogurt: Fact and Fiction," Colombo, Inc., states: yogurt is older than the Bible. I am not about to dispute this claim.

Prof. Frances James draws the same conclusion when she says, "nor can we say more precisely where laban (yogurt) originated than when."* She continues: "a great many peoples have claimed yogurt as their own invention. The Bulgarians are one. The Turks are another. It is by no means impossible that the Armenian area of Turkey is also home to laban." Everyone, it seems, has a finger in the pot.

A more fanciful version of the origins of yogurt (which I have seen in several publications) is this one from "The History of Yogurt" by Colombo:

We are told that yogurt originated when milk was carried by wandering nomads in leather bags made of sheep's stomachs. Bacteria contained in the bags combined with the milk as a result of the body warmth of the camels they were riding, and the heat of the sun. At nightfall the desert temperature dropped rapidly, cooling the milk and stopping the action of the bacteria.

This heating and subsequent cooling enabled the bacteria to convert

* From "Yogurt: Its Life and Culture," *Expedition* magazine, Fall 1975. Dannon has reprinted this article as a service to its customers.

the fresh milk into a custard-like consistency which became known as yogurt. The nomads then discovered that they could make yogurt by inoculating fresh milk with a small amount of already prepared yogurt.

Whether you believe this explanation to be authentic is up to you. We are, however, fairly certain of two facts about the origin of yogurt. One, yogurt is about as old as recorded history, and two, it began somewhere in the Near or Middle East.

Names: Here

In America, most of us refer to, and spell yogurt this way: Y-O-G-U-R-T. In the course of my reading I have also seen *yogourt*, *yoghurt*, *yohurt*, *yahourth*, *yourt*, *yaourt*, and *jugurt*. To keep both of us sane, I will use only *yogurt*, a simple Turkish word that, I think, is perfectly capable of holding its own.

Names: There

If you're planning to fly around the world, you may be interested in the Arabic word for yogurt. If not, there is no reason for you to plow through all these names. Unless, of course, you are like the explorer who, when asked why he had a burning desire to climb Mount Everest, replied quite simply, "Because it's there."

ARABIA   *laban**
ARMENIA   *madzoon, matsoon, mazun, mazoun*
BULGARIA   *kisselo-mleko, naja, tarho, yogurt*
CHILE   *skuta,* or *whey champagne*
DENMARK   *hocken milk*
EGYPT   *leben, leben raib, laban zabadi*
FINLAND   *glumse, plimae, fiili biima*
FRANCE   *yoghourt, yaourt*
GERMANY   *dicke milch, pumpermilch*
GREECE   *yiaourti, oxygala*
HOLLAND   *hangop*
ICELAND   *skyr*
INDIA   *dadhi, dahi, dahli, lassi, chass, matta*
IRAN   *mast*
LAPLAND   *pauira, taetioc*

* The name *Lebanon* comes from this Arabic word, which means "milk."

NORWAY   *kyael meelk, kaelder milk*
RUSSIA   *koumiss,* prostokvasha, varenetz, kefir, kuban*
SARDINIA   *gioddu*
SICILY   *mezzoradu*
SWEDEN   *filmjolk, taete, langemilk*
SWITZERLAND   *mezzoradu*

Yogurt in the United States

New York, I believe, gives one the chance to sample more exciting and delicious foods than any other place on earth. Even though I can't imagine it now—before I arrived in New York, I'd never eaten blintzes, bagels, lox, quiche, crepes, mousse, pita bread, moussaka, linzertorte, palacinky, wiener schnitzel or even—yogurt.†

No yogurt? Incredible. Now I eat it at least once a day, if not more. This brings us back to the question: How long has this food, which now plays such an important role in our daily diet, been around?

Whenever I have come across references to the origins of yogurt in the United States, the date 1784 usually pops up. Apparently, it was at this time that yogurt was brought to the United States by Turkish immigrants. However, how true any of this is I really can't say.

But from here on, I can vouch for the validity of my facts because I talked to a man who was making commercial yogurt thirty-eight years ago—long before it became the fad food it is today.

I interviewed Juan Metzger, a man who began making yogurt in 1942 and who is now the chairman of Dannon Milk Products, in an East Fifty-seventh Street restaurant one bright morning in September 1979. We discussed the beginnings and phenomenal growth of yogurt eating in the United States.

"The real start was in the early 1900s," Mr. Metzger said. "That was when Isaac Carasso, a businessman who lived in Barcelona, got cultures from the Pasteur Institute in Paris and began to make yo-

---

* In her *Expedition* article Prof. James wrote, "Unlike yogurt, koumiss is not started from the last batch, but from decaying animal or vegetable matter which contains the parent microbes. These produce a liquid combination of an acid and an alcoholic ferment—koumiss contains from 1.65 to 3.25 percent of alcohol when fully brewed." Keep this in mind when you visit Russia.

† On the other hand, since I left Canada I haven't had steak and kidney pie, sausage rolls, fish 'n' chips, and crumpets. You can't win.

gurt, which he sold mainly through pharmacies in Barcelona." In time Carasso's business grew, and eventually he extended his market to Paris. He called his yogurt Danone (believed to be named for his son, Daniel). This name was later anglicized to Dannon in the United States.

In 1940, Isaac Carasso died and left his thriving yogurt business to his son, who, when World War II broke out, decided to come to the United States. He bought a small yogurt factory called Oxy Gala, which was located in the Bronx. At that time, this small factory supplied yogurt to Turkish, Greek, and a few American customers— Americans who had become acquainted with yogurt while traveling in Europe. "Three months after Daniel bought the factory my father and I arrived in America and joined him," Mr. Metzger told me. "I was twenty-three at the time. Our total output was two hundred bottles of plain yogurt a day. We charged twelve cents a bottle plus three cents deposit." "How big was the factory," I asked. Mr. Metzger turned in his chair, gestured, and said, "From here to there," indicating an area approximately twenty by twenty-five feet.

"In 1947," he continued, "we added fruit preserves and made the first sundae-style strawberry yogurt.* Then, a couple of years later we came out with vanilla-flavored yogurt."

"But," I wanted to know, "when did the big break come for Dannon?"

"Well," mused Mr. Metzger, "our figures were in the red in forty-two, forty-three, and forty-four; then they started turning pinkish, and by 1950 we broke even. But our big break came when *Reader's Digest* published an excerpt from Gayelord Hauser's new book, *Look Younger, Live Longer.* He named yogurt as one of the five wonder foods†—all hell broke loose for us. Mind you, we were already on our way, but this just pushed it all up."

In the late fifties Dannon merged with Beatrice Foods and now, according to Mr. Metzger, "we are the first perishable food company with national distribution." I'd say that Dannon *and* yogurt have come a long way.

* Later on, in the late 1960s, Borden, Sealtest, and others introduced "Swiss style," or premixed, yogurts.

† Since I had never read this book, I decided to track down a copy of *Look Younger, Live Longer* (New York: Farrar, Straus, 1950) and read it for myself. I found a copy in the "outpost" branch of the New York Public Library (Forty-third Street between Tenth and Eleventh avenues). Sure enough, on page 24, Mr. Hauser names his five wonder foods: brewers' yeast, powdered skim milk, yogurt, wheat germ, and blackstrap molasses.

6

Yogurt in Canada

In 1932, two young teachers at a small Canadian school decided to set up an institute to make cultures—which would, in turn, produce cultured milk products. The two founders, Dr. José-Maria Rosell and Prof. Gustave Toupin, with their young assistant, Mr. Edouard Brochu, called their new enterprise the Rosell Institute.

In 1939 this small business made a big leap forward when a young businessman, Richard Tille, obtained a franchise from Rosell. His plan was to sell their cultures in the United States. Tille started his business in Chicago. Then, in 1942, he moved to Los Angeles and formed the Yami Yogurt Company (commercial) and the International Yogurt Company (home use).

I wrote to Mr. Brochu, who is now the president, and, after exchanging several letters, I decided to drive up to Montreal with my husband, Peter, and see the institute for myself.

Once at Rosell, which is about a forty-minute drive from downtown Montreal (the institute is no longer located at the school), we were greeted by Mr. Brochu who proceeded to give us a tour of the place.

"Here is where the cultures are freeze-dried," Mr. Brochu said, showing us into a spotless white lab. I peered into one of seven round glass windows that ran along one wall of the lab. Inside, I could see neatly stacked trays of freeze-dried cultures. "After this, the culture is broken into pieces, then ground up fine—to be used for both commercial and home use," explained Mr. Brochu.

Peter and I followed Mr. Brochu in and out of one lab after another—all light, bright, and spotless. In one, Mr. Brochu opened the door to one of the refrigerators and said, "Here, take a look. There are six hundred different cultures in this refrigerator." "Six hundred!" I gasped. "I didn't think there could be six hundred cultures in the world, let alone in this refrigerator." The cultures were in glass test tubes that stood upright in wooden stands. Mr. Brochu took out several and showed me. "Here is camembert, wine, beer, and cider," he said. Naturally, I couldn't tell one from the other.

After we finished our tour, Mr. Brochu decided to take us out to the Oka Agriculture School so we could see where Rosell* was founded forty-seven years ago.

* The Rosell Institute started in a very small way, but today it's quite a different story. Cultures from Rosell are now distributed in France, Australia, Mexico, South America—and, of course, Canada and the United States.

The school, which was originally started by a group of Trappist monks, is located near a monastery and a cheese factory—on 2,000 acres of land. On seeing all of this for the first time, I was impressed with the incredible quiet, the air of serenity and peace.

"Now you will see cheeses that are made from our cultures," Mr. Brochu explained. We threaded our way down, down, down into the cheese cellars. This journey ended with a remarkable sight: cyprus-wood shelves holding hundreds of small, round Oka cheeses—all in different stages of ripening. "Each cheese is washed by hand as it is turned over," our guide explained. "The process is repeated again and again until the cheese is ready."

Late in the afternoon, as we drove away from the school, Peter looked back and said, "What a view! Isn't that great?" I turned and saw the old gray stone monastery tucked into the lush green valley below. It was, I agreed, quite a sight.

The Future of Yogurt

These figures, which show the rapid growth of yogurt from 1955 to 1976, appeared in an article entitled "More Americans are Liking Yogurt More and More" in *Dairy Record* magazine by Dr. G. G. Quackenbush. They show per capita sales of yogurt in the United States for selected years, as published in the July 1977 issue of the USDA *Dairy Situation*.

1955	0.11 lb.
1960	0.26
1965	0.32
1970	0.86
1975	2.20
1976	2.40

Total sales in 1976 were estimated at 510 million pounds. Expanded introductions of soft-serve and frozen yogurt in 1977 speeded up the growth of the total market.

Or, as the New York *Daily News*, "largest circulation of any paper in America," reported on July 8, 1979: In 1960, there were 88 million cups of yogurt sold. In 1965, there were 122 million cups. By 1970, there were 344 million cups and by 1975, 890 million cups. This year, sales are expected to top one billion cups.

Yogurt

In Europe, especially in France, where it's eaten at the rate of a million cups a day, yogurt is more of a "known" food than it is here. However, that situation is rapidly changing. In the past five years, more Americans have eaten yogurt than ever before. Now, on the East Coast at least, you can buy yogurt at such disparate places as an off-Broadway theater during intermission, Yankee Stadium, Amtrak's Metroliner, and at the U. S. Open. In fact, during the Pan American Games in San Juan, Puerto Rico, in July 1979, officials providing food service at the Pan American Village, where the athletes and their trainers and coaches ate, reported that they served 385,000 meals. This included 17,400 pounds of ground beef; 10,000 pounds of fish; 352,000 half-pint containers of milk; *and* 100,000 containers of yogurt. That's a *lot* of yogurt.

Now, back to our original question: Just what—exactly—is yogurt? The best way to answer this is to analyze the look, taste, and consistency of yogurt and then briefly go into how yogurt is made.

In *The Dannon Book of Young Living* the authors, William and Ellen Hartley, give an excellent description of yogurt:

The taste of the end product is unlike anything other than—yogurt. It has a mild tang but is by no means sour. The consistency is about like that of excellent frozen custard, or chilled thick cream, but the taste is not so cloying, and the composition is, of course, entirely different except for the fact that yogurt is based on milk.

9

Keeping Dannon's definition in mind, let's take a look at the description that is currently being published by the U.S. Department of Agriculture:

Yogurt is a custard-like preparation made by fermenting concentrated whole milk. It is snow white in appearance, and differs from other fermented milks, in that it is consumed as a custard, rather than as a liquid.

Compared with the soft, friable curds of most common cultured buttermilks, yogurt curd is firm and somewhat tenacious. The texture of the finished product is fine and smooth, and the body is firm.

Both of these sources give, I believe, an excellent picture of the look, taste, and consistency of yogurt. But how does yogurt get this way? This question is answered in depth on page 27, in the chapter on commercial yogurt. However, for our purposes here, I will give a shorter, more succinct version of how yogurt is made.

First, you start with a certain quantity of warm milk. Then, you add the culture, which is made up of two "friendly" bacteria: *Lactobacillus bulgaricus* and *Streptococcus thermophilus*.

Both of these bacteria reproduce or multiply by breaking in half. Each half then grows to the size of its parent and the process is repeated all over again. (Think of how yeast acts in bread making.)

Both of these bacteria grow well at temperatures of between 100 and 115 degrees F. And as they grow, the milk sugar, or lactose, is changed into lactic acid. This acid causes the milk to curdle or thicken and creates the distinctive tangy flavor of yogurt. This "thickening" makes yogurt a more satisfying food than, say, a glass of plain "thin" milk.

Conclusion: We can say, then, that yogurt is (1) a snow-white substance that has (2) a tart, tangy taste with (3) a smooth, custard-like consistency and contains (4) two beneficial bacteria.

Curds and Whey Defined

Curds are the thick casein-rich part of coagulated milk. Whey is the serum or watery part of milk that is separated from the coagulable part, or curd, especially in the process of making cheese; it is rich in lactose, minerals, and vitamins and contains lactalbumin and traces of fat.

Milk Used in Making Yogurt

In this country, most yogurts sold in the supermarkets and health food stores are made from cow's milk.*

If you wish, you can buy goat's milk yogurt, at the Good Earth in New York City for seventy-nine cents (plain), or ninety-five cents (fruit-on-the-bottom). When I sampled this yogurt, I thought it had a slightly "salty" taste. Other than that, it looked like regular yogurt to me.

In other areas of the world, yogurt is made from the milk of reindeer, sheep, buffalo, camel, yak, and llama. Take your pick.†

Food Value

When I was a child growing up in British Columbia, my mother had two favorite things she would say to me. One was "Eat everything on your plate—children are starving in . . ." (the name of the country would change from week to week) and "Drink your milk, it will put curls on your head." I had great difficulty believing that a) my eating habits would help some poor waif halfway around the world, and b) milk would make my straight, blonde hair change into a mass of curls. At the present time, I have no proof as to the number of undernourished children I saved, but, I can tell you, unequivocally, that my hair still doesn't have even one trace of a natural curl or wave.

My mother's wishful thinking aside, I'm still a strong believer in milk and its benefits to the body. Since yogurt is made from milk, it follows that I have the same belief about yogurt. *But, be aware:* contrary to popular belief, milk is *not* a perfect food.‡ It has certain nutritional deficiencies, as does yogurt.

* If you make your own yogurt you can also use soy milk. Rodale's *Encyclopedia for Healthful Living* says "soybean milk has been used successfully as a substitute for cow's milk in the feeding of children who are allergic to cow's milk."

† One cup of milk from a goat is 163 calories; one cup of milk from a reindeer is 580 calories; cow's milk is 159 (whole), 88 (skim), 145 (low fat with 2 percent nonfat milk solids added) per cup, according to the Food and Drug Administration.

‡ Read "Milk: The Not-So-Perfect Food" in *Consumer Beware!* by Beatrice Trum Hunter, New York: Bantam, 1971.

However, one cup of yogurt (we will have to assume, for the sake of argument, that it's a fresh, natural yogurt) is a good source of protein (about eight grams per cup—or more, if nonfat milk solids have been added), calcium, and vitamin B₂ (riboflavin).

As far as the deficiencies of yogurt are concerned, let me quote from a letter I received, in response to my questions, from Dr. John Alford, laboratory chief of the Dairy Foods Nutrition Laboratory of the Nutrition Institute, U.S. Department of Agriculture, Beltsville, Maryland:

Yogurt, like milk, is deficient in iron, copper and Vitamin C. If yogurt is whole milk yogurt (i.e., has no milk fat removed and therefore contains

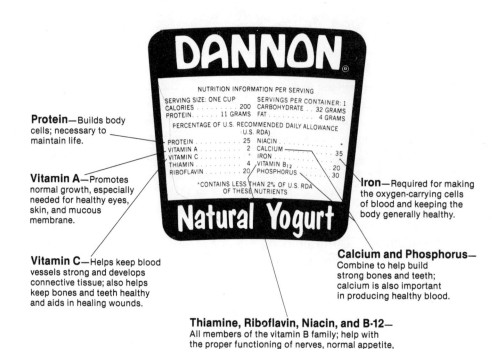

Protein—Builds body cells; necessary to maintain life.

Vitamin A—Promotes normal growth, especially needed for healthy eyes, skin, and mucous membrane.

Vitamin C—Helps keep blood vessels strong and develops connective tissue; also helps keep bones and teeth healthy and aids in healing wounds.

Iron—Required for making the oxygen-carrying cells of blood and keeping the body generally healthy.

Calcium and Phosphorus—Combine to help build strong bones and teeth; calcium is also important in producing healthy blood.

Thiamine, Riboflavin, Niacin, and B-12—All members of the vitamin B family; help with the proper functioning of nerves, normal appetite, good digestion, and healthy skin.

DANNON

NUTRITION INFORMATION PER SERVING

SERVING SIZE: ONE CUP   SERVINGS PER CONTAINER: 1
CALORIES 200   CARBOHYDRATE . . 32 GRAMS
PROTEIN . . . . . . 11 GRAMS   FAT . . . . 4 GRAMS
PERCENTAGE OF U.S. RECOMMENDED DAILY ALLOWANCE
(U.S. RDA)
PROTEIN 25   NIACIN . . . . *
VITAMIN A 2   CALCIUM 35
VITAMIN C . . . . *   IRON . . . . *
THIAMIN 4   VITAMIN B₁₂ 20
RIBOFLAVIN 20   PHOSPHORUS 30
*CONTAINS LESS THAN 2% OF U.S. RDA
OF THESE NUTRIENTS

Natural Yogurt

Courtesy of Dannon Milk Products, Long Island City, New York.

about 3.5 percent fat) it will be a good source of Vitamin A (a fat-soluble vitamin).

Low fat yogurt (1-1.5 percent milk fat) will have proportionately less Vitamin A, and skim milk yogurt essentially none.

Now, take a look at the label from a single eight-ounce serving of Dannon lemon yogurt. This will give you an even more complete picture of how yogurt can benefit you.

Sweet Dreams

Instead of a glass of warm milk before bedtime in order to relax, why not try half a cup of lemon yogurt?

Calories

HOW MANY ARE YOU GETTING IN

YOGURT?

Like it or not, we now have to talk about that curse of the civilized world: weight and how to control it. First, I'll tell you my loss-and-gain story.

In the past, I have taken off, and put on, the same ten pounds more times than I care to remember. At the moment I am at what I consider my correct weight for my height: 128 lb., 5′ 6″. Nice as this is, I'm positive I'll go up again.

But I'll be ready. Because over the years, in order to keep my weight from spiraling upward forever, I have devised a plain, simple diet that I'd like to share with you. Briefly, it goes like this:

BREAKFAST		A scoop of Friendship® pineapple cottage cheese
	3-4	Kraft unsweetened grapefruit sections*
	3	saltines
		Coffee with milk
LUNCH	1	container Dannon yogurt, any flavor
	3	saltines
		Coffee with milk
DINNER		Meat, fish, chicken, or eggs
	1	vegetable
		A glass of milk

* Chilled Kraft fruit, with no preservatives, can be found in sixteen- and thirty-two-ounce jars at your local supermarket.

14

Basically, this diet differs from my regular eating only in that I cut out potatoes, rice, bread, desserts, and wine. I do not give up milk. I've discovered that I must have a glass of milk now and then, and no matter how hard I try, I can't drink coffee black.

The point is, my simple diet, which is really a "cutting out or back" of high-caloried foods, includes eating yogurt every day. This works for me, and, as I'll explain later, it can work for you, too.

Of course, I would prefer to take these ten pounds off once and for all. But I, like you and everyone else, live in a world of endless temptations and, quite frankly, I can't do it. So when I notice that the extra pounds are on again, I go (about once a year) back on my diet.

Why You and I Gain

Have you put on an extra pound or two lately? Read through this checklist and if any of these apply, you'll know why.

1. *Too much food.* In particular, fattening delicacies. A chocolate eclair (360 calories) will taste great, but it won't do a thing for your waistline.
2. *Not enough exercise.* My friend Jackie says, "When I was in school in Canada, I played grass hockey and tennis—now I don't walk to the corner deli." When you drive, you don't burn up calories.*
3. *Too much TV.* Rockford munches, and you and I wait for the commercials so we can dash to the refrigerator and keep him company. Enough said.
4. *No time to eat.* A cup of coffee for breakfast, and nothing for lunch, leads to a huge meal at night. Three well-balanced meals equal fewer calories at the end of the day.
5. *Too much stress.* Everyone has to cope with life, but some do it better than others. If you reach for a Hershey bar every time the going gets tough, you'll never stay slim.

* Exercise *plus* dieting will enable you to lose weight. Here are the calories you'll use up per hour: bicycling (300–420), bowling (260), dancing (450–700), gardening (350), golf (210–300), housework (180–240), horseback riding (180–480), ice skating (360), Ping Pong (360), running (800–1000), skating (300–700), skiing (600), swimming (350–700), tennis (400–500), volleyball (210), walking (100–330). (Source: American Heart Association and the Nutrition Foundation)

Calories

When you buy yogurt, be sure to *read* the information on the carton. It is there for your benefit. You will notice, if you look carefully, that even though the flavor or fruit may be the same, the calorie count will vary from one brand to the next.

In its simplest form, this happens because of:

a) The type of milk used (page 11)
b) What is taken out of the milk, i.e., fat (page 29) and
c) What is added to the yogurt, i.e., milk solids, preserves, etc. (page 40)

If you are on a diet, you must keep this in mind and check before you eat. Plain yogurt has the lowest number of calories (150), followed by the flavored ones: vanilla, lemon, and coffee. Even here, the calories can vary. For example:

Lemon	*Calories (8 oz.)*
Breakstone	254
Dannon	200
Light n' Lively	229

In the fruit yogurts, the same rule applies: read before you eat.*

Raspberry	*Calories (8 oz.)*
Breakstone	264
Dannon	260
Light n' Lively	225
Maya	290

Note: In response to one of my questions about fat-free yogurt, Robert C. Finnie, Executive Vice-President of Venture Foods, replied: "While butterfat level does affect caloric content somewhat, the amount of the milk solids and, particularly, the sugar content of the fruit preserves control it much more."

Dieting

There is a "Yogurt Only Diet" on page 90 of Dr. Irwin Stillman's *Quick Weight Loss Diet* (New York: Dell Publishing Co., Inc., 1967). Here is what he says:

* In this section, we are only talking about commercial yogurt. Homemade yogurt is quite another matter (see page 43).

16

Quite a few patients have lost weight quickly and pleasantly on a yogurt only diet. For this diet take 120 calories of yogurt 5 to 6 times daily (total of 600–720 calories). You may vary the flavors as much as you please, keeping the total calories under 900 daily.

I question a few aspects of this diet, namely:

How does one measure 120 calories of yogurt? I suppose you could eat 80 percent of a carton (eight ounces) of plain commercial yogurt (150 calories). Or perhaps you could eat 60 percent of a carton of flavored yogurt (200 calories)—but this system is hit or miss at best.

What about the boredom factor? Eating yogurt three times a day, every day for a week or more, would surely affect even the most disciplined dieter.

Why eat "yogurt only," even for a short period? Yogurt (like milk) is not a perfect food—it has definite nutritional deficiencies (see page 11). I believe that any diet, long or short term, should be balanced, i.e., vegetables, meat, chicken, fish, eggs, milk, etc.

Yogurt is not the perfect diet food because one does not exist. Taking off weight and keeping it off is the result of discipline and effort. Here are the three ways you can use yogurt as a diet food:

1. In combination with a sensible diet (see page 14)
2. By itself for lunch or as a snack*
3. As a substitute for higher-caloried food

Short Stop

In a survey done by United Dairy Industries of America, the main reason most people gave for eating yogurt was not to lose weight or stay healthy, but simply because they like it.

Yogurt as a Substitute

The next time you have a baked potato, instead of topping it with sour cream (thirty calories per tablespoon), try plain yogurt with

---

* I eat *only* yogurt for lunch. However, here is another opinion on this. "Commenting on the current yogurt-for-lunch popularity, a New York City nutritionist, Barbara Premo, reported that yogurt is too low in protein to provide a full, balanced meal. She suggested yogurt as a dessert, after a sandwich of lean meat, fish or chicken." (Beatrice Trum Hunter, *Yogurt, Kefir and other Milk Cultures*, New Canaan, Conn.: Keats Publishing, 1973.)

chopped chives at only eight calories per tablespoon. It's just as tasty as sour cream, and much less fattening.

Or for dessert, instead of having a slice of apple pie (350 calories), substitute a cup of yogurt. The flavored kind can be sweet and satisfying—yet nowhere near the calorie count of apple pie.

And if you have a weakness for cream cheese, just remember that eight ounces of cream cheese are a whopping 848 calories. A better idea is "yogurt" cheese. You can make it yourself with a yogurt maker (page 55) or without (page 82), or you can buy it ready made.

In my opinion, the creamy, rich kefir yogurt cheese made by Continental Culture Specialists, Inc., in Glendale, California, is absolutely superb (try it on toast), and it's only 456 calories for eight ounces. I bought mine at the Good Earth health food store for $1.39.

Finally, you can substitute yogurt for high-caloried mayonnaise (sixty-five calories per tablespoon), or use half mayo and half yogurt. Idea: the next time you make yourself a tuna sandwich use lemon yogurt instead of mayonnaise. The lemon adds zest, the yogurt cuts calories.

Digestion

WHY YOGURT IS EASIER TO DIGEST THAN

MILK

About five years ago, my husband and I were staying at an apartment-hotel in Barbados. One Sunday night, instead of going to the hotel dining room, I decided to make dinner for us myself. I took the meat and vegetables out of the refrigerator, and discovered, to my dismay, that there was—*no milk*.

"Oh, God, now what," I said to my husband. I knew that every local shop was closed up tight. There's no place more dark and deserted than Maxwell Coast Road in Barbados on a Sunday night.

But I was determined to have our Sunday night dinner and I was not about to be put off because one item was missing. So Peter went off down the road in search of a quart of milk.

I waited for his return. And waited. And waited. Then I began to feel very guilty—I cursed myself for sending him on this mad expedition.

Just as I was beginning to despair, in walked Pete with a triumphant smile on his face. "Here," he said, "milk," and handed me a plastic bag that was sealed at both ends.

I held the bag flat in my hands and stared. It felt ice cold, and I could hear the milk sloshing back and forth inside. I thought it looked like a water bed for a whistling frog.*

"What's this?" I asked.

* The tiny whistling frogs of Barbados look like any other frogs you've ever seen. The only difference is the sound they make. Their soft, low "whistling" put me to sleep every night we were there.

19

"That's milk," he replied. "I got it from a guy who works out of a little window in his shack."

"You're kidding," I commented.

"Well," he replied, "all I know is that it's pitch dark. I knock on the window. A guy peers out. Then he opens the window about six inches and takes my money. A few seconds later, he hands out the milk and shuts the window. Not a word—nothing."

I had heard enough. I took the bag and carefully cut one corner. Then I poured the whole thing (the milk looked and tasted fine) into a container. Finally, at long last, I made our dinner.

My reason for telling this story is to illustrate the lengths to which some people will go to obtain milk. It is an essential part of their daily diet. On the other hand, there are many people in this world who *cannot* drink milk at all simply because they have great difficulty digesting it. This includes more people than you would think. According to Prof. Frances James:

From 80 to 99 percent of the Far Eastern peoples (depending on which immediate group you are examining) cannot tolerate it. Much the same percentage of African Negroes (again depending on the immediate group) are made quite sick by consuming milk.

She goes on to say that, in this country, figures for blacks "in whom a certain amount of white European blood now flows, show only about a 70 percent intolerance."

What is the cause of this? Briefly, tolerance or intolerance to milk depends on an individual's production of the enzyme lactase. In other words, lactase is needed to digest the lactose of milk.

Now we go from milk to yogurt. It has been found that some people who cannot digest milk *can* digest yogurt. And the reason? Yogurt is a source of predigested protein—or, put another way, the protein in yogurt is partially broken down in the fermentation process. Part of the digestive work (about 20 percent) is done before the yogurt ever reaches your stomach.

How much easier and faster yogurt is digested in relation to milk is a question of debate. I came across several different answers to this question in my reading—none of them quite agreed.

Colombo, in one of their information sheets, says: "milk converts into an absorbable form in three to four hours, whereas yogurt converts in only thirty to forty minutes." Dannon states: "nothing is lost in yogurt and much is apparently gained. One gain seems to be the ease with which yogurt is digested—*much faster* than milk according

20

to experiments conducted at a New York hospital." In *Therapeutic Uses of Yogurt*,* the author states, "yogurt is more easily digested than ordinary milk. On the average, one container is digested in about one hour as compared with three hours for the same amount of milk." And finally, the Rosell Institute says, "experiments conducted at Columbia University and Rosell Institute have shown that yogurt is nearly completely liquefied by stomach enzymes after one hour of digestion."

After reading through all these statements, I decided to consult an expert myself, so I wrote to Dr. Alford of the Dairy Foods Nutrition Laboratory. Here is his reply:

It has been shown that some of the milk protein in yogurt is partially broken down by the bacteria in it. Therefore, it should be *more easily* digested.

However, to say "much easier" overstates the extent of digestion. The rate of digestion of milk (or any food) depends upon the *amount of food in the stomach.* [The italics are mine.]

A glass of milk taken on an empty stomach will be digested more rapidly than a glass of milk taken with a meal. The time may vary from two or three hours to ten or twelve before it is all digested.

Conclusion: In brief, we can say, then, that (1) yogurt can be eaten by people who cannot drink milk; (2) yogurt is easier to digest than milk because it is partially digested before you eat it (due to the addition of a culture); and (3) you can digest yogurt faster than milk but just "how much faster" is difficult to say.

Don't Confuse Lactose and Lactase

Lactose is a sugar which only exists in milk. Lactase is an enzyme (or chemical substance) in your intestine. It breaks down or "splits" lactose into glucose and galactose.

If You Can't Drink Milk

I received an extremely interesting letter from Alan E. Kligerman, a senior partner of the SugarLo Company in New Jersey. In this letter, Mr. Kligerman describes a fascinating new product that his company makes called LactAid® brand lactase enzyme.

* Frederic Damrau, M.D., *Therapeutic Uses of Yogurt; A Review of Medical Literature* (New York: International Yogurt Foundation, 1954).

This product is, quite simply, for people who can't drink milk. In short, it makes milk digestible if one has an intolerance to lactose. Here's how it works: you squeeze out four or five drops of LactAid (it comes in a small plastic dropper bottle) into one quart of milk. Then you stir with a clean spoon or close the milk carton and shake —gently. After this you put the whole quart of milk into your refrigerator and leave it. After twenty-four hours (one full day) it will be ready to drink.

This sounds, to me at least, like a terrific product. Mr. Kligerman concluded his letter by saying, "I can only tell you that the response that we have had from thousands upon thousands of people, who have written us, and who buy it [LactAid] from us or through stores or distributors, has been little short of emotionally grateful."

If you're interested in this product, and you can't find it, write to: SugarLo Company, 3540 Atlantic Avenue, P.O. Box 1017, Atlantic City, NJ 08404 (phone: 609-348-3148).

Longevity

WILL YOU REALLY LIVE TO BE 100 YEARS

OLD?

If you eat yogurt every day, will you live to a ripe old age? And if you could—would you want to? For myself, living in New York as I do, I think it would be a bit of a hassle. Can you imagine trying to flag down a cab on a rainy Friday night or fighting one's way on the subway at, heaven forbid, the age of 100? I shudder at the thought.

However, the idea of eating yogurt to increase one's life span has been around for a long time. How did it start?

We have to go back as far as 1908. This was the year that Dr. Ilya Metchnikoff, a French physician of Russian origin and co-winner of the Nobel Prize, began studying the reasons for aging.

In brief, Metchnikoff believed that life could be prolonged by the use of "friendly" yogurt bacilli. He reasoned that the bacteria, carried in yogurt to the intestinal tract, produced lactic acid. This in turn inhibited growth of germs that produce intestinal disorders.

Then he took this even further and said that if the intestines were free of harmful bacteria, one would stay healthy and, as a result, live longer. He supported these views by citing the number of Bulgarians who ate yogurt every day and who lived past 100. (For every 1,000 deaths *recorded*, an average of 4 were of people over the age of 100.)

I decided to read Metchnikoff in the original, so one Saturday morning I trekked over to one of the "outpost" branches of the New York Public Library, on Forty-third Street between Tenth and Eleventh avenues.*

---

* A really deserted area on Saturday morning. You'll find trucks, warehouses, and one diner where, at least, you can get a good cup of coffee.

There I examined Metchnikoff—yellowish pages that fell apart in my hands, and more dust than I care to think about—but the real thing nonetheless. Here is what he has to say about old age:

If it be true that our unhappy old age is due to poisoning of the tissues (the greater part of the poison coming from the large intestine inhabited by numberless microbes), it is clear that agents [he means yogurt] which arrest intestinal putrefaction must at the same time postpone and ameliorate old age.

Now, the interesting part about Metchnikoff was that he was his own guinea pig. He planned to live to a ripe old age and executed this plan by eating yogurt practically *every day for eight years.* Or as he says:

For more than 8 years I took as a regular part of my diet, soured milk at first prepared from boiled milk, inoculated with a lactic leaven. . . . I am very well pleased with the result, and I think that my experiment has gone on long enough to justify my view.

Unfortunately, his experiment failed. Metchnikoff died at seventy-one (1845–1916)—admittedly a long life, but certainly not the extreme old age that he'd hoped for. (Of course, one could argue that, for that time, seventy-one was pretty good.)

Which brings us again to the question: Does the daily consumption of yogurt help one live longer? Since there are so many factors involved in health and aging, I remain a skeptic. So does Professor James, as she wrote in her article in *Expedition* magazine:

It is absolute irony, and poor science as well, to claim that laban [yogurt] gives long life when it is a basic food all over the Near and Middle East and India where *life continues to be shorter than anywhere else in the world.* [The italics are mine.]

I'd say that this is one of the strongest arguments against yogurt contributing to longevity. Professor James goes on to say that:

This claim was first made in 1910 by the Russian scientist, Metchnikoff, who associated the high consumption of yogurt in Bulgaria with statistics purporting to show that, of a population of about five million, some five thousand Bulgarians were centenarians. These figures can, however, point only to general illiteracy and an absence of birth certificates.

In summing up, we could say that the jury is still out. In this complex society of ours, with all its stresses and strains, it is very difficult to isolate one particular food and say that it can ensure a long life.* Yogurt is good for you—yes, undoubtedly—but ensuring that you'll live to be 100 years old is another matter. We'll have to wait and see what future scientific study will bring.

Long Shot

Yogurt was introduced into France by Francis I. The king had been failing in health. A physician from the court of Constantinople brought yogurt culture with him and prepared yogurt daily for the monarch. Francis I improved in vitality to such an extent that he named the milk food *lait de la vie éternelle*, or "milk of eternal life."†

Time Out

In Max Apple's book, *The Oranging of America* (New York: Viking Press, 1976), there is a humorous story about an old man called Vasirin Kefirovsky who, like our friend Metchnikoff, becomes obsessed with yogurt and eats nothing else. He says, "What is the promised land? Milk and honey and time. What is yogurt? Milk and bacteria and time."

* To illustrate the relationship between yogurt and longevity, Dannon has Bagrat Topagua, a Soviet Georgian, age eighty-nine, and his *mother* in one of their print ads. However, the copy reads: "Of course, many factors affect longevity, and we are not saying Dannon Yogurt will help you live longer."

† Adelle Davis, "Yogurt—America's New Food Discovery," *Life & Health*.

Commercial Yogurt

HOW IT'S MADE AND WHAT'S IN IT

Unlike, shall we say, the automobile industry, which is ruled by the "Big Three," yogurt is made by huge conglomerates employing thousands such as Kraft, smaller family-owned businesses such as the Alta-Dena Dairy in California, and tiny storefront operations like Yonah Schimmel's Knishery, which has been on New York's Lower East Side since 1910. Since it would be impossible for me to visit even a third of all the yogurt companies on the East Coast, I decided to pick one—Dannon—and describe their "yogurt-making" process to you.

On July 8, 1977, I wrote to Mr. Metzger and asked him "if it would be possible to interview you or a member of your staff." Three days later (companies that reply promptly always go up a notch or two with me) I received a letter from Mr. Metzger's secretary, saying, "I would suggest that you contact him during the second week of August when he will be returning from Europe."

I thought about her reply and decided I would take another approach. Several days later I wrote back and asked if it would be possible "to have a tour through one of your plants now, and interview Mr. Metzger later on." I also added that:

So far, all of my research has been with books. I've compiled a master list of 345 books from which I have culled the yogurt information I need. However, one of the gaps in my research is actually seeing for myself how commercial yogurt is made.

Four days later, I received another letter from Mr. Metzger's secretary, Lida Karyanin, saying that Peter and I could have a tour through Dannon's plant at 1145 Edgewater Avenue in Ridgefield,

New Jersey. She added that Leonard Hirsch, their manager, would escort us and explain the whole operation.

A Visit with Dannon Yogurt

On a hot Friday afternoon, July 22, 1977, to be exact, we started out from our apartment on Eleventh Street in Greenwich Village for Ridgefield—a trip, incidentally, that only takes thirty minutes from midtown Manhattan.

The Dannon building is a large, sprawling one-story brown-and-beige brick structure partially surrounded by a neatly trimmed green lawn. The name "Dannon Yogurt" is in big red letters on the front. Their neighbors, with the exception of the Ridgefield indoor pistol range in back, are mostly other companies in similar-looking low, modern buildings.

Inside

After waiting five minutes in Dannon's small reception room, we were escorted into a very large office area by Mr. Hirsch. The walls of this room have a display of close to 2,700 yogurt cartons (empty, of course) from all over the world—it is quite a sight.

From here, we went into the plant (one large room about the size of a football field) where the yogurt is actually made. The entire floor and all four walls were shining and spotless. Every piece of stainless steel machinery glistened and gleamed. Each worker wore a white apron and hat. "Can you believe this," Peter said to me. "I've never seen any place so clean."

Several of the workers were singing lustily (over the general noise which was, to my ears at least, quite high). I asked Mr. Hirsch why. "It's Friday afternoon," he replied. "On Fridays everybody likes to sing." I couldn't argue with that.

Step-by-Step: How Yogurt Is Made

This is how Dannon makes their yogurt (sundae-style and flavored) in their Ridgefield, New Jersey, plant. Dannon gave me this "step-by-step" material, which I have edited slightly. It took us two hours just to look at their whole operation—to write it down would have taken me two days.

1. The whole process begins with the dairies, which are located in rural areas—miles away from the Dannon plants. After the milk is taken from the cows it is put into stainless steel holding tanks. Then it is partly skimmed to reduce the cream or fat content (see page 29). Nonfat milk solids (4 percent) are added to this low-fat milk (99 percent fat free).

2. Within hours, the milk is transferred to refrigerated tank trucks. These trucks go to six Dannon manufacturing plants, one of which is the Ridgefield plant.

3. At Ridgefield (as with the other five) the milk is automatically pumped into special refrigerated stainless steel tanks for temporary storage. Each tank holds 60,000 pounds of milk.

4. As soon as the milk has been emptied from the tank truck, automatic cleaning devices wash and sterilize the truck storage compartment. Then the truck returns to the dairy to pick up another shipment of milk. Like many dairy jobs, the transfer and shipping of milk is an almost continuous operation—day and night.

5. Meanwhile, the milk that has just been delivered is moved from the holding tank through specially designed stainless steel piping to machines that homogenize and pasteurize it. Homogenization breaks up the particles of cream into tiny pieces so that they will not separate out and rise to the top of the finished product. This process guarantees a smooth, consistent yogurt.

6. During pasteurization the milk is flash-heated to destroy harmful bacteria. This safety procedure is used for all dairy products such as milk, ice cream, and cheese as well as for some wines, vinegars, and similar liquids.

7. Next, a special blend of two microorganisms, the rod-shaped *Lactobacillus bulgaricus* and the round-shaped *Streptococcus thermophilus,* is added to the homogenized, pasteurized milk. This particular lactic culture is used because it produces yogurt with the precise flavor and appearance qualities consumers want. While the cultured milk is still liquid, it is piped into fully automated cup-filling machines.

8. A special device on the processing line holds the 100 percent natural fruit preserves such as blueberry, strawberry, or red raspberry.

9. Four cups at a time go under the "preserve" spigot. About two tablespoons of fruit preserves are automatically dispensed into the bottom of each cup. The cup then continues to move down the filling machines.

10. The cultured milk is poured over the preserves to the top of the cup. Each cup is then automatically capped, date-stamped, and put into a cardboard tray.* Thirty-four trays, each with a dozen yogurt cups, are placed on a six-foot-high rolling cart.

11. Flavored yogurts such as vanilla, coffee, and lemon are made in a similar way except that the natural extracts that flavor the yogurt, and the sugar, are mixed with the cultured milk so that the taste is evenly distributed through the carton. Note: No human hands have touched the product and workers must meet precise sanitary standards.

12. The cups of yogurt are then stored for two and one-half to three hours in an incubator where the temperature is maintained at about 112 degrees F. During this time the bacteria continue to multiply and produce lactic acid, which causes the milk protein to coagulate and thicken. This is the action that transforms the liquid milk into the custardy yogurt.

13. From the incubators, the warm yogurt is wheeled into refrigerated rooms for overnight cooling to below 45 degrees F.

14. Early the next morning the yogurt is wheeled onto delivery trucks for shipment. Dannon's six production plants service almost all the United States. Since it has no artificial preservatives, Dannon yogurt must be shipped to stores within as few hours as possible after manufacturing. Dannon has one of the largest fleets of trucks in the United States to make these deliveries.

15. From the above, you will note that in the Dannon process, the milk is pasteurized before cultures are added. Some manufacturers pasteurize the product again, in order to prolong the shelf life. Unfortunately, the cultures are often deactivated this way. The result can be a yogurt without much in the way of yogurt cultures.

Note: To make Swiss-style yogurt, the mixture is incubated in vats before blending in the fruit.

The "Fat" Content of Yogurt

One of the first things I did, when I began the research on this book, was to go out and buy every carton of yogurt I could find. This

---

* Dannon stamps twenty-one days ahead. Some other brands stamp fifty days ahead because they add preservatives. Don't be misled. Whatever brand you buy, READ THE LABEL.

included shopping in both supermarkets and health food stores. When I had all the yogurt assembled, I noticed that there was a lot of information on the outside of each carton, most of which I did not really understand. So, after a lot of digging and questioning, my aim now is to make this information as clear as possible to you.

To start with, milk can be classified, as far as the cream (butterfat, milkfat, or just plain "fat") is concerned, in three ways: whole milk, lowfat milk, or nonfat or skim milk. If you look at your carton of yogurt and see *yogurt or whole-milk yogurt*, that simply means that *no* cream has been removed. This is explained on the carton two ways: 3.5% fat, or 96.5% fat free. Look for these names for whole-milk yogurts: Breyers, Colombo, Continental, and Maya.

Now, if you find your carton of yogurt says *lowfat yogurt*, that means the milk has been partly skimmed to reduce the cream by about half. This yogurt contains anywhere from 2 percent to 0.5 percent butterfat. To give you an example. Many yogurts in this category have 1 percent fat. Therefore, this is what you will see on the label: 1% fat, or 99% fat free. Look for these names for lowfat yogurts: Dannon, Sealtest, Lacto, Axelrod, Breakstone Stay 'n Shape, A&P Look Fit, Light n' Lively, Continental, and Alta-Dena Naja.

Keep in mind: 1 percent fat is 2 grams of fat out of 227 grams (227 grams is 8 ounces or 1 cup, which is the average size of a container of yogurt).

Lastly, we have *nonfat or skim milk* and this contains only 0.5 percent cream. It is seldom used to make yogurt.

When you see these descriptions and percentages spelled out this way, you realize the whole subject of milk/fat/yogurt* is really very simple. However, when you line up twenty different yogurts, all saying essentially the same thing twenty different ways, it looks very confusing. Remember, with yogurt the words may change but the melody stays the same.

Thin vs. Thick Yogurt

There is no right or wrong consistency to yogurt. Preference for a "thick" or "thin" yogurt is purely a question of personal taste. As far as commercial yogurts go, I prefer the consistency of Dannon.

* Fat content is a subject nobody seems to agree on, I've decided. Each person I talked to told me a different story. The above figures are very close, if not a bull's-eye.

To me, it's neither too thick or too thin—just a good "custardy" yogurt you can really dig into.

The thinnest or "loosest" yogurt I have ever eaten came from Yonah Schimmel's at 137 East Houston Street in Manhattan. This yogurt, prepared fresh every day, is, I understand, closer to the European or Middle Eastern idea of yogurt: a liquidy substance, almost like a soup. Offhand I'd say this particular yogurt is, like kippers and olives, definitely an acquired taste (especially to a palate like mine that's used to American-style yogurts). Make no mistake though, this *is* delicious yogurt. Buy a ten-ounce carton for 60¢ ($2.00 for a quart) and decide for yourself if this one is for you.

On the other hand, the thickest, richest yogurt I sampled didn't taste, to me at least, like yogurt at all. It struck me as tasting more like *coeur à la crème* (French cheese cream) or even American-made sour cream. I'm referring to sundae-style strawberry Maya Youghurt (their spelling) put out by the Alta-Dena Dairy in City of Industry, California. It's thick, rich, and creamy—*and* it's 280 calories. In New York you can buy Maya Youghurt at The Good Earth and Brownies health food stores for seventy-four cents a carton.

How Long Will Yogurt Last?

With commercial yogurt, I believe it's better to buy just the amount that you need. You may end up going to the supermarket more frequently—but, if you shop carefully, you'll know that the yogurt you're buying is fresh. Here's why.

All yogurt is open-dated. An "expiration date" is stamped on the top of each carton. "After this date," says Dannon, "the cartons are removed from sale in the stores."

How long will yogurt last after you get it home? Dannon believes that if your yogurt is properly refrigerated, "it should remain fresh, tasty and wholesome for at least a week beyond the expiration date."* On the other hand, The National Dairy Council states that "yogurt usually may be stored for ten days or longer after purchase." (*Yo-*

* This is the official FDA definition: *Pull or Sell Date*—the last date the product should be sold, assuming it has been stored and handled properly. The pull date allows for some storage time in the home refrigerator. Examples: cold cuts, ice cream, milk. *Expiration Date*—the last date the food should be eaten or used. Examples: baby formula and yeast.

gurt . . . Ancient Food with Modern Ways, National Dairy Council, Rosemont, Illinois 60018). This would work *only* if the yogurt was fresh when you bought it. Note: If yogurt is kept for an extended time, a sharp flavor may develop, but it will still be edible.

Conclusion: When you buy yogurt (1) look for a carton with an expiration date that is as far in the future as possible;* (2) remember the day or date when you bought your yogurt at the supermarket or health food store—in case there is no date on the carton; (3) if you are really concerned with freshness, make your own yogurt. *To repeat:* Watch the expiration date on yogurt when you buy it. Dannon says:

The fresher the yogurt, the higher the population of viable bacteria. The expiration date on the lid represents a time anywhere from 18 (for Dannon) to 28 days (for varieties that contain preservatives) after manufacture. The yogurt may taste all right after the expiration date, but it will be much less effective therapeutically than fresh yogurt with all its bacteria alive and jumping.

Is Commercial Yogurt a Natural Food?

I realize that this is a loaded question, so I'll be particularly careful with my answer. First of all, let's start with a definition of a natural food. Here's one which was sent to me from Dannon. They say that a natural food is one "which is manufactured without any man-made boosters to influence its size, shape, texture, flavor or shelf life." Or, put another way: "When a manufacturer has used natural ingredients at every stage of production, this type of yogurt can be classified as a natural food."

Of course, your next question is going to be, "Well, how would I know what ingredients are in the yogurt I'm eating?" All I can say is just read the information on the carton—it's all there.

And it's there for a very simple reason. The FDA, or Food and Drug Administration, requires that all the ingredients in commercial yogurt appear on the outside of the carton. Why? Because there is no "standard of identity" for yogurt. A standard of identity spells out "what" and "how much" of certain ingredients go into a product, and

---

* I am referring to a yogurt with *no* preservatives, additives, or stabilizers.

the FDA has not yet ruled on what exactly, in its opinion, constitutes yogurt.*

Now, to give you an example. Here is the list of ingredients for two cartons of strawberry yogurt:

Brand X	*Brand Y*
Cultured Pasteurized Lowfat Milk	Cultured Pasteurized Milk and Skim Milk
4% Nonfat Milk Solids Added	4% Nonfat Milk Solids Added from Condensed Skim Milk
Selected Strawberry Preserves	Strawberries
	Sugar
	Natural Strawberry Flavor
	Cellulose Gum
	Gelatin
	Starch
	Carrageenan
	Guar Gum
	Locust Bean Gum
	Artificial Color

It's not too difficult to see that Brand X qualifies as a natural yogurt while Brand Y barely deserves to be called yogurt at all.

Generally, when a yogurt says "all natural" ingredients, or "no artificial anything" you can be fairly sure there are no stabilizers or preservatives in it. However, read carefully; I've seen yogurts with "natural flavor" on the front and artificial ingredients listed on the back.

Conclusion: We can say, then, that with commercial yogurts (1) some are natural, some are not; (2) it pays to read the information printed on the front *and* back of a yogurt carton; (3) if you just want a milk-and-culture yogurt with absolutely *nothing* added, make your own.

---

* Dr. Ruth White of the FDA in Rockville, Maryland, wrote me: "At the present time, there are no standards of identity which regulate the recipes for yogurt in this country. However, on June 10, 1977 the FDA published Proposed Rules to establish a standard of identity for yogurt. Comments on this proposal are now being accepted by the Office of Hearing Clerk at FDA, and if the proposal is adopted, manufacturers of yogurt will be required to abide by these standards effective the end of 1979."

BUT WHAT DOES IT *REALLY* MEAN?

Or, Words That You Will See Associated With Yogurt

WHAT IT SAYS	WHAT IT MEANS	WHY IT IS ADDED TO COMMERCIAL YOGURT
Preservatives	Chemicals that can be either natural or synthetic. Are always added to Swiss-style commercial yogurt or to fruit. May be added to milk or, more frequently, to fruit portion of yogurt.	Increase shelf life. Prevent yeast and mold growth.
Stabilizers	Chemicals that are often added to commercial yogurt to produce a smoothness in texture and body. May be used with or without the addition of a culture.	Thicken and stabilize.
Preserves	A combination of fruit and sugar that is found in yogurt (the ratio of fruit/sugar is set by the FDA). The fruit and sugar are heated—then, pectin plus an acidulant (i.e., lemon juice) are added. Some fruit preserves with a low pH do not require an acidulant.	Add flavor and color.
Concentrate	A flavor that has been intensified through the removal of water. Can be natural or artificial.	Adds flavor and color.
Puree	A fruit-and-sugar combination found in commercial yogurt. Contains no pieces. (The best purees are made from preserves).	Adds flavor and color.
Pectin	A natural additive. Found in or obtained from fruits or succulent vegetables. Often added to the fruit in commercial yogurt.	Stabilizes the fruit.
Gelatin	A natural additive. A glutinous material obtained from animal tissues by prolonged boiling. May be added in place of culture.	Thickens and stabilizes. Gives a gelatinous texture.
Starch	A natural additive. A white odorless, tasteless granular or powdery complex carbohydrate. Obtained from corn and potatoes.	Thickens and stabilizes.
Cellulose gum	A synthetic gum product. Also called sodium carboxymethyl cellulose. Produced chemically in a lab.	Thickens and stabilizes.
Carrageenan	A natural additive. Extracted from carrageen, or Irish moss (a dark purple branching seaweed that grows off the	Thickens and stabilizes.

34

WHAT IT SAYS	WHAT IT MEANS	WHY IT IS ADDED TO COMMERCIAL YOGURT
Carrageenan (*cont.*)	coasts of Massachusetts and France). Used chiefly as a suspending agent in foods. Also used in fruit preserves.	
Guar gum	A natural additive. A carbohydrate that comes from a drought-tolerant legume grown in India. Its seeds produce a gum which is used as a thickening agent.	Thickens and stabilizes.
Locust and carob bean gum	Both natural additives. Basically a gum that is extracted from the locust bean and carob bean.	Thickens and stabilizes.
Alginate	A natural additive.* Extracted from giant ocean kelp that grow off the shores of California and Japan.	Thickens and stabilizes.
Artificial flavors Artificial colors	Flavors that are derived from aromatic chemicals. Colors that are produced chemically and added to the food.	Add flavor and color.
All natural ingredients. No artificial anything.	Means that the ingredients used in the product originate in nature in the form they are used (i.e., milk, fruit, pectin, lemon juice). Only companies with fast delivery (even their own trucks) from plant to store can operate with a short shelf life and no preservatives. No additives are used.	
Natural flavor on the front; artificial ingredients listed on the back of the carton.	Means that the flavor itself is natural but synthetic color and/or stabilizers have been added. Used as a come-on for yogurt eaters who do not read carefully.	

* I am using the word "natural" in a very loose sense. Seaweed, gum, etc., are natural in that they are not made by man in a lab. However, do they have any place in yogurt? Think about this.

2095046

Fast Start

Dannon suggests this delicious "Breakfast on the Run" for those who want a fast, easy, and nutritious breakfast:

1 egg	1 cup Dannon plain yogurt
2 tablespoons frozen fruit juice concentrate (orange, cranberry, grapefruit, tangerine, grape, or apple)	2 tablespoons wheat germ
	3¼ tablespoons Domino Brownulated sugar
	Dash grated nutmeg

Mix all ingredients in blender or beat thoroughly with electric or rotary beater. Pour into tall glass and serve very cold. Makes one serving.

Gourmet Hint

To get that extra touch of flavor into foods, do this: make a marinade with two cups of Dannon plain yogurt, lemon juice, salt; place chicken parts or meat into it overnight. You can season if you so desire. A truly distinctive taste.

Don't Confuse

Pasteurization is the heating of milk to assure its safety in consumption. Most milk is treated by flash pasteurization at 185 degrees F. for fifteen minutes. *Homogenization* breaks milkfat into particles that do not rise as a layer of cream, giving milk a uniform consistency and distribution of nutrients. Since the fat is broken up, the milk forms a softer, more easily digested curd in the stomach.

Down to Brass Tacks

In a fascinating *Dairy Record* magazine article, "More Americans are Liking Yogurt More and More," the author, Dr. G. G. Quackenbush, tells us that

In the Spring of 1977, a national sample of more than 4,000 people of both sexes, age 13 and over, returned questionnaires on use of various dairy products and attitudes toward these products.

This study came up with some very interesting findings. Here are the highlights:

- Of the 4,000 respondents, nearly one-half claimed that they never eat yogurt.
- Of the heavy yogurt users, 35 percent were female, 26 percent were male.

- The most users were females age seventeen to nineteen.
- The fewest users were males age twenty to twenty-four.
- In every age/sex group, more females were yogurt eaters than males.
- In the United States, more yogurt eaters were found in the Pacific area, followed closely by the Northeastern states.
- Both high- and low-income groups ate slightly more yogurt than middle-income groups.
- Lower-income groups have increased yogurt consumption the most in the last few years; higher-income people have consistently increased consumption.

Flavoring Yogurt

HOW COMMERCIAL YOGURTS ARE FLAVORED

—HOW TO FLAVOR YOUR OWN

The next time you're food shopping, take a minute to look at the range of yogurt flavors in your local supermarket. The variety, especially in suburban areas, is unbelievable. A yogurt fancier can never be bored.

Making a quick check over the vast array of possibilities, I've spotted: pineapple-orange, Dutch apple (Dannon), cherry vanilla, orange crush, peach melba (Colombo), strawberry/banana (Light n' Lively), cinnamon apple (Stay 'n Shape), vanilla bean (Breyers), and finally, flavors so exotic they bore no resemblance to yogurt as we think of it: Hawaiian salad, fruit crunch, date walnut, and peaches n' cream (New Country). A mind-boggling selection. Or, as Bob Finnie, Executive Vice-President of Venture Foods (New Country yogurt), writes: "Strawberry is fine, it appeals to a broad audience, but our objective is to please everyone's taste." The yogurt industry is, undoubtedly, motivated by profits: more flavors, more sales. But the customer benefits, too. With a little testing you can always find the yogurt flavor that's just right for you.

Keep in mind also—there's nothing static about the yogurt business in the United States. Flavors that don't sell vanish from the scene and new ones appear in their place. If you can't find a flavor that appeals to you now, next month may be different.

38

How Yogurt Is Flavored

You probably have a style and flavor you particularly like—and know what to expect when you flip open a carton of your favorite yogurt. But, just to give you an overview, here are the five ways you can buy yogurt at your local supermarket or health food store.

No fruit but flavored. This means no "chunks" or "pieces" of fruit, just a pleasant-tasting yogurt with a vanilla, lemon, or coffee flavor. I particularly like Dannon's vanilla-flavored yogurt. It's deliciously smooth on the tongue, mild-tasting, lightly flavored, and only 200 calories (versus the higher-caloried sundae styles).

Fruit-on-the-bottom. Or, as it's often called, "sundae-style" yogurt. The beauty of this type, with the fruit preserves or purees on the bottom of the carton and a plain yogurt on top, is that you can control the amount of fruit (let's just say calories) you want to eat. If stirring or mixing this form of yogurt seems tedious to you, just turn the entire carton upside down into a shallow soup bowl. The yogurt will be on the bottom and the fruit will be on top. The whole thing looks, I think, much more festive and special than yogurt-in-the-carton.

Fruit-on-the-bottom, flavored on top. This is also called Western-style yogurt. With this variety you get preserves on the bottom and flavored yogurt on top. You can eat "as is" from the carton or stir up the contents—whichever you prefer.

Fruit blended throughout. This is also referred to as blended, Swiss- or French-style yogurt. Here the work is done for you. Bits or pieces of fruit are blended throughout plain or flavored yogurt. There is one aspect of a premixed yogurt of which I feel you should be aware: all Swiss-style yogurts have either one or more additives to keep the fruit evenly distributed in the carton.

No fruit, no flavorings. The yogurt for purists, and for those who want to do it themselves. In short, you eat as-is or add your own fruits and flavorings. This version, also known as unflavored, natural, plain, or basic-style yogurt, has been around for hundreds of years and is how the ancients ate their yogurt. It's not a favorite of mine, but many yogurt eaters love it this way.

Don't Confuse: Puree and Preserves

A puree is a thick liquid. Preserves are bits of fruit cooked in a heavy syrup.

Preserves and Sugar

How much sugar you will eat if you have preserves in your yogurt is difficult to say. According to the Food and Drug Administration, "the amount of sugar will vary" from one yogurt manufacturer to another. The FDA also states that "some add preserves while others add sweetened fruit."

And what exactly is used to sweeten yogurt? Again, according to the FDA, yogurt makers may use "cane sugar, corn sugar, honey and sugar beet" (this is not a total list). But how much? They cite an example which, at least, will give you a general idea: "A recent report (March 1978) by Consumers Reports showed 13.7% sugar on a total sugar analysis of blueberry lowfat yogurt."

I received another letter that was more or less in agreement with this 13.7 percent figure. Alan Kligerman of SugarLo wrote me:

The standard of identity* for preserves indicates that as much as 60% of the fruit preserves is cane/corn sugar.

This means that in a regular fruit yogurt where the fruit content is approximately 20% of the cup, then the sugar content of the final product is going to be 60% of 20% or *12% of the entire cup.* [The italics are mine.]

In conclusion, then, I think we can say that the sugar in yogurt differs from one maker to another, and just exactly how much sugar one is eating is difficult to say.

The Most Popular Flavor

My friend Jackie has it all. She makes a whopping five figures as a Madison Avenue copywriter, turns up regularly in the latest St. Laurent, and has a husband who looks like a young Rock Hudson.

Four days out of five, unless she's roped into lunching with a client, Jackie sails through twelve-to-two with nary a thought about food. Lunch, to Jackie, is for mad forays into Bloomie's and Bendel's with wind-up stops at Tiffany's.

On Thursdays, she meets her husband, Rick, for lunch, and the two of them make a dash for a counter seat at Oscar's in the Waldorf Astoria. Once there, neither looks at the menu because they both

* Keep in mind that there is no standard of identity (as yet) for yogurt. However, there *is* one for preserves.

know what they want: yogurt. Or, more specifically, strawberry yogurt with a side order of melba toast and black coffee.

Jackie and Rick may be upper-income New Yorkers but they are like middle America in their choice of yogurt flavors. More people, from oldsters to teenagers, prefer strawberry yogurt than any other flavor. After this, it's a toss-up between blueberry, raspberry, and natural.

A word about price. If you do decide to stop by the Waldorf for your strawberry yogurt keep in mind that it's triple the price of your local A&P. But let's not fool ourselves. Supermarkets, to use an old cliché, are a dime a dozen. There's only one Waldorf Astoria.

Ways to Flavor Plain Yogurt

One afternoon several years ago, when I was working for one of the "top ten" New York advertising agencies, a group of about twenty women trooped through the office and headed for one of the large conference rooms. Since we were all a rather nosey bunch, we asked one of the account executives trailing along behind who the ladies were. "Oh," he said proudly, "those are *all* plain yogurt eaters. They're here for a focus group."* "Plain yogurt eaters," we chorused. All of us found it hard to believe that there were that many plain yogurt eaters in all of New York State, let alone on the fifth floor of our agency that afternoon.

Now, if you like the taste of plain yogurt, with nothing added, you can skip this section. However, if you don't, and you've happened to buy unflavored yogurt by mistake (as I did once), or if your Aunt Essie has just given you a new Salton yogurt maker for your fifth wedding anniversary, do read on.

Taste aside, plain yogurt has one big plus—there are only 150 calories in an eight-ounce serving. This fact alone means you can add a great variety of toppings, flavorings, or fruits and, unless you add with a lavish hand, the calorie count will still remain fairly low. Here's a partial list just to give you a few ideas:

* Big companies have their advertising agencies hold focus groups to determine what the consumer really thinks of their product. Generally, a moderator leads the group in a lively discussion, while the agency and company people observe the goings-on from behind a two-way mirror. There is nothing shady about this. The group is paid for their time, and they know why they were chosen (product users). More often than not, their answers are very straightforward and frighteningly honest.

Toppings	*Fruits*
Cinnamon	Fresh, whole:
Nutmeg	Raspberries
Brown sugar	Strawberries
Toasted coconut	Blueberries
Chopped walnuts	Fresh, sliced:
Sesame seeds	Apricots
Granola	Peaches
Wheat germ	Bananas
Grated orange rind	Pineapple
Maple syrup	Pears
Honey	

Flavorings

Dannon suggests flavoring one cup of plain yogurt with:

A dash of lemon juice and a teaspoon of sugar

1 teaspoon of chocolate syrup

1 tablespoon of liqueur (Curaçao, crème de menthe, or crème de cacao)

Making Your Own Yogurt

WHAT INGREDIENTS AND EQUIPMENT TO

USE PLUS STEP-BY-STEP DIRECTIONS

Why make yogurt at home? The four best reasons I can give you are (1) anyone can do it, unlike Coca-Cola,* there is no "secret formula" for yogurt; (2) your yogurt will be fresh; (3) you will know what is in your yogurt; and (4) you will save money.† However, I must confess that I don't make my own yogurt. Why? Quite simply, I'm a little lazy. It's just easier for me to dash to the supermarket and grab a few cartons.

Now, if I'm bent on converting you (and me) to making homemade yogurt, how do we start? First of all, there are two ways you can make your yogurt—with a yogurt maker (see page 51) or without. I believe you'll find that using a yogurt maker is easier, especially with one of the new electric ones. However, we'll get into that later. For now, let's start right at the beginning and discuss an area that applies to both methods. This is (1) types of milk you can use and (2) starter cultures you can use.

* The Coca-Cola Company says the secret formula for Coke's flavoring ingredients is kept in a bank vault, which can be opened only by a vote of the board of directors. What's in that Coke bottle? To start with, it apparently contains 99.8 percent water and sugar. After that, the mystery begins. (*New York Times,* April 9, 1978)

† One cup of homemade yogurt costs about ten to fourteen cents versus thirty-three to forty-five cents for store-bought yogurt. One cup of homemade skim milk yogurt is 85 calories; whole milk, 170.

Milk: What You Can Use

Frankly, when it comes to the type of milk needed to make yogurt, you can use just about anything. So, if you're stranded on a small island off the coast of Maine sometime—and food is running low—you can always make yogurt (provided you have the essentials, of course).

The milk one can use includes diluted condensed or evaporated milk; whole, lowfat, or skim (which can be raw, pasteurized, or homogenized). You can even try soy, goat's, or powdered whole or skim milk.

If you use whole or skim milk, add one-third cup dry milk per quart for a firmer yogurt. If you use evaporated skim milk, add one-third cup dry milk per quart for a firmer yogurt. If you use evaporated whole milk, add two cups of lukewarm water to two cups of evaporated milk. If you prefer an even richer yogurt, substitute plain milk for water.

Starter: What You Can Use

The two basic ingredients for all yogurts are milk plus the "starter," or bacteria, that is needed to change the milk into yogurt. When you make your own yogurt at home there are three ways you can "start" your yogurt: (1) with a dry yogurt culture, (2) with commercial yogurt, and (3) with your own yogurt.

The International Yogurt Company in Los Angeles has the "Improved Dry Original Bulgarian Yogurt Culture" which can be purchased in most health food stores in the United States.*

You use this culture only once—for your first batch. Then you can save a part of each batch for the next one. This can continue for one month (fresh batches twice a week). After a month the potency of the culture is weakened and you will have to renew your original culture. *Important:* Your culture may still work after a month but your yogurt will not be as effective in the body. (In fact, one large commercial yogurt company writes, "merely taking some plain yogurt, using it as a starter, and then transferring remainders day after day, is no guarantee that you will end up with viable yogurt. Your product may look and taste quite pleasant but too often it is not yogurt, just sour milk or clabber.")

* I bought mine at the Good Earth and at Brownies in New York. One envelope, or according to International, a full month's supply, is $2.50.

Remember also that it will require more time to incubate your first batch of yogurt from the dry culture (two and a half to ten hours) than it will take with subsequent batches (two to three hours).

In describing their product, International says, "Yogurt culture in powdered form is easy to handle, does not spoil, and requires no refrigeration." I noticed, however, that the Good Earth health food store keeps this product in their refrigerator. I may be overly careful, but I keep mine in the refrigerator, too.

Now, if you use a commercial yogurt as your starter, make sure it's *fresh*. In other words, buy a carton of plain yogurt with no preservatives that has an expiration date as far in the future as possible (preferably a week and a half to two weeks). You do this because you want to be sure the bacteria in the yogurt is *active*.

The same "freshness" rule applies when you're using yogurt you've made yourself—make sure it's not more than five to seven days old, and save at least a quarter of a cup as starter for your next batch of yogurt. Better to have a little too much than not enough.

Mild or Strong

Preference for a certain "taste" in yogurt is purely subjective. I may believe one type of yogurt is very tasty, while you think it's dreadful. This, of course, applies to other foods as well. My husband can eat a sandwich of sliced raw onion on buttered rye toast. Just thinking about this makes me ill. On the other hand, I once saw Peter turn positively green as he watched me eat curried goat in a beachfront restaurant at Doctor's Cave in Montego Bay, Jamaica. As I said before, there is no rational way to explain individual taste.

So, how "mild or tart" you want your homemade yogurt to be is entirely up to you. There are two main points you should keep in mind: (1) too much stirring will result in a tart yogurt, and (2) a long incubation period will result in a tart yogurt.

Stir gently if you do not want a sour, liquid yogurt. When you blend the yogurt starter into the milk, stir in a small amount first. Then add the remaining starter slowly—stirring, not beating—until all the starter is completely mixed in.

Incubate for a short period of time for mild yogurt, longer for stronger, sharper, tarter, or sourer yogurt. A mild yogurt can be obtained by placing your yogurt in the refrigerator just as soon as it begins to thicken (this means even if it's only "slightly" thick). For example, if you use a yogurt maker it will take five hours for a mild, delicate yogurt and up to ten hours for a thicker, tangier yogurt.

Thick or Thin

Keep in mind: if you have a richer milk, you'll have a thicker and richer yogurt. In fact, if you definitely want a yogurt with "body" add two tablespoons to one-third cup of powdered skim milk to each quart of "liquid" milk. Do this before bringing the milk to a boil. Let the milk simmer about fifteen minutes to evaporate part of the moisture. Result: a thicker yogurt.

Temperature

Making your own yogurt at home is simple to explain, but not that easy to do. The critical step in yogurt making—if you are not using an automatic yogurt maker—is keeping the yogurt at the correct temperature as it sets.

You *must* be sure to incubate your yogurt at the proper temperature. This is lukewarm, or 110 to 115 degrees F. (41 to 46 degrees C.). This heat is the reason why the yogurt culture reacts on the milk and converts it into yogurt.

Remember: if the temperature goes above 120 degrees F. it will weaken or kill the culture. On the other hand, if the temperature drops below 95 degrees F., the culture will again fail to react and no yogurt will develop.

Incubation Time

The length of time that your yogurt spends incubating is as important as keeping your yogurt at the right temperature. This time can go from three hours to ten hours depending on the (1) milk, (2) starter, (3) equipment—which includes the method of holding the temperature—and (4) weather.

As a general rule, if your incubation temperature is lower, you will have to incubate longer. And the reverse is true: if your incubation temperature is higher, the length of time needed to thicken the milk is shorter.

A high incubation temperature and a longer than necessary incubation may result in a "watery whey" forming on top of your yogurt. There is nothing wrong with this yogurt—it just doesn't look that

46

appetizing. You can pour the whey off or stir it back into the yogurt (there will be no change in taste—your yogurt will just be more liquid). For your next batch, just reduce your incubation time.

And remember, if your yogurt is wheyed off or has not thickened enough, *don't throw it out.* It will be perfectly all right as starter for your next batch of yogurt.

How to Make Your Own Yogurt

Step I

Heat a quart (4 cups) of milk to boiling (212 degrees F.) or just below (180 degrees F.) for one minute. This preheating is to wipe out competing strains of bacteria. Note: Add 1 to 2 tablespoons of skim milk powder for a more solid yogurt.

Step II

Cool the milk to 115 degrees F. You can do this by pouring the milk into a cold crockery bowl (not metal) or by placing the pot in which you have heated the milk into a bowl of cold water. You may even put the milk into the refrigerator for a short period of time.

You can test the temperature of the milk by using a candy or dairy thermometer.* Or you can put a drop of milk on the inside of your wrist. (Greek housewives test with the second joint of the little finger.) The milk should feel warm but not hot.

Step III

Put two tablespoons of plain, fresh yogurt or dry yogurt culture (follow instructions on the package) into the lukewarm milk. Stir gently, but well, with a wooden spoon. Make sure the culture is thoroughly mixed into the milk.

Step IV

Pour the inoculated milk into:
a) the containers that come with your yogurt maker (follow the instructions that come with your yogurt maker from here on)
or b) clean, sterilized cups, jars, or glasses. Place these containers in a large pot. Fill the pot with warm water—up to two-thirds (or necks) of the containers (can be with or without lids). Put

---

* If you use a candy thermometer make sure it registers low enough for yogurt.

a tight lid on the pot. Wrap a heavy towel around the pot and set aside (away from drafts). Or place the pot (without towels) over the pilot light of your gas range. Or put the pot in your oven—turn oven up to 275 degrees F., then turn off (it may be difficult to maintain the correct temperature with this "oven" method).

or c) a large crockery bowl. Cover the bowl with a dry dish towel and put the bowl-cover on. Then wrap all of this in two heavy towels (or a small blanket or several thicknesses of newspapers).

or d) a Thermos bottle (don't put the cover on tightly) and leave in a warm place

or e) cups, jars, or glasses that are placed in an electric frying pan. Set the temperature at 110 to 115 degrees F.

Step V

Whatever method you choose you *must* keep the temperature right (115 degrees F. for four to eight hours) so check it fairly often.

Step VI

Look at your yogurt. If it is thick—about the consistency of heavy cream—it is ready. (Yogurt should cohere if container is tilted slightly.) If it is liquid or watery, incubate longer.

Step VII

When your yogurt is ready put it in your refrigerator for three to nine hours or until it is the consistency you want. Your yogurt will continue to thicken as it cools in the refrigerator.

Step VIII

Eat your yogurt plain or add flavorings and fruits (see page 41). Stir in fruits or flavorings gently for a custardlike consistency, vigorously for a more liquid yogurt.

Why Your Yogurt Failed

The International Yogurt Company has drawn up this checklist for you to use when you find that your homemade yogurt hasn't come out "quite right." I think it's very comprehensive and I've made only minor editing changes for this book.

When the Milk Hasn't Thickened

- The incubation was made at a temperature that was too low.
- The jars containing the milk and culture were left standing in a cool place. Result: too rapid cooling and loss of heat that's needed to incubate yogurt.
- The culture was not put into the milk. (Yes, it happens.)
- The incubation time may have been too short.
- The starter culture was ruined because it was added to hot milk. The milk should have cooled to lukewarm.
- The starter was not mixed well enough with the milk.
- The thermometer used was not functioning properly.
- The soap or cleaning compound used in washing the jars and pots was not completely rinsed off. This can keep the culture from thickening the milk properly.
- Starter was old. Get fresh yogurt or powdered culture. (If you use a commercial yogurt it must be fresh, *plain* yogurt with an *active* culture.)

When Your Yogurt Is Watery (Wheyed Off)

- The incubation temperature was too high.
- The incubation period was too long.
- Too much starter was used.

When Your Yogurt Is Not Firm Enough or Is Lumpy

- The incubation temperature was too low.
- The yogurt was not incubated long enough (particularly if old yogurt culture was used).
- Not enough starter was used to culture the milk. Two tablespoons for one quart of milk are sufficient if the starter is fairly fresh. Use more if starter is older than four days.
- The milk was not heated to boil or near-boil.
- The yogurt was disturbed by shaking, tilting, or rattling during incubation.

Apron Strings

Elia Kazan, the famous director, was in Athens recently for a weeklong festival of his films. Speaking mostly in English to a crowded theater full of Greek movie buffs, Kazan (born Elias Kazanjoglou) told this story about his Anatolian Greek grandmother.

"The first thing she did on emigrating to the United States and entering the door of her new home in New York was to make a pot of yogurt," Mr. Kazan said. "And, because we ate yogurt three times a day . . . I tasted my ties with the old country at every meal." (*New York Times*, April 29, 1978)

Yogurt Makers

I have often read that the average American family doesn't realize what, or how much, it owns. Peter and I are no exception.

Several months ago, when we were filling out homeowner's insurance forms, I was amazed to learn that, in addition to five typewriters (two IBM electric, three manual), and four TV sets (three are broken), we had also managed to acquire, in the kitchen alone, over an eight-year period one Norelco coffee maker, a Waring blender, an Acme juicerator, a GE Toast-R-Oven, a Sunbeam mixer, a Salton automatic egg cooker/poacher, and a Rival electric can opener. Now, I ask you—do two people really *need* all this for two meals (lunch is always eaten out) a day?

Of course, I realize this is not the point. No one really *needs* any of these things—they just make life a little easier. The same reason could be given for owning an automatic yogurt maker. You don't *need* it, but don't say no to yourself if you really want one or if your mother-in-law decides to buy you one for Christmas. As far as small appliances are concerned, a yogurt maker is relatively inexpensive— the average price is between ten and twenty dollars, depending on where you buy it. (I saw one of the more popular models in a Fifth Avenue department store. Then I came across it later on in a discount place. The difference in price? $10.00.)

If you eat at least one carton of yogurt a day, a yogurt maker is a wise purchase. The electric ones are very inexpensive to operate and will take the guesswork out of your yogurt making.

Now, we are going to discuss seven yogurt makers. I wrote to the presidents of the firms making these products and asked them to send me their *best* models. They sent:

1. Salton "Thermostatically Controlled" Yogurt Maker
2. Salton Family Size Yogurt and Yo-Cheese Maker
3. Contempra "Natural" Yogurt Maker
4. Contempra Big Batch Electric Yogurt Maker
5. The International Yogurt Company "Yogotherm"
6. Hamilton Beach Culture Center
7. West Bend Electric Yogurt Maker

Salton "Thermostatically Controlled" Yogurt Maker

DESCRIPTION

- five dishwasher-safe eight-ounce opaque glass jars (3″ diameter, 3½″ high) with plastic lids
- a gray-and-yellow electrically heated base maintains a constant temperature. Base holds jars.
- a yellow Time-Out dial on top of the clear plastic cover which goes over the jars. You set this at "1, 2, 3, 4," etc., to remind yourself when the yogurt is ready. Note: Nothing "rings" or "buzzes" with this timer—it is simply a dial you look at.
- a yellow plastic spoon-thermometer that does *exactly* what the name says. First, you use it as a thermometer to test the temperature of the milk. When the temperature reaches "add starter," which is marked very clearly on the spoon-thermometer, you know the boiled milk has cooled to the correct temperature for adding the starter. Then you use the "spoon" to measure out *exactly* the amount of starter you need. Nothing is left to guesswork.
- economical to operate, 25 watts, 120 volts, UL listed.

SIZE

16″ long x 3¾″ wide x 4¾″ high

FROM

Salton, Inc.
1260 Zerega Avenue $13.50
Bronx, NY 10462   Model GM-5

Additional jars available for $6.50 per set of five.

Instructions for Making Yogurt

Ingredients

1. One quart of whole or skim milk. Or skim milk made from non-fat dry milk (make according to directions on the package but add an extra one-third cup of dry milk).
   Note: Add one-third cup of dry milk to the whole or skim milk for a creamier yogurt.
2. One heaping tablespoon of plain, unpasteurized yogurt or yogurt you've made yourself, or one envelope of dried yogurt culture.

Procedure

1. Put milk in pot and heat until it boils.
2. Cool milk until it reaches "add starter" level on the spoon-thermometer.
3. Add yogurt starter to milk in pot. Stir well.
4. Pour milk into jars and put lids on. Put the jars into yogurt maker.
5. Put on plastic cover.
6. Plug in the electric cord.
7. Set the Time-Out dial for ten hours later.
8. After ten hours, remove the jars and put them in the refrigerator for three to four hours.
9. Eat plain, or add your own fruits or flavorings (see page 41).

My Test

The above instructions are from Salton. When I tested the Salton Yogurt Maker I followed these directions—with some changes. I did *not* boil the milk. Instead, I heated the milk in a double boiler to just below the boiling point (tiny bubbles form around the edge where the milk meets the pot). For test purposes I used four cups of lowfat milk, one-third cup of dried milk (nonfat Carnation, bought at the local supermarket), and one tablespoon of plain commercial yogurt. In my first test, I incubated the yogurt for ten hours—too tart. The second test had an eight-hour incubation period and the results were excellent. Tip: when adding the starter I put the yogurt in a cup, added two tablespoons of warm milk—stirred both together—and *then* poured the whole thing back into the milk. This will prevent lumps from forming (as sometimes happens when cold yogurt is put directly into warm milk).

Salton Family Size Yogurt Maker with Yo-Cheese Maker

· five dishwasher-safe sixteen-ounce opaque glass jars (3¾″ diameter, 4¾″ high) with white plastic lids.
· a yellow-and-white "thermostatically controlled" base maintains a constant temperature. Base holds jars.
· a white Time-Out dial reminds you when yogurt is ready. This is not automatic; no buzzing or ringing.
· a white spoon-thermometer tests milk and measures yogurt starter.
· gives you a total of 2 liters (2.1 qt.) of yogurt.
· clear plastic cover included.
· 40 watts, 120 volts, UL listed.

SIZE

20″ long x 4¼″ wide x 7½″ high (at peak point).

FROM

Salton, Inc.
1260 Zerega Avenue $19.95
Bronx, NY 10462   Model GM-10

Additional jars available for $8.95 per set of five. If not in your local stores, order from Salton for $10.70 (includes handling and postage). Prices are suggested retail and subject to change without notice.

You can call Salton toll free at 800-221-8794 from anywhere in the continental United States if you have any problems with your yogurt maker (New York State, call 212-931-3907 collect). Look on the bottom of your yogurt maker and get your model and lot number *before* you call.

INSTRUCTIONS FOR MAKING YOGURT

Equipment
Yogurt maker, pot to heat milk, spoon thermometer.

54

Ingredients

1. Two quarts of whole skim, or skim milk made from nonfat dry milk (follow instructions on carton but use one-third cup more than directed per quart).
2. Two heaping tablespoons of plain, unpasteurized yogurt or two packages of dried yogurt culture.

Procedure

1. Heat milk in pot until it reaches "add starter" temperature. If you are using milk that has not been pasteurized, boil, then cool.
   2. Spoon two heaping tablespoons of starter into one yogurt jar.
   3. Add one-half cup heated milk and stir.
   4. Pour this mixture into pot of heated milk. Stir well.
   5. Pour milk into jars, put lids on, place in yogurt maker.
   6. Put plastic cover on, plug in.
   7. Set Time-Out dial for ten hours later.
   8. Remove jars, put them in refrigerator. Allow yogurt to cool four hours.

My Test

The above instructions are from Salton. When I tested the Salton Family Size Yogurt Maker I followed these instructions—with a few minor changes. I used eight cups of lowfat milk, two-thirds cup of dried milk, and two tablespoons of plain commercial yogurt for starter. I heated the milk in the top of a double boiler to just below the boiling point. I set the Time-Out dial for eight, not ten, hours and the results were excellent.

Salton Yo-Cheese Maker

Description

· included with every Salton Family Size Yogurt Maker
· lets you make a light, nourishing, easy-to-digest, and spreadable "cream" cheese from yogurt
· the white plastic Yo-Cheese Maker is flat. To assemble: press one end down until you hear a snap. Then press the other end down. You now have a stand with a round opening in the top. The cheese bag hangs through this opening.

Size

7¼" high x 7" wide

FROM

Salton, Inc.
1260 Zerega Avenue
Bronx, NY 10462   Model YO-1

Additional Yo-Cheese Makers are available at most stores in sets of two for $5.95. Or you can order directly from Salton, for $7.25 (includes postage and handling).

Additional Yo-Cheese bags are available from Salton at two for $1.95 post-paid in the United States. All of the above are suggested retail prices subject to change without notice.

INSTRUCTIONS FOR MAKING YOGURT CHEESE

Equipment
One Yo-Cheese Maker with bag, spoon, bowl.

Ingredients
Two cups or one 16-ounce jar from the Salton Family Size Yogurt Maker of chilled yogurt.

Procedure
1. Place the Yo-Cheese Maker in a bowl.
2. Spoon yogurt into the cheese bag.
3. Cover to keep clean.
4. Leave for twelve to twenty-four hours.
5. Take cheese from bag and place in a small bowl.
6. Mix with a fork to blend evenly and salt to taste.
7. YIELD: approximately one-half cup of yogurt cheese.
8. Chill to serve.

MY TEST

The above instructions are from Salton. After trying this little gizmo there's one thing I can say for sure—it's fun. And easy. I put a Pyrex pie plate under the cheese maker to hold the water that drained from the yogurt. (I was surprised at the amount of water that drained out—quite a lot.) After eight hours I felt that the bulk of the water had drained from the yogurt so I set the cheese maker and the pie plate in the refrigerator and let the yogurt drain for another eight hours. Result? Absolutely delicious yogurt cheese. I was really quite proud of myself!

FROM SALTON: RECIPES USING YOGURT CHEESE

Herbed Yogurt Cheese Dip

½ cup yogurt cheese
½ cup sliced almonds
1 tablespoon lemon juice
1 tablespoon Dijon mustard
2 teaspoons onion powder
1 teaspoon Worcestershire
    sauce
1 teaspoon dried basil
1 teaspoon parsley, chopped

1. Slightly crush sliced almonds, combine with cheese, lemon juice, mustard, onion powder, Worcestershire sauce, and basil. Chill.

2. When ready to use, sprinkle with parsley. Serve with raw vegetable sticks.

YIELD: approximately 1 cup

Blue Cheese Dip

¼ cup blue cheese
1 cup yogurt cheese
3 tablespoons mayonnaise
Few drops Tabasco sauce

1. Mash the blue cheese; add yogurt cheese and mayonnaise. Mix until smooth.

2. Add a few drops of Tabasco. Chill. Serve with raw vegetables.

YIELD: approximately 1¼ cups

Water Chestnut Spread

½ cup yogurt cheese
1 tablespoon onion soup mix
4 whole water chestnuts

1. Mix yogurt cheese with dried onion soup mix. Chop water chestnuts and add to cheese mixture.

2. Chill and serve spread on crackers or melba rounds.

YIELD: approximately ½ cup

Herring Spread

½ cup yogurt cheese
¼ cup herring tidbits, drained
1 tablespoon lemon juice

1. Put all ingredients in electric blender on medium speed; blend until smooth.

(cont'd)

2. Turn into a decorative bowl and serve on crackers or spread on toast.

YIELD: approximately 1 cup

Anchovy Spread

8 anchovy fillets
1 tablespoon lemon juice
½ cup yogurt cheese
2 tablespoons Piccalilli relish

1. Macerate or mash anchovy fillets with lemon juice. Mix with yogurt cheese and Piccalilli relish.
2. Chill and serve with crackers. Note: Heinz Piccalilli relish can be found in most supermarkets. Consists of red and green peppers, vinegar, onions, sugar, mustard seed, green tomatoes, salt, celery seed, allspice, and cinnamon.

YIELD: approximately ¾ cup

Curry-Cheese Loaf

½ cup yogurt cheese
4 ounces Cheddar cheese food
1 teaspoon onion powder
1 teaspoon garlic powder
1 tablespoon curry powder
½ cup walnuts, chopped

1. Mash yogurt cheese and Cheddar cheese food until blended. Add onion, garlic, and curry powders. Chill.
2. Put chopped walnuts on 12-inch piece of aluminum foil. Place chilled cheese mixture on nuts.
3. Shape into loaf and cover completely with nuts. Chill wrapped in foil. Serve with crackers.

Walnut Sandwich Filling

¼ cup walnuts, chopped
1 teaspoon wheat germ
Dash of cinnamon
½ cup yogurt cheese

1. Add walnuts, wheat germ, and cinnamon to yogurt cheese. Mix well and spread on bread.
2. Sprinkle with cinnamon. Raisin bread makes a delicious sandwich with this healthful filling.

YIELD: 4 sandwiches

Pineapple Sandwich Filling

¼ cup crushed pineapple,
   drained

½ cup yogurt cheese
1 teaspoon sesame seeds

1. Add pineapple to yogurt cheese. Mix well.
2. Spread on bread. Sprinkle with sesame seeds. Particularly good on raisin bread.

YIELD: 4 sandwiches

Strawberry Parfait

1 cup yogurt cheese
1 cup fresh strawberries,
   crushed

3 tablespoons honey

1. Have yogurt cheese at room temperature. Thoroughly mix all ingredients. Chill.
2. Serve in parfait glass or ramekin with a garnish of a whole berry or sliced berries.

YIELD: 6 servings

No-Bake Jamaica Cheesecake

Filling:

2 packages unflavored gelatin
1½ cups sugar
2 eggs, separated
1 cup skim milk
1 teaspoon lemon juice
1 tablespoon rum extract
3 cups yogurt cheese

Crust:

12 (2½-inch) graham crackers,
   crumbed
2 tablespoons butter, melted
¼ teaspoon cinnamon
¼ teaspoon nutmeg
¼ cup chopped nuts

To Prepare Filling:

1. In top of double boiler mix gelatin and 1 cup of sugar; add beaten egg yolks and milk, cooking over boiling water until mixture is slightly thickened (10 minutes).
2. Remove from heat; add lemon juice and rum. When mixture is cool add yogurt cheese and mix until blended.
3. In a separate bowl beat egg whites, slowly adding ½ cup

(cont'd)

sugar, until stiff. Fold into cheese mixture. Chill while preparing crust.

To Prepare Crust:

1. Mix crumbed crackers, butter, cinnamon, nutmeg, and chopped nuts.

2. Grease 9-inch springform pan lightly and dust crumb mixture on sides and press firmly on bottom. Put aside ¼ cup of mixture to use as garnish. Note: Springform pans have removable sides. Can be found in any hardware store.

3. Pour chilled cheese mixture into pan and sprinkle crumbs on top. Chill overnight in refrigerator.

YIELD: 12 servings

Sunny Italy Cheese Pie

Crust:

8 (2½-in.) graham crackers, crumbed
1½ tablespoons butter, melted
¼ cup walnuts, chopped fine

Filling:

1½ cups yogurt cheese
¼ cup flour
½ teaspoon orange extract
¼ teaspoon anise extract
Dash of salt
3 large eggs
1 cup sugar

To Prepare Crust:

1. Mix together crackers, butter, and walnuts. Lightly grease sides and bottom of 8-inch pie pan.

2. Preheat oven to 375 degrees F.

3. Press mixture on bottom and dust lightly on sides. Bake 5 minutes. Cool. Lower oven temperature to 350 degrees F.

To Prepare Filling:

1. With a fork mix together yogurt cheese, flour, extracts, and salt. Set aside.

2. In a mixer, beat eggs until foamy. Add sugar slowly until mixture is very thick.

3. Add cheese mixture to eggs in mixer and beat until blended. Pour into cooled crust and place pie pan in middle shelf of oven for 60 minutes.

4. Top usually cracks when cool. Dust with 2 tablespoons of confectioners sugar before serving.

Yɪᴇʟᴅ: 10 servings

Contempra Natural Yogurt Maker™ with Automatic Timer

Dᴇsᴄʀɪᴘᴛɪᴏɴ

- six 8-ounce clear glass jars (2⅞″ diameter, 3¼″ high) with white plastic lids. Glasses are dishwasher-safe; lids are not.
- modern-design electrically heated base, in yellow or white, holds the jars. A clear plastic cover goes over the jars.
- an automatic timer is on the front of the base. You can set the timer for the number of hours you want your yogurt to incubate (the timer goes from one to ten hours) and then the yogurt maker shuts itself off *automatically*.
- a short cord reduces the hazard of tripping or tangling; an extension cord may be added.

Sɪᴢᴇ

11″ long x 9¼″ wide x 5″ high

Fʀᴏᴍ

Natural Yogurt Maker™
c/o Contempra Industries, Inc.
371 Essex Road, Tinton Falls $22.50
(Neptune P.O.), NJ 07753   Model NYM-2T

To order an extra set of six jars with lids write above address (model NJ-6, $6.95—New Jersey residents add 5 percent sales tax).

Note: If the plastic dust cover is cracked or broken, your yogurt maker can still operate effectively. However, incubation time may be slightly longer than normal. Write to the above address on how to order a new cover.

In Canada: Braun Electric Canada Ltd., 3269 American Drive, Mississauga, Ontario L4V 1B9 (add provincial sales tax where applicable).

Other Models

The yogurt maker described is Contempra's deluxe model. They also have two other models which cost less and do not have automatic timers. Model NYM-1 has, like Salton, a "takeout" dial to remind you when the yogurt is ready to be put in the refrigerator. Model TY-66 does not have a clear plastic cover or takeout dial.

Instructions for Making Yogurt

Equipment
Yogurt maker, milk, plain yogurt for starter, pot for heating milk, tablespoon for stirring, measuring cup.

Ingredients
Four to five cups of whole, skim, or dry milk. (For skim milk add one-third cup dry milk powder. For dry milk, mix according to instructions on box, and add an extra one-third cup dry milk powder.)

Procedure
1. Plug yogurt maker into any 120-volt AC outlet.
2. Heat milk until it just begins to boil.
3. Remove milk from heat and cool to lukewarm (110 to 115 degrees F.).
4. Stir starter yogurt thoroughly. Put two-thirds tablespoon into each eight-ounce jar. (If dried starter is used, follow instructions on packet.)
5. Pour lukewarm milk into each jar and stir gently, until smooth, to distribute starter.
6. Put lids on jars. Set jars in the yogurt maker and put clear plastic cover over them.
7. Set timer (five to ten hours).
8. Remove plug from outlet.
9. Refrigerate yogurt for at least three hours before eating.
10. Save some of your newly made yogurt as starter for your next batch of yogurt. (Do not flavor starter.)

My Test

The above instructions are from Contempra. For test purposes I used four cups of lowfat milk, one-third cup of dried milk, and one tablespoon of plain commercial yogurt for starter. After heating the milk in a double boiler to just below the boiling point, I cooled it to 114 degrees F. I changed Contempra's steps 4 and 5 completely— this is extra work. I simply put one tablespoon of yogurt starter in one jar, added two tablespoons of warm milk, and stirred both together. Then I poured this mixture back into the milk in the pot. I set the timer for six hours later and the results were excellent. Note: Salton provides a thermometer; Contempra does not. I used a Taylor "Roast & Yeast" thermometer that worked perfectly. I bought it at The Professional Kitchen, 18 Cooper Square, New York, NY 10003 (phone: 212-254-9000) for $4.40 plus tax.

Contempra Big Batch™ Electric Yogurt Maker

DESCRIPTION

- two-quart capacity yellow-and-white plastic container with screw-off lid.
- an orange-colored nonautomatic Flavor Guide Reminder Dial is set into the lid. You simply turn the dial to a number (your starting time) and then look at the Flavor Guide. This tells you how long it will be before the yogurt is ready for refrigeration: mild, five to seven; tangy, seven to nine; and tart, nine to eleven hours.
- electric cord is removable; entire unit can be easily stored in refrigerator.
- easy to clean; electrical base must not be immersed in water.
- convenient and economical; 7 watts, 120 volts.

SIZE

11″ high, 5¼″ diameter

FROM

Contempra Industries, Inc.
371 Essex Road
Tinton Falls, NJ 07753 $17.95
201-922-9090   Model BB-2

Instructions for Making Yogurt

Equipment

Yogurt maker, milk, plain yogurt for starter, saucepan for heating milk, measuring cup, large spoon for stirring.

Ingredients

Two quarts of milk and one-half cup of starter (a half batch is one quart of milk, one-quarter cup of starter; timing will be about the same). Use whole, skim, or lowfat milk; evaporated milk; or reconstituted instant nonfat dry milk powder.

a) to use evaporated milk, add an equal amount of water
b) to use powdered milk, reconstitute according to package directions
c) for a firmer, creamier yogurt with any type of milk (particularly skim or lowfat), add one-third cup of nonfat dry milk powder per quart before heating.

Procedure

1. Heat milk in saucepan until it just begins to boil.
2. Remove milk from heat and cool to lukewarm. Test on your wrist; the milk should not feel hot.
3. Add one-half cup of yogurt starter to milk. Stir well.
4. Pour into yogurt maker and twist lid closed. Plug in and set Flavor Guide Reminder.
5. Disconnect at proper time. You may gently remove lid to check consistency. Note: Your yogurt will become firmer after chilling. Allow at least three hours in refrigerator before serving.

My Test

The above instructions are from Contempra. For testing purposes I used four cups of lowfat milk, one-third cup of dried nonfat Carnation milk, and one tablespoon of plain commercial yogurt. I changed Contempra's step 2. I did *not* test the milk on my wrist—this is not precise enough for me. I used a Taylor "Roast & Yeast" thermometer and when the milk cooled to 114 degrees F. I added the culture. I disconnected the Big Batch after five hours. Result? Delicious yogurt but a little too soft—six hours would have been better.

Evaporated milk, either whole or skim, makes a custardy, smooth yogurt.

Whole milk makes a more liquid type of yogurt. If you add one-third cup dry milk per quart, your yogurt will be firmer.

Skim milk, either dry or bottled, makes the most liquid yogurt. Add one-third cup dry milk per quart for more firmness.

CALORIES

Skim or nonfat milk yogurt made from bottled, evaporated, or powdered milk with one-third cup added powdered milk per quart contains about 110 calories per eight-ounce (one cup) serving.

Whole milk yogurt, made from bottled or evaporated whole milk with one-third cup added powdered milk per quart, contains about 180 calories per eight-ounce (one cup) serving.

International Yogurt Yogotherm® Yogurt Maker

DESCRIPTION

- a nonelectric yogurt maker or incubator that works on the principle of a Thermos.
- the "outside" canister is made of durable plastic and measures 9¼" high, 7¾" in diameter. When you remove the top of this canister and look inside, you will see (1) a one-inch removable Styrofoam lining and (2) a white plastic container (6½" high, 6¼" in diameter, ten-cup capacity) with a white plastic top. The container fits inside this lining.
- incubator will keep heat evenly distributed (no hot or cold spots) and hold it at the correct temperature.
- light in weight, convenient to use, and easy to clean.
- made by the Rosell Institute in Canada.

FROM

International Yogurt Company
628 North Doheny Drive
Los Angeles, CA 90069 $24.95

The Yogomatic electromatic incubator, in nonbreakable plastic, has a one-quart capacity and is imported from Europe. Simple to use—just plug it in. $14.95.

Instructions for Making Yogurt

Ingredients

One to one and a half quarts of milk. For a thicker consistency add one-quarter to one-half cup of nonfat powdered milk and one and a half heaping teaspoons of gelatin.

Procedure

1. Boil milk and cool to 115 to 118 degrees F. (47 to 48 degrees C.).
2. Add the yogurt culture and mix well.
3. Pour milk into plastic container (prerinsed with boiling water). Put lid on.
4. Incubate from three and a half to six hours.
5. When milk has thickened, take out the container and put in refrigerator for three hours.
6. Save one-quarter cup of yogurt as starter for your next batch.
7. Your next batches can be made with two to four tablespoons of starter per quart.

My Test

This was the only nonelectric yogurt maker I tried and, quite frankly, I was skeptical. How could it work? Well, I can assure you it works perfectly. I followed Yogotherm's instructions with minor changes. For testing purposes I used four cups of lowfat milk, one-third cup of dried nonfat Carnation milk, and one tablespoon of plain commercial yogurt for starter. After five hours' incubation time I found I had delicious yogurt (but a little on the soft side; six hours would be better). This yogurt maker is ideal for campers.

Hamilton Beach Electric Culture Center

Description

· six dishwasher-safe one-cup clear glass jars (3″ diameter, 3½″ high) with snap-on white plastic covers.

- an orange-and-white electrically heated base with a "consistency guide" and "hour reminder lever" on the front.
- the consistency guide (not on all models) tells you how long to incubate: three to six hours (soft and mild), eight to twelve hours (medium and tangy), fourteen to eighteen hours (firm and tart).
- the hour reminder lever tells you when to unplug the yogurt maker. This is *not* automatic; nothing buzzes or rings.
- a thermometer-spoon gives you the right temperature for adding starter to the milk. Spoon measures out correct amount of starter needed.
- a smoke-tinted cover goes over jars.
- 28 watts, 120 volts, 50-60 Hz.

SIZE

10¼" long x 7¼" wide x 5" high

FROM

Hamilton Beach Division
Scovill, Inc. $15.99
Washington, NC 27889   Model 726

INSTRUCTIONS FOR MAKING YOGURT

Equipment

A pot to heat the milk, a large bowl, and a measuring cup.

Ingredients

Six cups of whole or skim milk and four tablespoons of plain, fresh yogurt for starter. Or two cups of nonfat dry milk, five cups of water, and four tablespoons of starter.

Procedure

1. Put milk into saucepan and set heat at medium.
2. Bring temperature of milk to just below the boiling point, or when tiny bubbles form around the sides of pan. Do not boil.
3. Cool milk down to range marked on thermometer-spoon.
4. Using the thermometer-spoon again, add yogurt starter to a half cup of milk taken from saucepan. Stir until well mixed.
5. Stir yogurt mixture in cup back into saucepan of warmed milk. Recheck temperature.
6. Rewarm milk if necessary to top line (120 degrees F.) on

thermometer. Lower starting temperature means yogurt-making process will take longer.

7. Pour milk into glass jars. Fill to about one-half inch from top.

8. Put lids on jars, set them in yogurt maker. Put on smoke-tinted cover and plug in.

9. Set the hour reminder lever.

10. When the yogurt is ready, remove glass cups and chill for four hours or longer.

My Test

The above instructions are from Hamilton Beach and they are very accurate. For testing purposes I used four cups of lowfat milk, one-third cup of dried milk, and one tablespoon of plain commercial yogurt. I added the yogurt starter below 120 degrees F.—closer to 115 degrees—and unplugged the yogurt maker after six hours. Makes delicious, tasty yogurt.

Note

Fruit preserves may be added to the bottom of the glass jars *before* yogurt is incubated. However, *do not* stir. Incubate as for plain yogurt. Flavorings, extracts, or sweeteners should be added *after* the yogurt has been incubated and cooled. Stir in gently.

Hint

Be sure to use fresh, plain *natural* yogurt as starter. Some plain yogurts also contain modified starch and/or preservatives which may interfere with or hinder growth of the culture.

West Bend Electric Yogurt Maker

Description

· six dishwasher-safe one-cup clear glass jars (3″ diameter, 3½″ high) with snap-on white plastic covers.

· a white plastic holding tray fits into the yellow heating base. The tray allows you to handle six jars at one time.

· a smoke-tinted cover has a yellow take-out dial: for mild yogurt, process four to five hours. For a tart and tangy yogurt, process six to ten hours.

· if the lids for the glass jars are misplaced, 3″ to 3¼″ plastic snap-on lids found on cheese spreads or tubular potato chip containers may be used. For additional glass jars and lids, write to The West Bend Company, Customer Service Department, West Bend, WI 53095.

· 18 watts, 120 volts, AC only

SIZE

12″ long x 7″ wide x 5″ high

FROM

The West Bend Company
West Bend, WI 53095

$22.95
Model 5210

For service or repairs, you can take or send your yogurt maker to authorized West Bend repair and service centers in Canada, United States, Bermuda, Puerto Rico, and Venezuela.

INSTRUCTIONS FOR MAKING YOGURT

Ingredients

Four to five cups of whole or skim milk, one-third cup of instant nonfat dry milk (optional), and six tablespoons of plain yogurt containing live bacteria culture.

For yogurt made with whole or skim evaporated milk use two to two and one-half cups evaporated milk, two to two and one-half cups warm water (about 120 degrees F.), one-third cup instant nonfat dry milk (optional), six tablespoons plain yogurt.

Procedure

1. Heat milk in two-quart saucepan over medium heat to just below the boiling point (200 degrees F.).
2. If adding dry milk, combine with milk during the heating period.
3. Remove milk from heat and cool to lukewarm (about 110 degrees F.).
4. Place one tablespoon of yogurt into each jar.
5. Divide warm milk among jars, filling to within one-half inch of edge; stir gently.
6. Cover jars with lids and place jars in holding tray.
7. Set takeout dial; process four to ten hours.
8. After processing, unplug yogurt maker from wall outlet.
9. Transfer holding tray containing jars to refrigerator and chill at least three hours.

MY TEST

The above instructions are from West Bend. I used four cups of lowfat milk, one-third cup of dried milk, and one tablespoon of plain commercial yogurt. I cooled the milk to 115 degrees F., put the yogurt into one jar, added two tablespoons of warm milk, stirred well, and poured this mixture back into the pot. After stirring again, I poured the milk into the jars and set the takeout dial for six hours later. After chilling in the refrigerator, I had excellent yogurt.

Cooking with Yogurt

WHAT TO DO AND HOW TO DO IT

As you can see from the recipes in this book, the uses for yogurt in cooking are varied and many—everything from appetizers to desserts, and all that's in between. Just to keep you on the right track, here are a few general hints for cooking with yogurt.

Heating, when you use yogurt, boils down to (no pun) one basic rule: always heat for a short period of time, and use a low temperature.

When you add yogurt to other ingredients that are already heated, you'll find it can be done three ways:

1. At the beginning of the cooking period—to avoid curdling add a small amount of flour or cornstarch mixed with water. See recipe below.
2. At the end of the cooking period—just before removing from the flame.
3. Off the heat completely—purists say this results in less damage to the bacteria.

This recipe for stabilizing yogurt is from *A Book of Middle Eastern Food* by Claudia Roden (New York: Knopf, 1968):

Lengthy cooking causes yogurt made with cow's milk to curdle and stabilizers such as cornflour or egg white are required to prevent this.

4 cups yogurt	mixed with a little cold water
1 egg white, lightly beaten,	or milk
or 1 tablespoon cornflour	¾ teaspoon salt

(cont'd)

1. Beat yogurt in a large saucepan until liquid. Add the egg white or the cornflour mixed to a light paste with water or milk, and a little salt. Stir well with a wooden spoon. Bring to the boil slowly, stirring constantly in one direction only, then reduce the heat to as low as possible and let the yogurt barely simmer, uncovered, for about 10 minutes, or until it has acquired a thick, rich consistency.

2. Do not cover the pan with a lid, since a drop of steam falling back into the yogurt could ruin it.

3. After simmering, the yogurt can be mixed and cooked with other ingredients such as meat or vegetables with no danger of curdling.

4. If carefully handled, this process can also be carried out successfully after the yogurt has been mixed with other ingredients.

Mixing yogurt with other ingredients requires a light touch. The rule to remember is fold in gently, do not stir. If you mix too vigorously the texture of the yogurt will break down or separate. This, of course, only affects the looks, not the taste. Tip: To restore yogurt to its original consistency simply refrigerate for an hour or add a small amount of egg white.

Sauces using yogurt can be kept at the right "thickness" by adding arrowroot.

Salads that call for yogurt may "weep" or separate after a day or so. This won't happen if you add the yogurt just before you eat, and make only enough for one meal.

Baking with Yogurt

Sour cream, milk, and cream can all be replaced by yogurt when you're baking. Just be sure to add one-half teaspoon of baking soda for each cup of yogurt.

Yogurt Instead of

Like the Girl Scouts, a good cook should always be prepared. However, we've all experienced times when, halfway through a recipe, the discovery is made that one crucial item is missing. Therefore, keep in mind that yogurt is a good substitute for:

· *Buttermilk.* All you have to do is "thin" the yogurt with water or milk to make it closer to the consistency of buttermilk (i.e., one-half cup of yogurt and one cup of water).

- *Sour cream.* If you substitute yogurt for sour cream the end result will be a dish with a more "tangy" flavor (add one teaspoon of sugar to one cup of yogurt to sweeten).
- *Milk.* When making gravy (milk and flour) add yogurt and arrowroot* to the pan juices instead.

Savvy Secrets

Mix one tablespoon of yogurt to every two eggs. Beat well and cook as usual for omelets or scrambled eggs. Yogurt makes them extra light and moist.

Spoon yogurt over peach or apple pies before putting on the top crust, then bake.

Once Over Lightly

Yogurt will not only enrich many meats, but the lactic acid it contains helps to soften or tenderize the connective tissue. Yogurt can be added to veal, pot roast, liver, chicken, or lamb.

And, you can use yogurt instead of sour milk, buttermilk, or sour cream in making biscuits, breads, pancakes, waffles, and cakes. Yogurt adds a subtle flavor and insures a rich and tender texture. It makes particularly delicious chocolate cakes.

---

* I found arrowroot in New York at the Down To Earth health food store on Seventh Avenue between Twelfth and Thirteenth streets. According to the package directions Kuzu arrowroot "is made from the roots of wild plants of the arrowroot family which grow in the mountains around Kagoshima, Japan. It is used as a thickener for soups, sauces, desserts and beverages." I paid $1.74 for a four-ounce package.

Yogurt as a Sourdough Starter

HOW TO MAKE THIS FAMOUS SAN FRANCISCO

SPECIALTY FROM SCRATCH

For the past ten years of my life, I have been an advertising copywriter* in New York. One of the perks of this profession is to have one's name on the "comp"† lists of various magazines. Because of this practice, I'm able to read, I'd say, at least 80 percent of all the top magazines that come out each month.

One of the best magazines that I get is *Sunset*, "The Magazine of Western Living," published in Menlo Park, California. Each issue is packed with tips on travel, food, entertaining, building, remodeling, gardening—you name it.

In the May 1978 issue of *Sunset* there appeared a fascinating article entitled "Sourdough . . . the Breakthrough Continues." It begins:

Five years ago this month, we reported a breakthrough in sourdough baking—a more reliable sourdough starter made with yogurt.

The article goes on to say that *Sunset*'s original starter (from 1973) is "still alive and well and we use it often in our test kitchens." Since this was the first and only time I'd seen yogurt used this way,

---

* Copywriters do just that—write copy for print ads and TV commercials. A doctor once asked me who I "copy." Nothing could be further from the truth. It requires hard work and a lot of creative thinking to make your product stand out from twenty others on the market.

† "Comp" means complimentary copy. I still buy a number of magazines plus five newspapers a day to keep up with current news, trends, and ideas.

I decided to write to *Sunset* and ask permission to reprint their recipe for sourdough starter. I received a letter from them explaining that "our long-standing policy forbids the reprinting of our recipes by others." Naturally, I was disappointed.

Several weeks later, however, I came across recipes for this particular starter in several different publications, so I began to realize that yogurt starter is fairly well known in the sourdough world. Here, then, is how I make a sourdough starter from yogurt:

Yogurt Sourdough Starter

1 cup lowfat, skim, or whole milk	1 cup all-purpose flour, unsifted

2–3 tablespoons plain yogurt

1. Heat the milk in the top of a double boiler. Cool to 100-107 degrees (use a thermometer). Remove milk from heat and stir in yogurt.

2. Pour mixture into a clean container, cover, and let stand in a warm place for 12 to 24 hours. (I used an 8-ounce Yuban Instant Coffee jar and placed it in the "continuous clean" oven of my Modern Maid gas range. I *did not* turn the oven on, a continuous clean oven is always slightly warm.*)

3. Mixture is ready when it has the consistency of yogurt, i.e., should not flow readily when the container is tilted slightly. (The mixture in my oven was ready after 20 hours. The Yogotherm mixture was ready after 12 hours.) If whey or water is on top, stir it back in.

4. If starter or whey turns pink, discard mixture and start again.

5. After the curd forms, gradually stir flour into starter. Blend until smooth.

6. Cover top of jar (I used 2 layers of aluminum foil held by an elastic band, then I punched several small holes in the top to allow the gases to escape; Yogotherm was covered with its own lid) and let stand in a warm place (85-100 degrees) until mixture is full of bubbles and has a good sour smell, approximately 2 to 5 days. (The mixture in my oven was ready in 2 days; the Yogotherm mixture took longer and was ready only after I moved it to a warmer spot. *Important:* You *must* maintain correct temperature.)

* At the same time I also ran a second test using my Yogotherm yogurt maker from the International Yogurt Company of Los Angeles. I did not put the Yogotherm in the oven.

7. Again, if whey or water forms on top, stir it back into starter. Note: Each time you use part of your starter replenish by adding equal amounts of warm milk (100 degrees) and flour. Cover starter and let stand in a warm place several hours or overnight (until it is full of bubbles). Store in refrigerator.

YIELD: 2 cups

And, now that you have your sourdough starter, why not try these delicious sourdough recipes that were sent to me from Hickory Farms in Maumee, Ohio.

Sam's Sourdough Bread

2 cups yogurt sourdough starter*

5½–6½ cups all-purpose flour, unsifted

1 package active dry yeast

2 tablespoons sugar

1 tablespoon salt

2 tablespoons softened butter or margarine

1 cup hot tap water

1. Remove sourdough starter from the refrigerator 1 hour before preparing this recipe.

2. Preheat the oven to 375 degrees.

3. Combine 1 cup of the flour, undissolved yeast, sugar, and salt in large bowl. Stir well to blend. Add butter and hot tap water and beat with electric mixer for 2 minutes at high speed, scraping bowl occasionally.

4. Add sourdough starter and another cup flour. Beat at high speed for 1 minute.

5. With a wooden spoon, gradually stir in just enough of the remaining flour to make a soft dough which leaves sides of bowl. Turn out onto floured board. Knead 8-10 minutes or until dough is smooth and elastic.

6. Divide dough in half. Roll each piece into a 12 x 8-inch rectangle. Roll up tightly, beginning with 8-inch side. Seal edge and ends well. Place seam-side down in greased 9 x 5 x 3-inch loaf pans. Loaves may also be shaped into rounds about 8 inches in diameter and placed in greased 8-inch pie pans.

7. Brush dough lightly with oil. Cover with plastic wrap and a towel. Let rise in a warm place for 1-1½ hours or until doubled

* Note: A ready-to-use, 1½-oz. envelope of sourdough starter is made by Hickory Farms of Ohio, Inc.; 300 Holland Road; P. O. Box 219; Maumee, Ohio 43537.

in size. Cut an X in tops of round loaves with sharp knife just before baking.

8. Bake for 40-50 minutes or until golden brown. Remove from pan immediately. Cool on rack.

YIELD: 2 loaves

British Breakfast Rolls

1 cup yogurt sourdough starter	¼ cup yellow corn meal
2½–3 cups all-purpose flour, unsifted	1 teaspoon baking soda
	½ teaspoon salt
¾ cup buttermilk or sour milk	2 tablespoons yellow corn meal

1. Remove 1 cup of sourdough starter from the refrigerator 30 minutes before preparing this recipe.

2. Combine sourdough starter, 2½ cups flour, milk, ¼ cup corn meal, soda, and salt. Stir well. Turn out onto lightly floured board.

3. Knead until smooth (about 3 minutes), adding more flour if necessary. Roll dough to ½-inch thickness. Allow dough to rest 10 minutes. Cut with floured 3-inch biscuit cutter, making one sharp cut for each.

4. Sprinkle remaining corn meal onto wax paper. Place rolls on corn meal, turning to coat both sides. Cover with plastic wrap, then a towel. Let rise in warm place 1 hour.

5. Cook on lightly greased 350 degree griddle for 20 minutes, turning occasionally.

6. Cool. Split and toast; spread with butter or your favorite marmalade for an extra special breakfast treat.

YIELD: 8 rolls

Nob Hill Mocha Cake

1 cup yogurt sourdough starter	1 teaspoon baking soda
½ cup softened butter or margarine	1 teaspoon salt
	1 teaspoon instant coffee
1½ cups sugar	1 teaspoon cocoa
2 eggs	¼ cup milk
1 teaspoon vanilla	¾ cup finely chopped nuts
1½ cups all-purpose flour, unsifted	

1. Remove sourdough starter from the refrigerator 30 minutes before preparing this recipe.

2. Preheat the oven to 350 degrees.

3. With mixer, cream butter and sugar thoroughly until light and fluffy. Add eggs and vanilla and beat well.

4. In separate bowl, blend flour, baking soda, salt, instant coffee, and cocoa. Alternately, add the dry ingredients, sourdough starter, and milk to the creamed mixture, beginning and ending with the dry ingredients.

5. Mix well. Stir in nuts.

6. Pour batter into well-greased 10-inch Bundt pan or 9-inch square pan.

7. Bake for 50-55 minutes for the Bundt pan or 35-40 minutes for the 9-inch square pan. Cool on rack 10 minutes before removing from pan. Serve with Hard Sauce.

YIELD: One Bundt or 9-inch square cake

Hard Sauce

⅓ cup softened butter or margarine

1½ cups confectioners' sugar, unsifted

⅛ teaspoon nutmeg

2 teaspoons brandy or rum

1 teaspoon vanilla

Cream butter until light. Add sugar, nutmeg, brandy or rum, and vanilla. Beat until fluffy and smooth. Spoon on cake. Store remaining Hard Sauce in refrigerator.

YIELD: 1 cup

Cinnamon Rolls

2 cups yogurt sourdough starter

5½–6½ cups all-purpose flour, unsifted

1 package active dry yeast

½ cup sugar

2 teaspoons salt

⅓ cup softened butter or margarine

1 cup hot tap water

Melted butter

1. Remove sourdough starter from the refrigerator 1 hour before preparing this recipe.

2. Preheat the oven to 375 degrees.

3. Combine 1 cup flour, undissolved yeast, sugar, and salt in large bowl. Stir well to blend. Add butter and hot tap water and beat

with electric mixer for 2 minutes at medium speed, scraping bowl occasionally.

4. Add sourdough starter and 1 cup of flour. Beat at high speed for 1 minute.

5. With a wooden spoon, gradually stir in just enough of the remaining flour to make a soft dough which leaves sides of bowl.

6. Turn out onto floured board. Knead 8-10 minutes or until dough is smooth and elastic.

7. Divide dough in half. Roll each piece into a 15 x 9-inch rectangle. Brush each rectangle lightly with the melted butter and sprinkle each with 1 cup of Cinnamon Filling, covering all the dough. Press filling lightly into dough.

8. Roll each rectangle of dough, beginning with long side, jelly-roll fashion and seal edges. Cut the rolled dough into 1-inch slices and place, cut side up, close to each other in a greased 13 x 9 x 2-inch pan.

9. Cover with plastic wrap and a towel. Let rise in a warm place for 1½-2 hours or until doubled in size.

10. Bake for 20-25 minutes or until golden brown.

YIELD: 2½ dozen rolls

Cinnamon Filling

⅓ cup melted butter or margarine
1 cup light brown sugar

1 teaspoon cinnamon
⅛ teaspoon cloves
1 cup finely chopped walnuts

Combine butter or margarine, brown sugar, cinnamon, cloves, and walnuts. Mix well.

YIELD: 2 cups

Old West Biscuits

1 cup yogurt sourdough starter
2 cups all-purpose flour, unsifted
3 teaspoons baking powder

1 teaspoon salt
¼ cup shortening
⅓ cup milk

1. Remove sourdough starter from refrigerator 30 minutes before preparing this recipe.

2. Preheat the oven to 450 degrees.

3. Combine flour, baking powder, and salt. Stir to blend.

(cont'd)

4. Cut in shortening with pastry blender until mixture resembles coarse meal.

5. Add sourdough starter and milk. Stir with fork until dry ingredients are moistened.

6. Turn out onto lightly floured board. Knead gently about 20 times. Roll dough to ½-inch thickness. Cut with floured 2½-inch biscuit cutter and place on ungreased baking sheet.

7. Bake for 10-12 minutes or until golden brown.

Yield: 1 dozen biscuits

Prospector's Pancakes

1½ cups yogurt sourdough starter	½ teaspoon baking soda
1 cup all-purpose flour, unsifted	½ cup milk
	1 egg, slightly beaten
3 tablespoons sugar	3 tablespoons cooking oil
1 teaspoon salt	

1. Remove sourdough starter from the refrigerator 30 minutes before preparing this recipe.

2. Preheat griddle to 375 degrees or until drops of water skitter on surface.

3. Combine flour, sugar, salt, and baking soda in a large bowl. Stir well to blend. Add the sourdough starter, milk, and egg. Mix well. Batter may be slightly lumpy.

4. Grease hot griddle for first pancakes and as needed. Pour about ¼ cup batter onto griddle for large pancakes, about 1 tablespoon batter for silver dollar-size pancakes.

5. Bake until edges are dry, then turn and bake other side (about 2 minutes per side for large pancakes and 1 minute per side for small pancakes).

Yield: 1 dozen large or 2 dozen silver dollar-size pancakes

Sourdough Wheat Germ Buns

¾ cup yogurt sourdough starter	1 cup warm milk (115 degrees)
1 cup all-purpose flour, unsifted	1⅓ cups all-purpose flour, unsifted
1 cup wheat germ (Kretschmer regular)	1½ teaspoons baking powder
	1 teaspoon salt
2 tablespoons firmly packed brown sugar	2 tablespoons cooking oil

1. Remove sourdough starter from the refrigerator 30 minutes before preparing this recipe.

2. Preheat the oven to 375 degrees.

3. Combine sourdough starter, 1 cup flour, wheat germ, sugar, and milk in large bowl. Stir well to blend.

4. Cover bowl loosely with plastic wrap. Let stand in warm place about 6 hours until very thick, bubbly, and spongy looking.

5. In another bowl, combine 1⅓ cups flour, baking powder, and salt. Stir to blend. Add to wheat germ mixture. Stir until all ingredients are moistened. Stir in oil.

6. Turn out onto lightly floured cloth-covered board.

7. Knead gently 20 times. Pat dough into a 9-inch circle. Cut with floured, 2-inch biscuit cutter.

8. Fit tightly into greased 9-inch round pan. Let rise in warm place 30 minutes.

9. Bake for 25-30 minutes or until golden brown.

YIELD: 1½ dozen buns

Yogurt Cheese

Are you a cheese eater? I certainly am. One of my favorite shopping trips is to go down to Balducci's (the gourmet's haven in Greenwich Village) and check out their cheeses. I'm particularly fond of the Norwegian Jarlsberg, while Peter favors their California Monterey Jack. And, as I said earlier (page 18), kefir yogurt cheese, especially the one made by Continental in California, is also a real taste treat.

Should you decide to make yogurt cheese yourself, this is how you do it. To begin with, your "starter" can be either (1) fresh plain yogurt or (2) a yogurt cheese culture that is sold in a packet ($2.50) at your nearest health food store. This culture (the same one is used for making homemade buttermilk and sour cream) is from Rosell Institute, Inc., 8480 St. Laurent, Montreal, Quebec. It is distributed in the United States through the International Yogurt Company, 628 North Doheny Drive, Los Angeles, CA 90069.

Making Yogurt Cheese at Home from a Culture

These instructions are from the Rosell Institute.

1. Heat a quart of milk to boiling for at least 1 minute. Cool the milk down to 115-118 degrees F.

2. Inoculate the milk with one envelope of yogurt culture. Mix well.

3. Incubate* the inoculated milk in the saucepan at a temperature of 105-115 degrees F., until solid curdling of milk, which requires from 2¾-4 hours.

4. Drain the curd. Do this by pouring the curd in a small sterile sugar or flour bag. Hang the bag for 20-24 hours.

5. When the curd has a soft butter texture, take it out of the bag and work it with a spoon or spatula. Salt lightly.

6. Pour the cheese into a clean glass or jar and keep refrigerated. It is now ready to be eaten. (Can be easily kept over 10 days in a cool place.)

Note: You use the Rosell yogurt culture only once—preferably as soon as you get it. For each additional batch of yogurt cheese use (as your new culture) a small quantity of curd from your previous preparation. This curd should *not* be drained. Just pour into a sterile glass or bottle and keep in the refrigerator until you are ready to use it.

My Test

I heated the milk to just below boiling in the top of a double boiler. Then I cooled the milk to 115 degrees F. and added the cheese culture. After this I incubated the milk in an electric yogurt maker for six hours (Yogotherm works equally well). Finally, I drained the yogurt for eight hours at room temperature and eight hours in the refrigerator. Makes delicious, low-caloried cheese.

Making Yogurt Cheese at Home from Yogurt

This is an excellent way to use up yogurt that's a few days old. To make yogurt cream cheese:

1. Take plain unflavored yogurt and pour off the liquid whey (water that may collect on top). Put the yogurt in 2-3 layers of cheesecloth. Gather up the corners and tie in a knot.†

---

* To incubate, place the pan containing the inoculated milk in a large container filled with water at a temperature of 105-115 degrees F. Keep the temperature of the water between this range. (However, in a letter to me Mr. Brochu, President of Rosell, states, "the easiest way to incubate is with the Yogotherm incubator." He also advises use of a new culture once a month.)

† In Wadeeha Atiyeh's *Scheherazade Cooks* (Great Neck, N.Y.: Channel Press, 1960) the author tells how she makes her own cheesecloth bag by "taking a 24-inch square of doubled cheesecloth, giving it a 1-inch hem and adding a drawstring." She also wets the bag before using.

2. Place bag in a strainer or colander over a pan to catch the liquid or tie your bag over a faucet to drain for 3 or 4 hours. If even thicker cheese is desired, drain for 8 hours or overnight. The consistency should be similar to cream cheese.

3. Use the cheese in the same way you would cream cheese or flavor it with salt, herbs, or spices. Serve as a dip or spread. Note: The older the yogurt is, the more tart it will become, so flavor your cheese accordingly.

Ways You Can Use Yogurt Cheese

- Serve plain as a spread on toast or crackers (or season with curry powder).
- Mix with chopped onion, minced chives, pickles, pimento, chopped green or red pepper, or sesame seeds and use as a tasty sandwich filling.
- Serve with fresh papaya, peaches, avocado, melon, or pineapple.
- Roll into balls (walnut size) and sprinkle with olive oil and paprika.

Frozen Yogurt

ALL ABOUT THIS NEWEST WAY TO EAT

YOGURT

After nearly ten years on the American scene, frozen yogurt is not about to melt away. If anything, the number of frozen yogurt products, and where you can buy them, is growing day by day.

All over New York, from Wall Street to Eighty-sixth Street on the upper East Side, people of all ages—from grandmas to grade schoolers—are going into yogurt shops with names like Yogurt Emporium; Everything Yogurt, Inc.; Dannon Yogurt Store; Yogurt Chalet; Yogurt Hut; Yogurtland—and on and on. These places offer an endless variety of hard and soft frozen yogurts in the form of sandwiches, parfaits, and sundaes (with or without toppings) that can be eaten in the store, on the street, or taken home.

Next to a yogurt shop, the best place to buy frozen yogurt is at your supermarket or health food store. Our local Sloan's Supermarket on Sixth Avenue between Twelfth and Thirteenth streets has hard frozen yogurt in cartons, cups, and pops. One of my favorites is Dannon's yogurt-on-a-stick or "the world's first yogurt pop" in uncoated or coated versions (chocolate or carob).

As far as health food stores go, Brownies on Fifth Avenue between Sixteenth and Seventeenth streets has an incredibly delicious soft frozen yogurt, which it sells right from an open window. In other words, you don't even have to step inside the store to feast on frozen yogurt.

Frozen Yogurt Flavors

Do you like soft frozen yogurt? I absolutely love it. When I get the urge, I dash to Bloomingdale's and their 40 Carrots* restaurant (one of my favorite spots in New York) for a dish of "Frogurt"† soft frozen vanilla yogurt.

So far, the only flavors I've tried in frozen yogurt are strawberry, chocolate, and vanilla. But, for those who like variety, Frogurt also has blueberry, peach, raspberry, and—would you believe—passion fruit. (The name alone must do wonders for one.)

Even more fanciful are the yogurt flavors made by one large company that's known primarily for their delicious ice cream. Their public relations representative in Burbank, California, told me, "We make hard frozen yogurt in a variety of flavors which are rotated in much the same way as our ice cream flavors are rotated." A quick check in the Village revealed that this month's flavors "with the fruit in each and every scoop" included Apricot Brandy yogurt with juicy chunks of apricot, Very Strawberry yogurt with nuggets of strawberries, and Blueberry Cheesecake yogurt with bite-size bits of blueberry cheesecake. One would be hard-pressed, I believe, to top any of these flavors.

The Culture in Frozen Yogurt

On Third Avenue in New York, there was a frozen yogurt shop between Fifty-second and Fifty-third streets that I walked by at least twice a week at lunchtime for about a year. Without fail, this small, nondescript place would always be crowded. Everybody there knew that a soft frozen yogurt sundae for lunch was fast, easy, cheap, and delicious.

All of this is well and good, of course, but how about the crucial question: Does frozen yogurt provide the same benefits as "regular" yogurt? In the *New York Times* of August 10, 1977, Dr. Robert L. Bradley, a professor in the University of Wisconsin's food science department, explained that it depends on how "frozen" it is.

* According to *Nation's Restaurant News*, 40 Carrots has been so successful that it "has been expanded three times, from an original twelve seats two years ago, to its present forty. Now, it's looking for a major chain with which to share the wealth."

† Frogurt frozen yogurt is made by H. P. Hood, Inc., the 131-year-old Boston dairy. The big three in frozen yogurt in the East are Frogurt, Dannon, and Colombo.

86

Dr. Bradley explained that while one bacillus, the Streptococcus thermophilus, remains impervious to freezing, the lactobacillus is broken by ice crystals and can be destroyed in the freezing process.

He goes on to explain:

In soft frozen yogurts, particularly those made at home, I suspect that the lactobacillus population is almost at its top. But the rate of destruction depends upon the length of time it is frozen. In the commercial, hard-frozen yogurt, most of the beneficial bacteria is probably destroyed.

All I can say is that with or without a culture that's alive and jumping, I still think frozen yogurt is the greatest thing that's come along in some time.

Calories: Frozen Yogurt vs. Ice Cream

I'd be the first to admit that soft ice cream is delicious, but then, so is frozen yogurt. However, the difference between the two, according to Vasa Cubaleski, president of Continental Culture Specialists, Inc., in California, is that "frozen yogurt is better for you than ice cream. It has less fat, fewer calories, and is cultured to make it more digestible."* This is true, but keep in mind that *fewer calories* does not necessarily mean that frozen yogurt is low caloried. For example, a cup of Continental's frozen soft-swirl chocolate yogurt is 270 calories. The average calorie count for one cup of ice cream is 500 calories. But, like "regular" yogurt, once you add toppings (for example, fruits, nuts, honey, liqueurs—see page 41) the calorie count takes a licking.

On the other hand, Dannon's frozen yogurt-on-a-stick is only 60 calories—provided you stay with uncoated vanilla. Switch to chocolate-coated vanilla and the calorie count shoots up to 120.

Seven Uppers

Whether you buy it or make it yourself, frozen yogurt is more fun to eat if you add a favorite fruit or topping. Here are seven delicious frozen yogurt combos from Frogurt.

- A crisp, golden waffle topped with either strawberry, raspberry, or plain frozen yogurt.

* One ounce of Continental's mix contains 1.0 grams of protein, 3.75 grams of carbohydrate, and 1.5 grams of fat.

- A generous slice of honeydew melon (in season) topped with frozen yogurt and a dollop of pure honey.
- Fresh sliced banana with milk and frozen yogurt. Serve with a vanilla wafer.
- Crepes filled with frozen yogurt and topped with fresh fruit.
- California cling peaches served with frozen yogurt and shredded coconut.
- Generous slices of avocado and either plain, vanilla, strawberry, or raspberry frozen yogurt. Serve with lime wedge and a vanilla wafer.
- Strawberry shortcake: fresh or frozen strawberries over plain cake topped with vanilla frozen yogurt.

Nitty Gritty

I think that this short piece (a spoof of a much-loved nursery rhyme), which appeared in the Children's Book Review section of the *New York Times*, is absolutely delightful.* It begins as a letter to "Dear Ms. Goose" and goes on to say:

A number of us have now had a chance to read your nursery rhymes, and I am happy to report that, on the whole, we find them charming and imaginative. As you will see, we have made some small suggestions for improvement.

The letter is signed, "Sincerely, The Editors." The nursery rhyme in question is this old chestnut:

> Little Miss Muffet
> Sat on a tuffet
> Eating her curds and whey
> There came a great spider
> And sat down beside her,
> And frightened Miss Muffet away.

And what changes do the editors suggest? Read on.

Too many difficult words here: tuffet, curds and whey. How many youngsters would know, for example, that curds are the coagulated part of the milk, from which cheese is made? Would consider substituting frozen yogurt. Also, spiders don't sit; they dangle.

* From "Little Jennifer Has Lost Her Sheep" by Charlotte Pomerantz, *New York Times Book Review*, April 30, 1978.

Making Frozen Yogurt

Why make frozen yogurt? Why not? Making frozen yogurt can be a family project—like having an old-fashioned taffy pull. It's fun to do, and even more fun to eat the results. Of course, the best reason for making your own frozen yogurt is that you will know exactly what is in the finished product. To the yogurt itself you may add some, or none, of these: corn syrup, unflavored gelatin, sugar, eggs, or evaporated milk. Now, look at (keeping in mind that each commercial frozen yogurt differs from the other) the ingredients in these two leading soft frozen yogurts:

Brand X	Brand Y
Cultured pasteurized milk	Cultured Grade A pasteurized
Nonfat milk	skim milk
Sugar	Cream
Fruit purees	Fruit concentrate
Corn sweetener	Corn syrup
Natural flavors	Honey
Egg yolks	L. Bulgaricus
Juice concentrates	Alginate
Gelatin	Guar gum
Carob bean gum	Locust bean gum
Citric acid	Carrageenan
Viable yogurt micro-	Lactose
organisms	

Of course, to be fair, I must point out that commercial frozen yogurt has farther to travel than your homemade variety. For example, most soft frozen yogurt "mixes"* are packaged in half-gallon or gallon containers, shipped frozen to the store (some are shipped fresh and frozen at the store), thawed, and then poured into a soft serve freezer (which works in the same manner as a soft serve ice cream freezer).

On the other hand, your homemade frozen yogurt, made from "scratch" with a few natural ingredients and an ice cream maker, is not going to have the "holding power" of a commercial frozen yogurt. In all probability, your frozen yogurt will be almost as smooth, tangy, and flavorful as the commercial version—but it may melt fairly quickly. Your best bet is to be prepared to eat your homemade frozen yogurt shortly after it's made.

Ice Cream Makers for Frozen Yogurt

Are we, as the experts say, becoming a nation of people with weak-muscled bodies? Personally, I detest all forms of exercise except walking in Manhattan in winter and swimming on Long Island in the summer.

Because of my outlook, I found it rather interesting to observe that, when I asked six manufacturers of ice cream makers to send me "the model that would lend itself to making frozen yogurt," not one sent a hand-cranked machine. I suspect that, even though a hand-cranked model would be indispensable in a rural area with no electricity, the trend these days is to let the electric company do all the work.

Therefore, two types of electric ice cream machines are talked about here: (1) the bucket ones that are similar to their hand-cranked sisters and (2) the small-capacity type that will make frozen yogurt in your freezer. Generally, the bucket types use table or rock salt and crushed or cracked ice, while the in-freezer one uses no salt and no ice.

---

* Most soft frozen yogurt "mixes" are made for commercial use. However, Alta-Dena tells me that they sell their mix (in half-gallon containers) to health food stores in the East. "Our mix has been used, and does make an excellent frozen yogurt using a home ice cream freezer," they say.

90

Salton Frozen Dessert Maker

Description

- a small (1-quart capacity) machine that is operated by an electric motor. The top of the unit comes in two colors: chocolate or strawberry. The bottom is white and both are made of plastic.
- when you take the top off (which holds a fan to keep the machine from overheating) and look inside, you will see a small, round tinned-steel container (3¼″ high, 6¼″ diameter) with a transparent plastic lid.
- when you remove *this* lid, you will see the white plastic dashers that do the mixing.
- this machine requires no crushed ice or rock salt.
- it uses only a penny's worth of electricity per quart of frozen yogurt, ice cream, ice milk, or sherbet.
- in order to operate, the machine has to be put into a freezer. You should have a roomy separate freezer or a large double-door refrigerator and a very low temperature (zero or below).
- 120 volts AC, 60 Hz, 55 watts.

Size

8″ high, 8″ diameter

From

Salton, Inc.
1260 Zerega Avenue
Bronx, NY 10462

$22.95
Model IC-3

Basic Vanilla Frozen Yogurt

½ cup evaporated milk
½ cup sugar
Dash of salt
1 envelope unflavored gelatin, softened in ¼ cup water

2½ jars* Salton whole milk plain yogurt
2 teaspoons vanilla

1. Scald evaporated milk over low heat, stirring occasionally to avoid the "skin" formation over the top of the milk. Add sugar, salt,

(cont'd)

* Jars furnished with Salton yogurt maker. Note: Each jar holds 8 ounces, or one cup.

and softened gelatin. Stir until thoroughly dissolved and mixture is completely smooth. Cool.

2. Add yogurt and vanilla. Mix well. Chill thoroughly in refrigerator for 2 hours or longer. Pour into Salton ice cream machine and freeze.

My Test

I decided to use a rich, full-bodied yogurt for this recipe so I bought two containers of Alta-Dena Maya Plain Youghurt (4 percent milk fat minimum) at our local health food store. One two-cup container costs $1.25. I heated the evaporated milk in the top of a double boiler and stirred constantly. As a result, I had no trouble with a "skin" forming. After cooling the yogurt mixture I assembled the entire unit and put it into the freezer compartment of my refrigerator. *Important:* The ice cream maker is *inside* the refrigerator but the cord comes *outside.* In other words, you shut the door on the cord (which is covered in a heavy protective plastic) and plug it into the wall. I unplugged the unit after fifty minutes and found I had a delicious (though not quite as "airy" as I would have liked it) frozen yogurt.

Hints

1. *Only* whole milk yogurt should be used to make frozen yogurt. (No skim milk or skim milk products.)
2. After chilling in your refrigerator for two hours or longer the yogurt mixture will resemble a pudding.
3. If you have hardened the frozen yogurt in your freezer, allow it to soften before serving for optimum flavor.
4. It is very important to stir the evaporated milk while heating it over a low heat. This is to avoid the "skin" formation over the top of the milk, which will affect the product. Once a "skin" has formed over the milk it cannot be dissolved.
5. The gelatin in the recipes is a natural food product and helps to smooth the consistency of frozen yogurt.

Waring Ice Cream Parlor™

Description

- a white plastic ice bucket fits snugly on a white base with chocolate trim which holds the motor.
- when you look down into the ice bucket you will see four parts:

1. a clear plastic support arm
2. a clear plastic lid. This goes on
3. a metal cream can that's 6½" high, 5" diameter. Inside this can is
4. a plastic dasher.

- the clear plastic top on the can lets you keep an eye on whatever frozen dessert you happen to be making. Note: Plastic parts are not dishwasher-safe.
- the motor in this appliance cannot burn out. A thermostat shuts the motor off automatically when your yogurt or ice cream is ready (twenty to fifty minutes).
- uses four trays of ice cubes from your refrigerator, one standard twenty-six-ounce box of ordinary table salt, and two cups of cold water. In other words, no special ice or salt is necessary.
- makes one-half gallon of frozen sherbet, yogurt, ice cream, ice milk, and other frozen desserts.

SIZE

12¾" high, 9" diameter

FROM

Waring Products Division
Dynamics Corporation of America $40.00
New Hartford, CT 06057   Model CF 520-1

Plain Low-Calorie Frozen Yogurt

2½ pints (4½ cups) plain   1½ teaspoons flavoring extract,
natural yogurt   optional

Spoon yogurt directly into cream can. Add vanilla or other flavoring if desired. Note: Waring says, "Frozen yogurt is a variation of ice milk or sherbet in which most or all of the milk has been replaced by cultured yogurt, which lends a characteristic 'tangy' flavor. The use of the low-fat variety of yogurt makes true low calorie frozen desserts possible."

MY TEST

The above recipe will give you delicious, tasty frozen yogurt. I found the Waring ice cream maker simple and easy to use. After putting the yogurt (I used Alta-Dena again) into the cream can I plugged in the machine and added the water, salt, and ice. Specifically, here is how it goes: one cup of chilled water, a layer of ice *cubes* (*not* crushed ice), six level tablespoons of table salt. Then repeat: ice, salt, ice, salt, ending at the top with one more cup of chilled water. Waring recommends using three-fourths of a carton of table salt; this is about two and a quarter cups. Warning: get your ice (and plenty of it), salt, and water assembled ahead of time.

Tips

Ingredients. If you use your own recipe with the Waring ice cream maker be sure to adjust the ingredient quantities for a maximum two-quart yield.

Prechilling. If you make up your mixture well ahead of time and prechill for an hour or two in your refrigerator's milk storage area, the subsequent processing time will be reduced. (This is not an absolute necessity, however, except in cases where the recipe calls for boiling or cooking, in which case the mixture *must* be cooled before attempting to process.)

Texture. The texture of the finished product depends largely on how fast it is processed. The slower the freezing process, the smoother the texture. (You can easily control the processing rate, and hence the finished texture, by varying the amount of salt you use in the "freezing mixture.")

Amount of salt. Using about three-fourths of a standard twenty-six-ounce box of salt will result in a reasonably fast-acting freezing mixture, and produce a relatively smooth-textured finished product. Use of *more* salt, up to a full box, will shorten the processing time and produce a coarser, more granular "icy" texture. Use of *less* salt, down to one-half box, will lengthen the processing time and produce a finer, smoother texture.

Note: The directions given for the Waring recipes are based on the use of three-quarters of a box of salt, and it is recommended that you try this quantity—at least the first time you use your Waring Ice Cream Parlor.

To sum up: More salt (up to a full box)—faster processing, coarser texture. Less salt (down to half a box)—slower processing, finer texture.

Deluxe Electric Proctor-Silex Ice Cream Maker

DESCRIPTION

- four-quart capacity ice cream maker has simulated "wrought iron" bands and an American Eagle on the bucket.
- the bucket itself is made of durable "polywood" and has a heavy, corrosion-resistant polypropylene liner.
- a black steel bridge holds the motor and its chrome-finish cover.
- inside the bucket you will find the ice cream can (8" high, 6¾" diameter), which has a clear plastic lid and white plastic dashers.
- this machine requires crushed or cracked ice (ice cubes cannot be used) and rock or table salt (rock salt is preferred).
- 120 volts, AC only, 130 watts, 60 cycle, UL listed.

SIZE

10¾" high, 11½" diameter

OTHER MODELS

Proctor-Silex has four other models (six- and four-quart capacity) ranging in price from $40.95 to $17.95. Two of these are electric; two are hand operated.

FROM

Proctor-Silex
SCM Corporation
1016 W. Ninth Avenue $43.95
King of Prussia, PA 19406   Model F801F

Frozen Strawberry Yogurt

1 envelope unflavored gelatin	¼ teaspoon salt
1 cup pureed strawberries, divided	1 tablespoon lemon juice
1 cup sugar	3 containers (8 oz. or 1 cup) strawberry yogurt

1. In medium saucepan sprinkle gelatin over ½ cup strawberry puree. Place over low heat and stir constantly until gelatin dissolves, about 3 minutes. Stir in sugar and salt; stir until sugar dissolves. Remove from heat; stir in remaining puree and lemon juice.

(cont'd)

2. Cool slightly. Stir in yogurt. Turn into can of four-quart Proctor-Silex ice cream maker. Insert dasher, cover, and freeze according to Proctor's directions. Turn into container, cover, and ripen about 2 hours in your freezer.

YIELD: approximately 2 quarts

MY TEST

For this recipe I used strawberry "Royal Taste" yogurt from Continental (a thick, rich yogurt I bought at Brownies for 77¢ per eight-ounce carton). To operate the Proctor-Silex ice cream maker you need crushed ice and rock salt. And where do you buy rock salt? At the hardware store, of course. You didn't know that? Neither did I until I went looking for it (costs $1.60 for a ten-pound bag). For a four-quart Proctor-Silex you need two and a half cups of rock salt and crushed ice (our General Electric refrigerator churns out crushed ice so I got off easy). Specifically, I put in two inches of ice, three heaping tablespoons of rock salt, and then repeated the process over and over until I reached the top. This machine works fast—and makes excellent frozen yogurt.

HINTS

Consistency. It may vary. Firmness of ice cream or frozen yogurt depends on the type of ice cream or frozen yogurt mixture used, room temperature, size of ice, temperature of brine, and temperature of mix before it is churned. By observing the frozen yogurt and noting texture, it is possible to improve each batch you make.

Too soft. If the motor did not stall in thirty minutes, the brine did not get cold enough. Remedy: after thirty minutes, continue churning and add six tablespoons of salt. This will reduce the brine temperature and cause the product to stiffen. Depending on the temperature of the brine, two or more applications of six tablespoons salt to an inch of ice may be required. This should result in the motor stalling within a few minutes.

Too hard or lumpy. If the motor stalled in less than twenty minutes, the brine got too cold too fast. This results in coarse, textured ice cream or frozen yogurt, lumps found throughout the product, or inconsistent texture (hard lumps floating in cream). Remedy: The problem could be anything relating to too much salt for the amount of ice. If the ice is too large or you added too much salt in each layer of ice, this cold brine froze the product nearest the outside of the can and made lumps of ice or frozen ice cream or yogurt in the mix. These lumps snowball into big lumps and ruin the texture. Try adding less salt, more ice, or finer ice.

The Ultimate: White Mountain Electric Four-Quart Freezer

DESCRIPTION

- handsome maple-finished pine bucket or tub. Motor and frame fasten securely on top of the bucket.
- inside the bucket you will find a tin-plated steel can (11" high, 5½" diameter) with a cover.
- inside the can are tinned cast-iron mixers that have self-adjusting beechwood scrapers.
- every part of the machine that touches the ice cream is tin-plated.
- uses crushed ice and rock salt.
- this model also comes in a six-quart capacity.
- 115 volts, AC or DC.

SIZE

20" high, 11" diameter

OTHER MODELS

White Mountain has a wide range of ice cream makers—fourteen in addition to the above two. Their selection includes both electric and hand-crank units at $56.50 to $672.90 (a twenty-quart commercial freezer).

FROM

White Mountain Freezer, Inc.
Winchendon, MA 01475
"Makers of ice cream freezers $114.20
for over 100 years"   Model 69204

MY TEST

The White Mountain recipe booklet with this four-quart freezer has fifty-five recipes that cover everything from butter brickle mousse to golden glow ice cream—but there are no frozen yogurt recipes. To test this machine I used three 8-oz. cartons of Dannon strawberry yogurt, three cups of rock salt, and thirty-two to thirty-six cups of chipped ice. I put the yogurt in a bowl, mixed well, and then placed the yogurt in the refrigerator to chill (about twenty minutes). Then I put the cream can (with the dasher in it) in the tub, poured the yogurt in, put the top on the can, locked the gear frame, which holds the motor, in position, and plugged in the freezer. As the cream can rotated I put in three inches of crushed ice, one-half cup of salt, and kept repeating this process until I reached the top. This machine is powerful and fast. In fifteen minutes the yogurt was ready. In our own, highly subjective I'll admit, taste test, Peter and I agreed that this combination of machine and yogurt produced the best frozen yogurt.

RCW Frost King Five-Quart Electric Ice Cream Freezer

DESCRIPTION

· makes two to five quarts of frozen yogurt, ice cream, sherbet, or any other frozen dessert in only twenty to thirty minutes.
· takes one and a third cups of table salt or, if you prefer, two cups of rock salt, and ten to fifteen pounds of crushed ice.
· electric motor and gear frame fasten on top of the wood pail or bucket. The motor has an automatic reset device. This protects the motor when it stops at the end of its intended running time of twenty to thirty minutes.
· inside: can (7¼″ high, 7¼″ in diameter) with plastic top and plastic beater or dasher.
· the can fits easily in most refrigerator freezer compartments for ripening or storage after freezing.
· one-year warranty from date of purchase.
· also available in four- and six-quart capacity.
· 120 volts, 60 cycles, 1.4 amps, AC only.

SIZE

15″ high, 11¼″ in diameter.

FROM

Richmond Cedar Works
Manufacturing Corporation
400 Bridge Street
Danville, VA 24541

$34.95
Model EFKW5-41651

My Test

Since the RCW booklet does not provide any frozen yogurt recipes, I improvised (as I did with White Mountain) and used three 8-oz. cartons of strawberry yogurt. Again, the results proved to be very good. Note: With both the yogurt makers and the ice cream makers that I tested, I noticed they all had one thing in common— very short cords. This is done on purpose for safety reasons. However, I found it inconvenient and with every machine (especially the ice cream makers where I had to work by the kitchen sink) I ended up using an extension cord—make sure you have one on hand. Warn your family if you think someone will trip on it. Also, with the ice cream makers make *sure* you have *plenty* of ice and hand. I underestimated the amount of ice I'd need each time I tested a machine.

Note

The five-quart electric wood tub ice cream freezer model 1985 that is sold by Sears, Roebuck and Company is almost identical to the model described above and is, in fact, made by the Richmond Cedar Works. The only difference between the two, as far as I can see, is the addition of the name "Sears" on the motor of model 1985 and the deletion of the name "Frost King." (In a letter to me, Sears pointed out that theirs has "a bail type handle with wooden grip; Richmond Cedar Works does not.")

Hints (from Sears)

Location of ice cream maker. Decide where you want to put the freezer while it is churning. Salt water drains from the small opening at the top of the tub, so it is advisable to freeze away from grass and plants. Also, evaporated brine leaves a salty residue if spilled on pavement. A large shallow container placed beneath the freezer works well to catch the brine, or the freezer can be operated in or near a sink. Don't operate an electric ice cream maker out of hearing range —motor pitch signals when freezer is completed.

On ice. Of course, ice will be needed to freeze your cream mix. Twenty-five pounds should suffice for four- or -six-quart freezers. You can make ice in your refrigerator freezer compartment or buy it. Liquor stores almost always have the kind you'll need or can tell you where to get it. *The ice must be chipped or crushed*—cubes will not melt properly and can jam the revolving can, damaging the motor on electric units. If you can find only ice cubes, they are readily crushed by placing them in a *heavy* cloth bag and pounding with a mallet or hammer. Continue until all cubes are crushed fine.

About salt. About two pounds of rock salt are necessary to freeze ice cream, more for ices, sherbets, and frozen yogurt. Rock salt is more easily handled than fine table salt, and much cheaper. It can be purchased at most grocery or hardware stores. You may want to buy in bulk, for use in future freezing.

Cleaning. Always wash your can, dasher, and can lid with soap and hot water before adding the cream mixture. Chilling the mix for about four hours (or even overnight) before pouring it into the can will make your ice cream or frozen yogurt's texture even smoother, and will hasten freezing.

Some simple items to make freezing easier are a scoop for handling the salt and crushed ice, a sponge to keep freezer and surrounding area neat and dry, and the cork packed with the unit (this should be saved to plug the lid after the churning process).

Plain Talk

The taste of your homemade frozen yogurt will depend, to a large degree, on the type or brand of plain yogurt that you use. Choose with care.

Superior homemade frozen yogurt can be made from plain yogurt by Continental. In its nonfrozen state, this yogurt tastes like a thick, rich sour cream. Continental is available in quart cartons in health food stores and select supermarkets.

Sundae-style or fruit-on-the-bottom commercial yogurts (i.e., Dannon's red raspberry) can be poured straight into your home ice cream machine and frozen. The results are surprisingly good.

Whipping your yogurt mixture will add the air necessary for a lightly textured frozen yogurt.

Refrigerating it for about two hours before freezing allows the flavors to blend—and shortens the freezing time.

Frozen dessert will result if you simply pour the mixture into a container and freeze for a few hours. However, you won't have a light "soft ice cream" texture unless you use an ice cream machine.

Kefir

A DELICIOUS CULTURED DRINK—

EVERYTHING YOU NEED TO KNOW

I remember, quite distinctly, the first time I tasted kefir. Peter and I had driven from Manhattan to Chittenango, New York, a distance of about three hundred miles, to interview Daniel Gates of the Gates Homestead Farms. Our trip had taken us past Woodstock, through Albany, and almost to Syracuse. I don't wish to carp, but this stretch of highway is—if you're not on a leisurely holiday jaunt and are in a bit of a hurry—extremely tedious. For some reason, the exits are miles and miles apart. You pass, say, Exit 21 and think, "only four more to go." And then—shock. After traveling simply forever you see "Exit 21 N or S" and you say to yourself, "My God, at this rate we'll never get there."

But, to return to my original story. After this long trip, we arrived in Chittenango and met Mr. Gates. He offered to give us a quick tour of the farm—house, barn, animals, equipment—before we sat down to talk.

It was a blistering hot day in August, and we were seated on an open porch. In the middle of our conversation, Mr. Gates said, "Would you like to taste some of our kefir?"* We both said yes, so Mr. Gates jumped up and went back to one of his huge walk-in re-

---

* Mr. Gates calls his product Rifek™, which is kefir spelled backwards. He explains why: this product is known as kefir in other states, but since the genuine kefir of Europe and Asia possesses fermenting, effervescing alcoholic characteristics and the product known as kefir in the USA does not, the use of the generic name "kefir" has been prohibited in New York State. (This changed as of July 1979. I've heard that there is now a Moondane kefir in New York State that has effervescing alcoholic characteristics.)

frigerators. A few minutes later he returned with several quarts of strawberry kefir.

What can I tell you? After the first sip I thought I was in heaven. The kefir was icy cold, tangy, and rich. A hint of strawberry flavor— yes, but just right, not too sweet. It was a perfectly delicious drink for a summer's day.

What Is Kefir?

In this country, the kefir you buy in your local supermarket or health food store is nonalcoholic. And in contrast to yogurt, kefir is a liquid, not a custardlike yogurt. You can drink kefir the same way you would milk, except that kefir is, I believe, much richer-tasting than milk. By comparison, the genuine European kefir contains from 0.5 to 1.5 percent alcohol.

The Alta-Dena people say kefir is a "cultured milk drink that is thick like buttermilk, and tastes similar to yogurt, but is different from either of these products." An apt description, but I would like to add one comment. When it comes to taste, I hate buttermilk, like yogurt, and love kefir. You figure it out.

Calories

For 3.5 ounces or 100 grams (that's just under one-half cup), kefir made with:

Whole milk	70 calories
Low-fat milk	53 calories
Skim milk	36 calories

Who Makes Kefir?

The Gates Homestead Farms. Their kefir is known as Rifek and is made with pasteurized whole certified milk. Flavors are made by adding natural fruit puree to plain kefir. No sugar or artificial sweetener is used (fruit flavors are sweetened with a little fructose). Comes in peach, plain, strawberry, pineapple, black cherry, and red raspberry. Location: Manlius-Chittenango Road, Chittenango, NY 13037. (In Georgia, according to a recent phone conversation I had with Mr. Gates, kefir is made by R. L. Mathis Certified Dairy, 31 81 Rainbow Drive, Decatur, GA 30034.)

Alta-Dena Dairy. Uses no sugar or artificial sweetener (fruit flavors are sweetened with a little fructose) and is made from whole pasteurized milk. Flavors are red raspberry, black cherry, peach, pineapple, apple, strawberry, lemon, and boysenberry. Location: 637 S. Hambledon, City of Industry, CA 91744.

Continental Culture Specialists. Made with pasteurized grade A whole milk and available in plain, boysenberry, cherry, peach, pineapple, raspberry, and strawberry. The sweetening agents for fruit flavors are honey and fructose. At P.O. Box 9285, 1354 East Colorado Street, Glendale, CA 91206.

Where to Buy Kefir

At Down To Earth, 33 Seventh Avenue (between Twelfth and Thirteenth streets) in New York, you can buy Gates Farms plain or flavored Rifek. The price is $1.85 for a quart of flavored, $1.65 for plain, and 60¢ for a half pint. Also at Brownies, 91 Fifth Avenue (between Sixteenth and Seventeenth streets), New York, NY 10003 (phone 212-242-2199); Good Earth, 1334 First Avenue (between Seventy-first and Seventy-second streets), New York, NY 10021 (phone 212-472-9055).

And recently I spotted Continental kefir at our local supermarket. It comes in a half-pint "pedestal" container which was, according to Continental, "designed and patented" by the head of the company, Mr. Cubaleski.*

Kefir Grains

This product, as I understand it, gives you the benefits of kefir-fermented milk—in a freeze-dried form. International Yogurt sent me a six-ounce sample (suggested price is $6.50). Their description reads, "Kefir grains contain four species of lactic bacteria and two species of lactose fermenting yeasts. All of these are important in maintaining a predominantly lactic flora in the intestines, or in restoring lactic bacteria when it is needed." You can take kefir grains

* Shortly before publication of this book I was informed by Continental that they are no longer allowed to sell their "kefir" in New York State. California and New York have regulations concerning this product that are mutually exclusive. No yeast is allowed in kefir in California; yeast is allowed in New York *but* a no-yeast product cannot be called kefir. Continental has discontinued their pedestal container and currently packs their kefir in an eight-ounce dairy container (all over the United States except New York).

by simply stirring a teaspoonful into a glass of cold milk. (This will *not* give you the same-tasting kefir as the ones made by Gates, Alta-Dena, and Continental.)

How to Make Kefir at Home

These instructions are from the Rosell Institute.

1. Heat one quart of pasteurized or homogenized milk (whole or skim) up to 180 degrees F. or 82 degrees C. Then, let it cool down to room temperature (70 to 80 degrees F.).

2. Mix the contents of an envelope (net weight 0.33 ounce) of Rosell kefir culture* to the cooled milk and pour the inoculated milk into a suitable container or divide in small jars of four to six ounces. *Important*: Containers must be sterilized in boiling water.

3. Let the milk stand at room temperature until curdling occurs (about twenty-four hours). Keep in the refrigerator.

4. Stir the curd with a spoon or an eggbeater, if a liquid kefir is desired.

5. For your next batch of kefir, inoculate each quart of milk (previously heated up to 180 degrees F. or 82 degrees C. and cooled) with one ounce or three tablespoons of the last batch of kefir.

6. Renew the kefir culture monthly. According to Gates Farms "a new culture of kefir must be used to eliminate the foreign microbes which have developed due to the gradual contamination caused by air, utensils and handling—as well as to restore the balance between the five microbe species which constitute the culture of kefir."

7. Your first batch of kefir will be quite liquid, subsequent batches will jell. For a more solid kefir add one-half cup of powdered milk.

My Test

I used four cups of low-fat milk and one envelope of kefir culture that was given to me by Mr. Brochu when Peter and I visited Rosell. I used Rosell's Yogotherm to incubate the kefir. (*Important:* Be sure to wash all yogurt equipment *thoroughly* after each use. I had inadvertently left a very tiny residue in the Yogotherm from a previous experiment and—let's just say I was aware of it when I opened up

---

* You can buy kefir culture from the International Yogurt Company of Los Angeles at any health food store.

the Yogotherm for this test.) After approximately eighteen hours I had delicious, refreshing kefir.

Ways You Can Serve Kefir

- Drink it plain or sprinkle with pepper.
- Mix with honey or maple syrup.
- Add brown sugar or vanilla flavoring.

Kefir Is Good for

The Rosell Institute believes that kefir, apart from tasting good, is beneficial for certain types of people. Here are Rosell's suggestions:

1. For children: it tastes delicious, is easy to digest, and provides nourishment for no-appetite or "picky" eaters.
2. For expectant mothers who often find it hard to eat anything at all.
3. For older people, or for anyone recovering from an illness.
4. For all persons treated with antibiotics such as penicillin or aureomycin (see page 123).

Kefir Recipes

Here are several recipes, using kefir, from Alta-Dena Dairy (created by Patricia Connolly of San Diego). All of them call for Alta-Dena kefir—naturally—but I imagine they'd work equally well with any kefir, commercial or homemade.

Party Dessert

2 cups kefir, any flavor	1 tablespoon gelatin
1 cup fresh or frozen fruit	¼ cup water
⅛ cup honey	Whipped cream

1. Place the kefir in your blender with the fruit and sweetening.
2. Dissolve gelatin in water and melt over lowest heat.
3. Turn on blender and pour the melted gelatin into the whirlpool in the center of the blender.
4. When well mixed, pour into custard cups or a serving bowl and chill until the gelatin sets.

(cont'd)

5. Serve topped with whipped cream and a strawberry or other fruit.

Fruit Salad

2 cups kefir, any flavor
1 tablespoon gelatin
¼ cup water

1½ cups diced mixed fruit (any combination of bananas, peaches, cherries, apricots, plums, pears, grapes, apples, papaya, or berries).

1. Place kefir in blender.
2. Dissolve gelatin in water; melt over lowest heat and add to the kefir, which is whirling on low speed.
3. Pour into serving bowl or mold and add fruit.
4. Chill in refrigerator and unmold onto a bed of lettuce or alfalfa sprouts. Garnish with cottage cheese or kefir cheese.

Kefir Freeze

Freeze any flavor kefir in ice cube trays or any plastic mold. Remove cubes and place in plastic bag in your freezer to have a variety available. These cubes make a delicious and nutritious freeze.

Kefir Shake

Kefir cubes, any flavor

Equal amounts of milk and kefir (same flavor as cubes)

Place all of the above in your blender and blend until you have a thick kefir shake.

Kefir Ice Cream

½ cup kefir, any flavor
1 egg
2 tablespoons honey, optional

1 cup frozen or fresh fruit
2 cups kefir cubes, same flavor as fruit

1. Put kefir, egg, and honey in blender. Blend to mix honey well.
2. Add fruit and kefir cubes until you have ice cream consistency. (Much thicker than the shake.)

106

3. Or, place the mixture (using 2½ cups liquid kefir rather than cubes) into a Salton ice cream maker which slides into your freezer and will turn the mixture into ice cream.

Don't Confuse

Certified milk is raw or pasteurized fresh fluid milk produced under the Methods and Standards for the Production of Certified Milk by the American Association of Medical Milk Commissions. It may be homogenized and fortified with vitamin D. Certified milks are on the decline, made obsolete by the high standards of production and processing now followed by the dairy industry. (*Milk . . . Ageless Food with National Appeal*, National Dairy Council, Rosemont, IL 60018)

Goat's Milk Yogurt

A YOGURT FOR THOSE WHO WANT

SOMETHING DIFFERENT

One day, when I was shopping in the Good Earth health food store, I spotted goat's milk yogurt made by Pure Goat Products in Pennsylvania.* Since I had never tried this type of yogurt before, I decided to buy a carton. As I said earlier, other than tasting a little salty, it seemed like "regular" yogurt to me.

I decided, after sampling this yogurt, that I'd like to know more about the company that made it. The address on the side of the carton read "Pure Goat Products, Inc., Rd. 3, Boyertown, Pa. 19512."

On June 13, 1977, I wrote my first letter of inquiry. Then, after waiting over a month and receiving no reply, I wrote a second one. Again, no reply. Finally, on February 22, 1978, I wrote my third and last letter. When I again received no response, I decided that the direct approach would be best—just show up and politely request an interview.

A Visit with Pure Goat Products

Peter and I started out for Boyertown, Pennsylvania, and Pure Goat Products one blustery day in March. The distance to Boyertown, according to our AAA Triptik, was 126 miles. Note: Our return trip was 131 miles (plus 10 miles extra when I headed straight north to Scranton—courtesy of a toll collector who told me the wrong turn

* You can also buy goat's milk by Pure Goat Products. One quart of pasteurized goat's milk is $1.35.

108

for New York. Sartre's *No Exit* is a dream compared to the nightmare of traveling for miles in the wrong direction on a turnpike). Since we had driven 600 miles round trip in one day when we visited Gates Farms in Chittenango I felt we could do this 267-mile trip with ease.

When at last we parked our station wagon near a cluster of large stone buildings with a sign on one that read "Pure Goat Products" I realized that, since it was Saturday, there was a possibility no one would be there. We knocked on the doors to several of the buildings. I peered around a couple of them, hoping to see, at least, a few goats.

Finally, I spotted a stone house several hundred yards down the hill and decided to try there. We were in luck. Mrs. William Wagner, the owner of Pure Goat Products, invited us in and offered to give us as much information as she could.

When we began to discuss Pure Goat products, Mrs. Wagner told me that her company made not only goat's milk yogurt but also goat's milk ice cream and cheese. "And we make a goat's milk frozen yogurt dessert," she added. "It's not as rich as ice cream, but it's smoother than a sherbet. I really like it."*

I asked her to tell me as much as possible about goat's milk yogurt. "Well," she said, "there are no goats here because we buy all our milk from dairies in New Jersey, Maryland, and Pennsylvania. And ours is a pure yogurt—no sugar, no preservatives. We don't use anything artificial at all. We make blueberry, peach, strawberry, and raspberry fruit flavors but our plain yogurt is the most popular. And we make nothing ahead of time—our yogurt is made only after an order has been placed" (from distributors and health food stores). She added that Pure Goat products can be shipped anywhere in the United States.

I quizzed Mrs. Wagner about the benefits of goat's milk. "You can digest it faster than cow's milk," she said. "Goat's milk can be digested in just half an hour [for approximately one cup]. I'm talking about the milk now," she stressed. "I don't know about the yogurt."

"Are you sure of this?" I asked.

"Yes," she replied, "we've had research done in Philadelphia—at the Children's Hospital."

As we got up to leave, I asked Mrs. Wagner if she had anything

* You can buy this product in New York at Brownies for $1.20. It contains "condensed and whole goat milk, yogurt culture, honey and pure fruit." Look for it in the freezer.

more she'd like to say about her yogurt. She laughed and said, "Well, we think it's good." Then she added, "Make sure you say we're the only ones in the East doing this kind of work." I promised her I would.

Acidophilus Yogurt

THE YOGURT MADE FROM A "DIFFERENT"

CULTURE

On the East Coast there is an acidophilus* yogurt that I shall refer to as Brand Z, made by an Armenian family who operate their ten-year-old company from a brick building that is smaller than my living room. I wrote a letter of inquiry to Brand Z in June 1977 and received a short, hand-written note saying that they did not wish to reveal "any details of our company" and that "even though only two or three line comments have appeared in national magazines in the past, it resulted in more mail than our small company could answer." The note ended by saying that "if you still have not yet published your book at the beginning of next year—-write to us again at that time."

I wrote one more letter in July 1977 asking for a few short answers to questions I had about acidophilus yogurt but received no reply. So, I decided to get on with other things and did not write again until February 1978. Again, no reply. It was at this point that I decided to call. But—surprise—there's no listing for Brand Z yogurt. No phone.

---

* *Lactobacillus acidophilus* is a bacterium that is normally found in the large bowel of a healthy person. There, it performs many vital functions. One is to make B vitamins—these are crucial for the production of antibodies that protect us from infection.

A Nonvisit with Brand Z

In March I drove to central Pennsylvania and tracked down the owner at her home from a phone number on a piece of paper that was taped to the door of the plant. When I got her on the phone, she said that she would not answer any questions on the phone, would not allow a face-to-face interview, and did not want any publicity—at all. Now, I believe in being persistent to get what one wants in this world, but even I decided to give up at this point.

When I got back to New York, I decided to sample Brand Z yogurt again. I noticed that it had, for lack of a better word, a "skin" or cream layer on top. This unusual characteristic is explained in the copy on the carton, which says "the top cream proves the milk has not been exposed to the extra processing of homogenization." I would say this yogurt is in the same category as other "special" yogurts that I tried (apart from the obvious health benefits, of course)—it's definitely an acquired taste.

Brand Z acidophilus yogurt is available in health food stores on the East Coast. I bought an eight-ounce carton at the Good Earth for 69¢ (a sixteen-ounce carton is $1.25).

Yami Acidophilus Yogurt

On the West Coast, a large company called Foremost Foods makes Yami* lowfat acidophilus yogurt in thirteen flavors—including pineapple and papaya. Dr. Brochu of the Rosell Institute, which supplies Yami with their cultures, told me that this yogurt is sold in "the western United States, Canada, Hawaii, Guam, and Australia."

How to Make Your Own Acidophilus Milk

The International Yogurt Company in Los Angeles has an acidophilus milk culture that you can buy for $2.50 per packet (a month's supply). According to them, this culture will enable you "to make acidophilus milk from homogenized milk, skim milk, partially skim milk or reconstituted skim milk. The lactic bacteria strains in this culture can curdle milk in a few hours."

* *Yami* means "yogurt acidophilus milk."

Directions

1. Heat a quart of milk to boiling or close to boiling for about five minutes. Cool to 105-110 degrees F.

2. Pour in the acidophilus milk culture. Mix well, then pour the milk into a clean container.

3. Place the container in a pan filled with lukewarm water (105-110 degrees F.) up to the level of the milk. Cover. Incubate, keeping milk at lukewarm temperature until milk is curdled (four to six hours). Refrigerate until cold.

4. Liquefy the solid acidophilus milk by stirring and eat it plain or add sugar, honey, or preserves.

Important: Next batches are made by culturing each quart of lukewarm milk with two to three tablespoons of acidophilus milk from the last batch. This practice may be continued for about a month. A new culture should then be used to eliminate contamination.

Note: The acidophilus milk culture sold by the International Yogurt Company can also be used to make acidophilus yogurt. Here are additional—more enlightening—instructions which International sent me in April 1978.

When you put the envelope of acidophilus culture into one quart of milk —you make one quart of acidophilus that sets up exactly like yogurt. If you want it even more solid add a few tablespoons of powdered milk.

However, even though it sets up like yogurt, you can turn it into a *liquid* by vigorous stirring. Your acidophilus milk will be like a heavy buttermilk.

My Test

For this experiment I used lowfat milk which I heated in the top part of a double boiler to just below boiling, then cooled to 115 degrees F. After it had been six hours in an electric yogurt maker, I placed the yogurt in my refrigerator and allowed it to cool. At this point the result is acidophilus yogurt. However, after vigorous stirring, this acidophilus yogurt does, indeed, turn into an acidophilus milk which, as International said, has the consistency of "heavy buttermilk."

Short Stop

Should the acidophilus bacteria be added to yogurt? Here's a counterargument from Dannon: "Yogurt cultures require a certain level of temperature and amount of time to develop properly. These conditions are quite different from those required by acidophilus. The two types of culture, yogurt and acidophilus, are not compatible in production. As we see it, normal, healthy people eat yogurt for its high nutritional value, reasonable calorie content and satisfying taste. Acidophilus cultures make no contribution in these areas."

Don't Confuse

Acidophilus milk with its high acid content and harsh taste has not been well received by consumers. To overcome the taste problem, flavors such as chocolate, coffee, strawberry, and lemon have been added. *Sweet acidophilus milk* is a new product that has eliminated the harsh acid flavor of regular acidophilus milk; it tastes like lowfat pasteurized milk.

Yogurt in the Medical World

SCIENTIFIC STUDIES THAT SHOW YOGURT

WORKS

Is yogurt the magic cure-all for half the diseases one finds in a medical dictionary? Or is 90 percent of all the literature on "yogurt remedies" pure bunk? Personally, I suspect that the truth lies somewhere in between. There is a lot of nonsense written about yogurt, I agree, but on the other hand, some highly regarded individuals in very reputable medical institutions have done thorough scientific studies on yogurt and its effect on the human body.

Here, then, is a brief chapter on yogurt in the world of medicine. I make no judgments and offer no hard-and-fast conclusions. I am asking you to simply read and decide for yourself.

Cholesterol

On Sunday, June 23, 1974, the *New York Times* published an article by Jane E. Brody entitled "Study Hints That Yogurt May Reduce Cholesterol." This piece was based on a report that was published in the *American Journal of Clinical Nutrition* in May 1974.

I have tried many times to obtain a copy of this report and, for one reason or another, I've failed. (I even wrote the author who replied, "Sorry, I have exhausted my supply of reprints.") However, Ms. Brody has written the best "for-the-layman" piece that I've seen on this yogurt/cholesterol report (and, in the course of my research for this book over the past four years, I've seen many). Here, then, is Ms. Brody's *New York Times* article.

STUDY HINTS THAT YOGURT MAY REDUCE CHOLESTEROL

The long-standing popular belief that yogurt is good for you may have a stronger base in scientific fact than has heretofore been realized, according to the accidental findings of recent nutritional study among primitive African tribesmen.

The study indicates that some subsance in yogurt may be capable of lowering the level of cholesterol in the blood by lowering the amount the body produces, and this in turn may help protect against the development of atherosclerotic heart disease, which is epidemic in this country.

Although at the moment this is a tentative conclusion based on preliminary findings of an experiment originally designed for another purpose, the investigators say that they have already reproduced the cholesterol-lowering effect in adult Americans who are consuming large amounts of homemade yogurt as part of a continuing study at Vanderbilt University of Tennessee.

The effect is occurring even though the yogurt diet is high in cholesterol. Yogurt, like fresh milk, is a relatively high-cholesterol food. If made from whole milk, a quart contains from 120 to 150 milligrams of the fatty substance notorious for its ability to clog arteries.

STUDY OF SURFACTANTS

The interrelationships between the amount of cholesterol in the diet, the amount the body itself produces and the level of cholesterol in the blood are at best poorly understood. However, it is widely believed that excessive dietary cholesterol, while shutting off the body's production to some extent, generally results in an excess in the blood and eventual clogging of the blood vessels.

The African study was conducted by Dr. George V. Mann, associate professor of biochemistry and medicine at Vanderbilt who is a career investigator for the National Heart and Lung Institute, and Anne Spoerry of the African Medical Research Foundation. It was originally intended to explore the effects surfactants, a widely used class of food additives, have upon blood cholesterol levels.

Surfactants make oil or water more mixable and are commonly used in this country in such commercially produced foods as mayonnaise, ice cream, chocolate and baked goods, as well as in detergents. In earlier experiments in rabbits, monkeys and dogs, Dr. Mann found that blood cholesterol levels rose when surfactants were added to the animals' diets

116

in levels ordinarily used in American foods. He then went to East Africa to test this observation on human beings.

Nomadic People

Dr. Mann chose for the study a group of Masai tribesmen, a primitive nomadic people he has studied intensively for the last decade because they are unusually resistant to heart disease despite a milk-and-meat diet heavily laden with animal fats and cholesterol.

Ordinarily the Masai have very low blood cholesterol levels, averaging 135 milligrams per 100 milliliters of blood, against an American male average of 240, and since the Masai have no other exposure to surfacants, they were good candidates for a carefully controlled study of the chemicals' effects upon cholesterol.

The regular Masai diet consists of about a gallon a day of fermented whole milk, a kind of homemade yogurt, and a once-a-week feast of meat, with a daily cholesterol intake of nearly twice that recommended by the American Heart Association.

The twenty-four young Masai men chosen for the study were divided into two groups, a treatment group that received surfactant in their yogurt and a control group that got yogurt without the additive. Since the food was free, the men kept asking for more and soon were consuming twice their normal amount of yogurt. Not surprisingly, they also began to gain weight, and since weight gain by itself is known to raise cholesterol levels, Dr. Mann decided to end the experiment after three weeks.

The big surprise came, however, when the men's cholesterol was measured. In both the treatment and the control groups, blood cholesterol levels had dropped significantly since the start of the study. In fact, the more weight gained (and thus, presumably, the more yogurt consumed), the greater was the cholesterol drop. This drop occurred despite a tremendous increase in dietary cholesterol, so it must have resulted from a dramatic decline in the body's own production of cholesterol, Dr. Mann concluded.

Americans Studied

Results of the African study, which was supported by the National Live Stock and Meat Board, were published in the May issue of the American Journal of Clinical Nutrition.

Dr. Mann is now studying twelve adult Americans who are being given two liters (slightly more than two quarts) of yogurt daily plus enough of their regular diet to maintain their normal weight. Thus far, he said in a telephone interview, yogurt made by adding a commercial

American yogurt culture to whole milk or to skimmed milk has been found to lower cholesterol, although the same amount of fresh, unfermented milk had no such effect.

Dr. Mann suspects that the yogurt bacteria produce a substance, probably a small fatty acid, that blocks cholesterol production in the liver. He is now testing various fractions of yogurt to isolate the precise substance that has this effect.

But whatever the results of his study, Dr. Mann emphasized that diet was certainly not the only factor that protected the Masai from heart disease. The average young Masai walks up to 25 miles a day, and even the old men cover distances of seven or eight miles, his studies have shown. In general, the typical Masai is as physically fit as a trained American athlete, the doctor reported.

Effect of Yogurt with Prune Whip on Constipation

This study, the results of which appeared in the *American Journal of Digestive Diseases*, September 1955, was conducted by Drs. Francis P. Ferrer and Linn J. Boyd at a New York hospital.

One hundred ninety-four chronically ill patients, suffering from constipation, were selected for this investigation. The group included men and women ranging in age from fifty-three to ninety-one. Out of the whole group, ninety-one were diabetic.

All of the patients were given prune whip yogurt as a night feeding from September 30 until November 20. No laxatives were given during this period and no other changes were made in the patients' regular diet.

At the conclusion of the two-month study, it was found that 187, or 95.8 percent of the patients required no laxatives during the time they were eating prune whip yogurt.

Yogurt for Diarrhea in Infants

I first heard about yogurt as a remedy for diarrhea in babies from my Armenian friend, Mrs. Attarian. "I gave it to both my boys when they were babies," she told me.

I then found out that research had been done in this area. After some digging, I obtained a copy of the article "Yogurt in the Treatment of Infantile Diarrhea," published by Drs. Molly Niv, Walter

Levy, and Nathan M. Greenstein in the July 1963 issue of *Clinical Pediatrics.*

The study begins by making the point that although yogurt has been used for years as a remedy for diarrhea in infants (in countries along the Mediterranean Sea and the Balkans) its effectiveness as a treatment has been given little or no heed in medical literature.

The research itself was conducted at Jewish Memorial Hospital with forty-five children, 75 percent of whom were infants under one year old, who had "severe cases of diarrhea, whose treatment at home had failed."

The children were divided into two groups: one group was fed 100 ml. of yogurt three times daily; the second group received one teaspoon of Neomycin-Kaopectate three times daily. Other than this, both groups had the same diet: 5 percent glucose in water, weak tea, and half-diluted boiled skim milk. Here are the results:

DAYS TO RECOVERY DEPENDING UPON TREATMENT	YOGURT	NEOMYCIN	TOTAL
1–3	21	7	28
4 and over	4	13	17

As can be seen, more children in the yogurt group recovered within three days, while the opposite was true in the Neomycin group.

Under Comments in the original report a cautionary note is added: "Although too definite conclusions cannot be drawn from the small, heterogenous group of patients studied, significantly faster recovery from diarrhea was obtained with yogurt than with Neomycin-Kaopectate."

A Brief Comment: Children and Yogurt

In one of their many publications, Dannon says, "Recent studies show that a child who is overweight at the age of six has an 80 percent chance of being overweight all his (or her) life." We can say, then, that an awareness of good eating habits should begin very early in a child's life.

Suggestion: why not serve yogurt as a snack (better than pretzels) or lunch for your child? If you have an infant, start him or her on plain yogurt or lightly flavored yogurts like vanilla and lemon. For older children, try the fruited yogurts such as cherry, strawberry, raspberry, or peach.

Plain Yogurt and Bananas for Babies Six Months and Older

Combine mashed ripe bananas with one-half container of plain yogurt.

For a quick, tasty beverage, blend one cup plain yogurt, one cup orange or apple juice, and one ripe banana in a blender. Sweeten to taste.

A simple dessert for your baby: Crush one or two graham crackers. Mix half of the graham crackers, one-half ripe mashed banana, and one-half container of plain yogurt together. Sprinkle remaining graham cracker crumbs on top.

My Study: Babies and Yogurt

In April 1978 I decided to do a very small research test on babies and yogurt. I drafted a simple two-page questionnaire and sent it to my sister, Karen, who is a nurse and lives in Vancouver, British Columbia.

Karen asked eight of her friends, all mothers of babies ranging in age from seven to twenty-two months, to (1) feed Baby yogurt, (2) watch and listen to Baby's reaction, and (3) write it all down.

Nine babies—this included Karen's daughter Lisa—were involved in the study. In my questionnaire I asked the mothers to grade Baby's reaction, verbal or nonverbal, this way:

1. Wow, this is fantastic—gimme more!
2. Okay, but I've tasted better.
3. What is this stuff you're feeding me?

Here are the results. I find them both humorous and interesting.

The three boys, Jonathan, Geoffrey, and Sheldon, all scored 1. In fact, Geoffrey's mother writes, "He smacked his lips and had his mouth open for more. Geoffrey eats everything. If he *really* likes something he says, 'Mmmm.' If he doesn't like something he pretends to gag—but he still keeps on eating."

Of the six girls, Katy and Kelly thought that yogurt was the greatest. Kelly cried "more, more" after it was all over. The other four split the vote 50-50: two, by their reactions, let Mother know that yogurt was "okay, but I've tasted better" and the other two, Shelley and my niece, Lisa, just didn't like it. However, I asked the

120

mothers to use *only* plain or lemon yogurt. Karen reports, "After one spoonful of plain yogurt, Lisa just wouldn't open her mouth. Then I mixed the yogurt with some stewed prunes and down the hatch it all went—as fast as I could spoon it up." Results? Only one baby (Shelley) out of nine definitely did not like yogurt. So I'd say yogurt wins. Hands down.

Fever Blisters, or Cold Sores, and Canker Sores

Some of the first case studies on yogurt for treatment of fever blisters (also called cold sores) and canker sores were presented by Dr. Don J. Weekes in 1958 when he was associated with the Department of Otolaryngology at Harvard Medical School and the Department of Surgery at Peter Bent Brigham Hospital in Boston.

In the *New York State Journal of Medicine* (Vol. 58, No. 16, August 15, 1958) Dr. Weekes describes how treatment with a living culture of *Lactobacillus acidophilus* and the related *L. bulgaricus* affected his patients.

Among his early cases was a thirty-nine-year-old woman who had been complaining of almost continuous aphthous* stomatitis (canker sores). After suffering for two years, she began taking two Lactobacillus tablets dissolved in the mouth with milk four times a day and her symptoms were promptly relieved.

Another patient, a forty-two-year-old graduate nurse, was so plagued by canker sores that she was unable to take proper nourishment. She was admitted to the hospital suffering from severe dehydration. "Forty-eight hours after treatment with Lactobacillus therapy all ulcers had healed, she was taking fluids well, and urine volume returned," Dr. Weekes reports.

Dr. Weekes continued with his research and again reported his results—this time in the December 1963 issue of *E.E.N.T. Digest.* Here, he goes on to describe clinical tests of the Lactobacillus preparation involving 174 patients. The results? Ninety-five percent showed either complete relief or dramatic improvement of painful blisters or sores in or about the mouth.

To conclude: no one is sure exactly how the yogurt culture works

* The Greek word *aphthae* originally meant "to set on fire."

in relieving the pain and inflammation of canker sores and fever blisters. One theory is that the lactic acid in yogurt somehow kills the bacteria responsible for these flare-ups.

My Test

This was a tough one to test. After all, I could hardly ask my friends if they had canker sores and may I run a yogurt test on them. However, one day in August 1979 Peter happened to get a particularly nasty canker sore in his mouth. It lasted for five painful days. On the morning of the sixth day I watched him bite into a piece of toast and almost hit the roof with the pain. "Look," I said in desperation, "at least *try* the yogurt remedy." "Okay, okay," he replied. For two days he ate vanilla yogurt four times a day. By the morning of the third day the pain from the canker sore was completely gone and shortly after the canker sore itself disappeared.

Interesting Facts About Canker Sores and Fever Blisters

Where do they appear? Canker sores usually appear inside the mouth—on the lining of the cheeks, on the edge of the tongue, or in the groove at the base of the gums. Fever blisters, or cold sores, often occur outside the mouth and usually erupt on the skin adjoining the lip.

Who is susceptible? Canker sores affect between 20 and 50 percent of the population. Women are twice as likely to have them as men. About 90 percent of the time the problem is found to run in the family. Another indication of a strong genetic factor is its rarity in racially unmixed Negroes. The disease is not contagious. It is not limited to any climate or economic conditions.

What causes canker sores? They tend to appear when one has experienced some physical or emotional stress. A study of a group of college students revealed that canker sores were more likely to develop during examination periods than during vacation. Food allergies may be a factor. Some people avoid *acid foods* such as citrus fruit, walnuts, vinegar, and tomatoes because they trigger problems.

What causes fever blisters? Fever blisters often follow lowered physical resistance; illness, particularly upper respiratory infection; trauma; or emotional stress. They are also associated with temperature increases due to illness or too much sun. The disease tends to run in certain families and probably has some hereditary component. (Source: U.S. Department of Health, Education, and Welfare)

Yogurt and Antibiotics

On a recent visit to my doctor, I was given a prescription for an antibiotic. "Eat a little yogurt after you have this," Dr. Walden said. "It will take care of your tummy." (This translates, as I learned later, into "restoring the bacterial flora" in one's intestine.)

Several months later, when I decided to explore this subject further, I came across a book of my husband's, *A New Breed of Doctor* (New York: Pyramid House, 1972). In it, the author, Dr. Alan Nittler, states, "If drugs must be given they should be given in combination with nutritional supplements." He goes on to say that "antibiotics kill valuable intestinal flora" and recommends that one take yogurt "with and following" ingestion of antibiotics.

Since my curiosity was aroused, I decided to check into this area a little further by writing to six of the largest drug companies in the United States (Eli Lilly, Pfizer, Warner-Lambert, Squibb, Lederle, and Upjohn) to get their opinions on the yogurt/antibiotics question.

Of the six, I received replies from five. Two said that they had no information on this particular subject, one sent a list of three sources that I could look up in a medical library, and two gave me complete answers.

Of these last two, Dr. James Vavra of the Upjohn Company in Kalamazoo, Michigan, said that if an antibiotic reached the large intestine it could "upset the bowel ecology" and as a result "diarrhea can occur." To counteract this, Dr. Vavra said, "ingestion of yogurt could reasonably be expected to hasten establishment of a normal flora."

Dr. Robert Buchanan of Warner-Lambert in Ann Arbor, Michigan, also agreed that yogurt can theoretically correct an intestinal imbalance caused by an antibiotic. However, he also added that "the newer antibiotics have been improved" so that "changes in the intestinal flora rarely occur." Therefore, Dr. Buchanan concludes, "the addition of yogurt is unnecessary."

My conclusion? I'd say the vote was in favor of taking yogurt "with and following" antibiotics. And, of course, you can always look at it this way—if taking yogurt with an antibiotic doesn't help you, it certainly won't hurt.

Yogurt and Alcohol

I will be the first to concede that alcohol has no place in this chapter. However, I really don't know where else to put it, and I'm not about to discard this subject simply because it doesn't fit into a neat category. So, as I've said many times before when faced with quizzical looks, "Humor me."

I heard about alcohol and yogurt for the first time from Mrs. Attarian. She told me that she had, on occasion, given her husband a cup of yogurt on mornings after he'd had too much to drink. I forgot completely about her comment until I came across this sentence by Prof. Frances James in her article "Yogurt: Its Life and Culture":

Yogurt has been shown by London University investigators to reduce peak blood alcohol levels by 67 percent if ten ounces (that's slightly over a cup) of yogurt are consumed before drinking.

She concludes with this interesting comment: "That is to say, so much yogurt has an effect on alcohol similar to that of a substantial meal, but leaves considerably more space for the alcohol."

So now you know. If you want to prep for your next "night on the town," just eat an eight-ounce carton of yogurt an hour or so before you go.

Sunburn and Freckles

DOES YOGURT WORK?

Have you ever had a *real* sunburn? One that's so unbearable you can't stand the touch of a lightweight cotton sheet against your skin? Believe me, it's a painful experience.

The worst one I ever had happened at St. Thomas in the Virgin Islands about ten years ago. How it came about is so totally lacking in common sense that I'm almost embarrassed to tell you about it.

However, here goes. We were staying at the Mafolie Hotel, which is located high in the hills overlooking Charlotte Amalie, the capital of the islands. Needless to say, the view is breathtaking.

At that time, the Mafolie had a small bar down by the pool which they kept open all day. (Six years later when we returned, the bar was closed down completely.) However, if you can believe this, on my very first day in the Caribbean—I, with fair skin and freckles— sat by the pool for *five hours* sunning and drinking Bloody Marys. It was my very first trip to the Caribbean and I was totally enchanted with the entire scene.

Of course, I was constantly being reminded by my husband that I was overdoing it. But I wouldn't listen. We had just left New York —ten degrees and snowing—and I was determined to get as much sun as possible. All in one day.

Need I tell you what I looked like the next morning? A bright pinky red, of course. But, worse than this, I couldn't open my eyes. Both of them were swollen shut—I looked like I'd been slugged by a heavyweight boxing champion. (On reading this paragraph, my husband reminded me that I'd left out one important part. That was when I leapt out of bed yelling, "I'm blind, I'm blind—my God, I'm too young to be blind.")

125

This tale, fortunately, ends on a happy note. Peter took me to the emergency room of a local hospital where an East Indian doctor gave me a lecture and a prescription—in that order. "Even with my skin I wouldn't sit in the sun for five hours," he said. I looked at the floor.

Of course, once it was established that no real damage was done, Pete found the whole incident rather amusing, and offered to take my picture. I made my feelings known, very quickly, as to how I felt about *that* idea.

Later, we went to the pharmacy, had the prescription filled, and within hours I was back to normal. Never again.

Yogurt for a Sunburn

I have read, several different sources, that yogurt is good for a sunburn. My husband also told me that his barber once remarked, "In Greece, mothers use yogurt on their children as protection against the sun."

I wanted to verify some of the uses I'd come across for yogurt (sunburn, freckles, and wrinkles) so I talked to my Armenian friend, Hilda Attarian, whose name I'd seen in an article on yogurt that appeared in the *New York Post* of October 2, 1976.

I interviewed Mrs. Attarian one evening in a small coffee shop on Manhattan's East Side. She told me that, at the time of the publication of the article, she owned a small boutique on West Twenty-third Street. The *Post* gave the name of her shop and many people mistakenly thought she sold homemade yogurt there. "The phone rang every day for weeks," she said. "I didn't get any peace—everyone wanted me to tell them how to make yogurt." (The article had stressed that Mrs. Attarian always made her own yogurt. "It's so easy to make," she was quoted as saying.)

I asked Mrs. Attarian whether it was true that yogurt was, indeed, used for sunburn. "Yes," she assured me, "it was. But, of course, today we have all these modern things—lotions and such." Then she added, "Armenian women do dab a bit around the eyes for wrinkles" (see page 132). American women, I might add, dab *a lot of things* on for wrinkles. My personal theory is that a well-balanced life-style does more to fight wrinkles than anything one may put on.

But back to yogurt for a sunburn. Does it work? I admit I have no scientific data on this, but I'm inclined to believe it does. So, file this info under useful trivia. Someday, if you're in the Mojave Desert with one flat tire, no hat, and a cup of yogurt, it may come in handy.

126

Yogurt for Freckles

I have had freckles all my life. Up until the sixth grade I hated my freckles with all the passion a child can muster. Then one day Timothy Lewis told me that he thought freckles on a girl's nose were "neat." Since Timothy had given me twenty-two cards for Valentine's Day his remark made a noticeable dent in my attitude toward freckles.

As an adult, I have accepted the fact that every winter my freckles will fade—and every summer I will have a fresh crop on my nose, shoulders, and back. I think they look "healthy" and I see no reason to try to get rid of them.

Which brings us to the question: Is there, if one should want to, a way to remove freckles permanently—or, at least, "bleach" them out temporarily?

Let's look at *The Yogurt Book: 100 Things to do with Yogurt Besides Eating it out of the Container* (New York: Grosset & Dunlap, 1977). The authors, Connie Berman and Susan Katz, prescribe yogurt as a freckle bleach:

Yogurt Freckle Bleach—Simply apply yogurt to the blotchy or discolored areas of the skin, wherever you want a more uniform skin tone. When the yogurt is dry, rinse off with cool water.

Regular use should help to achieve even skin coloration. If skin feels dry after the yogurt bleach, dab on a few teaspoons of oil to prevent irritation.

I decided to seek out opinions from reputable sources on how effective yogurt could be as a freckle bleach. The results were rather interesting. Two doctors didn't reply, four said that they had no information on the subject, and Dr. Albert M. Kligman of the dermatology department at Monell Chemical Senses Center in Philadelphia responded with an answer that could in no way be misconstrued. His one-word reply? "Hokum."

As for myself, I'm inclined to be a bit skeptical. But if you feel you want to try using yogurt as a freckle bleach—by all means go ahead. You've got nothing to lose but your freckles.

Milk

DIFFERENT TYPES OF MILK DEFINED

From the age of six until I was thirteen I spent all my summer vacations on a small island located at the mouth of the Skeena River, which is about sixty miles south of Alaska. My family (parents and four children) thought it was a great place to visit for three months out of every year. My sister, brothers, and I would fish, swim, sail, hike—and generally exhaust ourselves every day until six o'clock in the evening. Then it was time for dinner, and if we were lucky we had one of our favorites—abalones* prepared by my father.

We were always aware that this treat was in the offing because, invariably, my father would announce the night before, "Well, it's zero tide tomorrow, who wants to come with me and pick abalones?"

The next morning we'd all crawl out of bed at some ungodly hour to go with my father on his abalone hunt. After a two-mile hike we'd reach the right spot on the beach. Then we'd have to move fast. The abalones clung like barnacles to large, wet rocks that were only exposed at zero tide. We usually had about half an hour to gather our supply—then the tide would come rushing in.

To gather the abalone, we had to grab its shell and pull hard. They have the ability to fasten themselves, very tightly, with small suction cups to the rocks. My father would carry a long screwdriver in his back pocket to use as a wedge in case one got a little stubborn.

* The foot of this delicious shellfish—contraband if shipped from California—comes to our markets canned or frozen from Mexico and Japan, shelled, pounded and ready to cook. If you get it in the shell, remove the edible portion by running a knife between the shell and the meat. Abalone needs prodigious pounding to tenderize it—the meat is ready to cook when it looks like Dali's limp watch. (Irma S. Rombauer and Marion Rombauer Becker, *Joy of Cooking* [New York: Bobbs-Merrill, 1975])

128

After we had enough abalones for six people (or if the tide cut off our search) we'd head for home. There my father would remove each abalone from its shell, clean it under cold, running water, and flatten it with a wooden mallet. Then the meat would be dipped in beaten egg, rolled in bread crumbs, and put into sizzling butter in a hot frying pan. When it turned golden brown it was ready. Delicious? All I can tell you is that my father would say, grandly, every time, "A feast fit for a king."

Now, what do abalones have to do with milk? Not very much, I'm afraid. Except for the fact that I really like milk,* and I really like abalones. The only difference is that I drink milk every day and I haven't had an abalone in years.

Know Your ABC's

Grade A milk is the grade of fresh fluid milk generally sold retail to consumers. It is pasteurized and homogenized and includes whole and skim milks, buttermilk, and flavored milk drinks. Grade B milk is used only to make manufactured dairy products such as butter, cheese, and evaporated milk. (Source: National Dairy Council)

Holy Cow!

A high-producing dairy cow may weigh 1,200 pounds or more and consume many times that weight in feed yearly. The total could include 3,100 to 5,000 pounds of concentrated feeds such as farm grains and seed oil cake. These are called concentrates because they are compact sources of energy.

Also on the cow's yearly menu are two and a half tons of hay; six and a half tons of silage made of chopped green corn, sorghum, and grass legume mixtures; and the grass of two or more acres of good pasture. Yearly water consumption may range from 4,000 to 7,000 gallons—the equivalent of forty to seventy very large bathtubs filled to capacity.

Depending on her care, and inherited ability, the cow will then produce anywhere from 8,000 to 30,000 pounds of milk a year. This is approximately 3,700 to 13,950 quarts. (Source: *Milk . . . Ageless Food with Natural Appeal*, National Dairy Council)

* The real reason I'm including a chapter on milk is because the relationship between yogurt and milk is so close. Don't want to leave any loose ends.

Don't Confuse

Evaporated milk is canned milk that is made by removing part of the water from whole milk. It is then processed by heat to prevent spoilage. Open evaporated milk can be kept in its can, covered and stored in the refrigerator, for three to five days. *Condensed or concentrated milk* is similar to evaporated milk because it is also made by the partial removal of water from whole milk. Unlike evaporated milk, concentrated milk is usually not heat processed to prevent spoilage. *Sweetened condensed milk* is, again, a canned milk that is made by removing part of the water from whole milk. It is mixed with sweetener to help prevent spoilage. This milk should be covered and refrigerated after opening, but its sugar content prolongs its freshness. *Dry whole or skim milk* is made by the removal of all water from pasteurized whole or skim milk. It should be stored in a cool, dry place with container resealed after opening. Humidity causes powdered milk to lump and change flavor, but it can still be used in cooking and baking. Properly stored skim dry milk will keep up to a year or longer. Dry whole milk will keep at least three months. (National Dairy Council and the U.S. Department of Agriculture)

Your Quick Guide to Dairy Foods*

A. Fluid or market milk
   Homogenized whole milk
   Vitamin D whole milk
   Fortified milk
   Flavored milk
   Lowfat milk
   Skim milk or nonfat milk
B. Fermented milk and milk products
   Cultured buttermilk
   Sour cream
   Yogurt
   Acidophilus milk
   Kefir
C. Market creams with varying amounts of fat

* From: "Composition and Nutritive Value of Dairy Foods," *Dairy Council Digest* 47(5):25, 1976. (Note: For material from the National Dairy Council I contacted the Dairy Council of Metropolitan New York, 60 East 42nd Street, New York, NY 10017. Phone: 212-682-7961.)

D. Butter, butter oil, and spreads
E. Concentrated milk products
   Evaporated whole or skim milk
   Plain and sweetened condensed whole, lowfat, and skim milk
   Condensed buttermilk
F. Dried milk products
   Nonfat dry milk
   Dry whole milk
   Dry buttermilk
   Dry cream
   Malted milk powder
G. Over 400 varieties of cheese
H. Frozen desserts
   Ice cream
   Frozen yogurt
   Frozen custard
   Ice milk
   Sherbet

Yogurt Products

WHAT YOU CAN BUY

I've discovered that research, if done in depth, is not only a pains-
taking process but a highly physical one as well. I've logged miles
(on foot, in cars, cabs, subways, and trains) checking out information in libraries, dairies, plants, restaurants, supermarkets, health
food stores, frozen yogurt shops—you name it. The end result is that
now I am able to give you a pretty good idea of everything that's
available in the way of "yogurt." My original plan (and I hope I
have succeeded) was to make this book as broad as possible. That is
the reason I have included this chapter on yogurt products.*

Yogurt Face Cream Concentrate

This comes in a small one-ounce tube (like toothpaste) and contains "living yogurt culture, protein and yeast extracts." It looks
almost like a salve to me, and has a nice "clean" smell. The benefit
of this product, according to the pamphlet that goes with it, is that it
"should decrease the size and appearance of wrinkles." This is
printed in bold type, so it's obviously one of their main selling points.
They go on to say that this product is a "hydrophilic—it can absorb
two to three times its own weight in water."

How to Use. Apply a tiny dab on your skin. Remember, this is a
concentrate, a lot goes a long way. You will find that the cream is
slightly grainy at first. According to International, this is "due to
active yogurt cells." And apparently these cells need water to multiply, so you emulsify this cream concentrate by using a circular
motion with *wet hands* until the cream is absorbed into the skin.

* All products are from the International Yogurt Company in Los Angeles.

Yogurt Face and Body Powder

This lightly scented powder comes in a two-and-a-half-ounce size and contains "unlike other powders—living yogurt bacteria, protein, and yeast extracts."

How to use. International recommends that this product be used by adults, and for babies, after a bath or shower.

Comment

Does the face cream concentrate really get rid of, or diminish, wrinkles? Quite frankly, I don't know. My theory about skin care is that the most important factors are diet, sleep, and exercise. And I believe that stress has a great deal to do with aging and one of its most visible signs, wrinkles. (The sun is also supposed to be reponsible for wrinkles and crows feet, but I will *never* give up sunbathing.) However, we all use cosmetics and skin care products to some degree, and I believe if you think that a product is good for you—by all means use it. In this book, my function is to let you know what is available. Then, you can choose for yourself. (The cost is $4.50 per tube—a sixty-day supply—for the face cream concentrate, and $3.50 for a container of the powder.)

Yogurt Tablets

Some people just do *not* care for the taste of yogurt—no matter how cleverly it's disguised. On the other hand, these same people realize that yogurt has very definite health benefits. If you are in this category, why not try yogurt tablets.

The International Yogurt Company sent me a sample bottle of theirs (120 tablets, two months' supply for $4.95). Taken twice a day—one tablet after breakfast, the other after dinner—ensures, according to International, "a good supply of beneficial or friendly lactic bacteria in the intestines."*

---

* In *Yogurt, Kefir and Other Milk Cultures*, Beatrice Trum Hunter states, "Yogurt can be a good precaution against picking up dysentery when traveling abroad. If no yogurt is expected to be available abroad, or there is any uncertainty about being able to obtain it, the traveler is advised to take along some yogurt in tablet form. Each tablet supplies several million bacteria. Two or three tablets can be taken daily."

Ordering by Mail

All products from the International Yogurt Company (cultures, beauty products, tablets, yogurt makers) are available, according to Wayne Barnette, "throughout the United States and in some other parts of the world." However, he also stresses that "all of the health food stores in this country do not carry *all* of our products. For example, approximately 95 percent sell our yogurt culture, but not all sell our other cultures [i.e., kefir], tablets, cosmetics and so forth."

On the last page of a long four-page letter that I received, Mr. Barnette says: "We offer all our merchandise via mail order to those individuals who do not have access to health food stores. This is particularly good in remote areas, and even in cities, where older people may have trouble with transportation." By the way, International has been in business for over thirty-eight years—a remarkable feat in itself.

What You Can Order from International Yogurt

CULTURES

1	International yogurt culture (for making yogurt)	$ 2.50
1	International kefir culture (for making kefir)	$ 2.50
1	fresh cheese culture (also buttermilk and sour cream)	$ 2.50
1	acidophilus milk culture	$ 2.50
6	cultures shipped one a month for 6 months, Service "A"	$11.85
12	cultures shipped one a month for 12 months, Service "B"	$20.85

134

Yogotherm nonelectric incubator (2-quart capacity) $24.95
With culture $26.95
Yogomagic electromatic incubator (1-quart capacity) $14.95
With culture $16.95

Products

Yogurt concentrated tablets (ready to eat)
   2 months' supply $ 4.95
Kefir grains (6 ounces ready to eat as directed) $ 6.50

Yogurt Beauty Products

Yogurt face cream concentrate $ 4.50
Yogurt face and body powder $ 3.50

Other Products

Yogurt thermometer $ 3.50

Address

The International Yogurt Company
628 North Doheny Drive
Los Angeles, CA 90069
Phone: 213-274-9917

Please add 50¢ for handling order, except cultures.
(California residents add correct sales tax.)

In Canada

If you live in Canada, you can order yogurt products from the Rosell Institute in Montreal.

Cultures

Yogurt $ 2.00
Kefir $ 2.00
Cottage cheese, buttermilk, and sour cream $ 2.00
Acidophilus milk $ 2.00
6 cultures of your choice $10.50
12 cultures of your choice $18.00

PRODUCTS

100	Yogurt tablets (bottle)	$ 2.50
50	Yogurt capsules (bottle)	$ 3.50

YOGURT BEAUTY PRODUCTS

Yogurt face cream	$ 3.50
Yogurt body powder	$ 3.50
Yogurt shampoo	$ 2.75

YOGURT MAKERS*

Yogotherm in avocado, gold, orange, white	$15.00
Yogotherm, a dairy thermometer, 12 yogurt cultures plus an extra one free	$30.00

OTHER PRODUCTS*

Dairy thermometer	$ 4.20
Steel cheese strainer with cloth bag	$ 5.25
Cloth bag for cheese strainer	$ 2.45

ADDRESS

Rosell Institute, Inc.
8480, boul. St. Laurent
Montreal, Quebec H2P# 2M6
Phone: 514-381-5631

Rosell adds that their cultures are "very stable. They will maintain their effectiveness for 12 months if stored in your refrigerator, or 18 months in the freezer."

To Order LactAid Lactase Enzyme

For a 12-quart supply of $2.50
    LactAid Lactase Enzyme   (includes postage
                              and handling)

Make check payable to:
LactAid
P.O. Box 1017R
Atlantic City, NJ 08404

* In Quebec add 8 percent tax.

136

To Order Yogurt Makers

S<small>ALTON</small>

1. Family Size Yogurt Maker
   "Thermostat Controlled" $19.95
   with Yo-Cheese Maker
   Model GM-10

2. Additional jars available $10.70 per set of 5

3. Additional Yo-Cheese
   Makers available   In sets of two for $7.25

4. Additional Yo-Cheese   Two for $1.95 postpaid
   bags available   in the U.S.

5. "Thermostat Controlled"
   Yogurt Maker Model GM-5 $13.50

6. Additional jars available,
   RJ-5 $6.50 per set of 5

All prices include handling and postage. All of the above are suggested retail prices subject to change without notice.

Address: Salton, Inc.
            1260 Zerega Avenue
            Bronx, NY 10462

C<small>ONTEMPRA</small>

1. Natural Yogurt Maker with
   Automatic Timer (deluxe)
   Model NYM-2T $24.95

2. To order an extra set of $7.95
   6 jars with lids,   (New Jersey residents add
   Model NJ-6   5 percent sales tax)

3. Natural Yogurt Maker
   (without automatic timer;
   has a takeout dial)
   Model NYM-1 $12.95

4. Thriftee Yogurt Maker
   (without automatic timer,
   takeout dial, or plastic
   cover) Model TY-66 $11.95

5. Big Batch Electric Yogurt
   Maker (2-quart capacity)
   Model BB-2 $17.95

A 96-page recipe book is included with all yogurt makers. All Contempra prices include postage and handling. New Jersey residents add 5 percent sales tax.

Address: Contempra Industries, Inc.
             371 Essex Road, Tinton Falls
             (Neptune P.O.), NJ 07753

In Canada: Braun Electric Canada Ltd.
             3269 American Drive
             Mississauga, Ontario L4V 1B9
             (For current prices write to above address)

HAMILTON BEACH

Culture Center $15.99 (includes postage
(electric) Model 726   and handling)

Address: Hamilton Beach Division
           Scovill, Inc.
           Washington, NC 27889

Additional jars and lids can be ordered from the above address.

WEST BEND

Electric Yogurt Maker
Model 5210 $22.95

Address: The West Bend Company
           Customer Service Department
           West Bend, WI 53095

Additional jars and lids can be ordered from the above address.

To Order Ice Cream Machines

SALTON

Salton Frozen Dessert Maker $22.95
with Scoop Model IC-3   (plus New York tax if applicable;
                                  includes postage and handling)

Address: Salton, Inc.
           1260 Zerega Avenue
           Bronx, NY 10462

WARING

Waring Ice Cream Parlor $39.95
Model CF 520-1   (no charge for shipping or
                                 handling)

Address: Waring Products Division
           Dynamics Corporation of America
           New Hartford, CN 06057

WHITE MOUNTAIN

White Mountain electric 4- $114.20
quart freezer Model 69204   (postage and handling extra)

Address: White Mountain Freezer, Inc.
           Winchendon, MA 01475

SEARS

Sears 5-quart electric ice
cream freezer Model 1985 $25.99

In Sears Summer "J" catalog and at most Sears retail stores.

To Order from Health Food Stores

ALBUQUERQUE, NEW MEXICO

Radiant Health Products
35 Winrock Center
Albuquerque, NM 87110
Phone: 505-883-5406

Yogurt Cultures
Handles International, Richlife, Pima, and Yogamet

Yogurt Products
Has yogurt chips, tablets, crackers, crunchy yogurt, and more

Yogurt Makers
From $12.50 and up (shipping not included in price)

AUSTIN, TEXAS

Austin's Natural Foods
2606 Guadaloupe Street
Austin, TX 78705
(Mail order in Texas only)

Yogurt Cultures	
International Yogurt Co.	$ 2.25
Yogurt Beauty Products	
LeLord Kordel's special soap	59¢ each
Other Yogurt Products	
International yogurt tablets, 120	$ 5.00
Yogurt Maker	
Salton	$12.95

Postage will be added to each of the above.

DETROIT, MICHIGAN

Health Supreme, Inc.
1334 Gratiot Avenue
Detroit, MI 48205

Stocks yogurt, cultures, yogurt beauty products, and yogurt makers. Add UPS to retail prices.

LINCOLN, NEBRASKA

Lincoln Health Foods, Inc.
122 N. 14 Street
Lincoln, NB 68508

Also located at:
5629 "O" Street
Lincoln, NB 68510

140

Yogurt Culture
International $2.50 plus postage

Yogurt Products
International yogurt tablets, 120 $ 4.95
Various acidophilus capsules and tablets
Schiff goat milk acidophilus capsules, 100 $ 4.50

Yogurt Makers
Salton
Yogomagic 1-quart unit

NEW YORK, NEW YORK

Down To Earth
33 Seventh Avenue
New York, NY 10011
Phone: 212-924-2711

Yogurt Cultures
Rich-Life yogurt $1.35
International Yogurt Co. kefir culture $2.50

Yogurt Products
TwinLab crunchy yogurt $4.95
International yogurt tablets $4.95
Schiff acidophilus capsules   50 for $2.50
Solgar acidophilus capsules   50 for $2.20, 100 for $3.70

Yogurt Makers
Salton, family size, and Yo-Cheese $17.95
Sunpot yogurt and cultured food cooker $10.95

Down To Earth calls their store "a natural food supermarket."
Prices are subject to change without notice. C.O.D. charges and
freight collect. On international shipments must have money and
freight with order.

Miracle Exclusives, Inc.
P.O. Box 347
3 Elm Street
Locust Valley, NY 11560
Phone: 516-676-0220

Yogurt Cultures

Yalacta	$2.45
Yalacta kefir culture/milk	$3.75
Yalacta kefir culture/fruit	$3.75

Yogurt Makers

Yalacta, standard	$65.00
Yalacta, deluxe	$75.00

Miracle Exclusives, Inc., is the exclusive importer and distributor of the above mentioned products (Yalacta/France).

PORTLAND, OREGON

Healthway Food Center
524 S.W. 5th Avenue
Portland, OR 97204

Yogurt Cultures

International, dry Bulgarian	$ 2.50
Daisyfresh Dairy, Bulgarian	$ 2.50
Yogourmet, freeze-dried yogurt starter	$ 2.25
International kefir culture	$ 2.50

Yogurt Products

International kefir grains, 6 ounces	$ 6.50
International yogurt tablets, 120	$ 4.95

Yogurt Makers

Contempra Big Batch	$12.95
Contempra Thrifty	$11.95

Above prices do not include handling and postage. Healthway reports: "We have five stores; our mail order is done from 524 S.W. 5th Avenue."

SALT LAKE CITY, UTAH

Scheibner's Foods
158 State Street
Salt Lake City, UT 84111

Yogurt Culture

International, dry	$ 2.50

142

Yogurt Beauty Products

Soap	$1.50 for 3 bars
Cream	$4.50 a jar

Yogurt Makers

Manfood	$ 9.98

SAN JOSE, CALIFORNIA

The Bee Hive Country Store
5807 Winfield Boulevard
San Jose, CA 95123
Phone: 408-225-3531

Yogurt Cultures

International, dry	$ 2.50
International kefir culture	$ 2.50
International acidophilus culture	$ 2.50
International buttermilk culture	$ 2.50

Add 50¢ to each of the above items for handling and postage.

Yogurt Makers

Salton, GM-5	$12.95
Salton, family size, GM-10	$19.95
Yogotherm	$24.95

Shipping charges will be added to each of the above.

Francis LeBaron, owner of the Bee Hive Country Store, writes: "We also sell a great number of home dehydrators—a favorite use is to produce yogurt—and, of 17 brands we've carried in the last 8 years, the Excalibur is the most popular."

RECIPES

Appetizers

Banana Pachadi

2 cups sliced bananas	¼ teaspoon salt
¼ cup grated unsweetened coconut	Juice of ½ lime
	Pinch of cayenne pepper
2 teaspoons sugar	1 teaspoon clarified butter
1 cup plain yogurt	¼ teaspoon mustard seeds

1. Combine banana slices, coconut, sugar, yogurt, salt, lime juice, and cayenne pepper.
2. Heat butter and fry mustard seeds until they crackle. Stir into banana mixture.

YIELD: 6 servings

Anchovy-Stuffed Eggs

6 hard-cooked eggs	Dash of Tabasco sauce
⅓ cup plain yogurt	Dash of white pepper
1½ tablespoons anchovy paste	12 chopped ripe olives
1 tablespoon chopped scallions	

1. Cut cooked eggs lengthwise and remove the yolks. Mash with a fork and blend with the yogurt, anchovy paste, scallions, Tabasco, and pepper.
2. Fill egg white shells with the mixture and top with chopped ripe olives. Chill before serving.

YIELD: 12 hors d'oeuvres

Seafood Coquille

1 pound fresh bay scallops
3 tablespoons minced scallions
½ cup butter or margarine
3 tablespoons flour
1 pound small cooked shrimp
2 cups plain yogurt
½ teaspoon rosemary leaves
1 tablespoon lemon juice
Salt and pepper to taste
1 cup canned mushroom pieces, drained
½ cup fine bread crumbs
½ cup grated Parmesan cheese

1. Cook scallops in a little water until tender. Drain. In a skillet sauté the scallions in the butter, adding the flour and blending well.

2. Add the shrimp, scallops, and yogurt and blend well over very low heat. Stir in the rosemary, lemon juice, salt, and pepper. Last, add the mushrooms.

3. Turn into individual ramekins or a shallow baking dish. Sprinkle with bread crumbs, then Parmesan cheese. Place under the broiler until the cheese browns.

YIELD: 6 servings

Onion Raita

2 large onions, thinly sliced
½ teaspoon cumin
½ teaspoon salt
1 cup plain yogurt
1 tablespoon chopped mint leaves
Dash of Tabasco sauce

Combine onions, cumin, salt, yogurt, mint, and Tabasco sauce. Chill until ready for use. Stir well to mix before serving.

YIELD: 6 servings

Cauliflower and Pea Raita

1 cup cauliflower flowerets, cut in small pieces
1 cup green peas
1 cup plain yogurt
½ teaspoon salt
¼ teaspoon cumin
Chili powder

Cook cauliflower and peas in salted water. Drain and chill. Mix with yogurt, salt, and cumin. Sprinkle chili powder over top.

YIELD: 6 servings

Potato Raita

3 medium potatoes
2 cups plain yogurt
½ teaspoon cumin
½ teaspoon chili powder

1 teaspoon salt
3 fresh or pickled green chilies, chopped
1 bunch mint

1. Boil potatoes. When cold, peel them and cut into thin slices.

2. Combine yogurt, cumin, chili powder, salt, green chilies, and half of the mint sprigs, which have been finely chopped. Add to the potato slices and mix well. Garnish with remaining mint sprigs.

YIELD: 6 servings

Eggplant Caviar (Melitzanesalata)

This dip or puree is typical of the Balkans and Near East, but to be really delicious, the eggplant must be locally grown in season. The whole eggplant should be toasted over a charcoal fire, turned frequently, until the outer skin is wrinkled and the eggplant noticeably soft. This can also be done over the flame of a gas burner or in the oven, but the flavor is not as good as when the vegetable is toasted over charcoal.

1 large eggplant
1 small onion, grated or finely minced
2 garlic cloves, crushed
2–3 tablespoons olive oil

1 teaspoon lemon juice
Salt to taste
1 tablespoon minced parsley
½ cup plain yogurt, optional

1. Roast or toast eggplant. When soft, peel away the outer skin. Place the pulp in a sieve to drain.

2. Blend the drained pulp with grated or minced onion, crushed garlic, oil, lemon juice, salt, and parsley. Add the optional yogurt.

With an Electric Blender:

1. Cut the onion into quarters; place in blender with a cup of water and beat at high speed until finely chopped, almost pureed.

2. Drain the onion and blend with the pulp of eggplant and crushed garlic, oil, lemon juice, salt, and parsley. Return mixture to blender and beat at slow speed until pureed. If yogurt is to be added, stir in after removing puree from blender.

YIELD: approximately 2 cups

Spinach Raita

1 bunch spinach
1 tablespoon vegetable oil
1 teaspoon ground cumin
1 teaspoon mustard seeds
1 teaspoon fenugreek seeds

1½ cups plain yogurt
½ teaspoon salt
¼ teaspoon cayenne pepper, optional

1. Wash and chop spinach. Steam. Squeeze out any excess moisture.

2. Heat vegetable oil and fry the ground cumin, mustard seeds, and fenugreek seeds until they crackle.

3. Add to yogurt along with spinach, salt, and cayenne pepper. Mix thoroughly.

YIELD: 4 servings

Cabbage Raita

2 cups cabbage, shredded
1 cucumber, peeled and grated
2 tablespoons minced green pepper

¼ teaspoon cayenne pepper
½ teaspoon black pepper
1 teaspoon salt
2 cups plain yogurt

Soak cabbage in ice water for 1 hour. Drain and dry thoroughly. Combine cabbage, cucumber, green pepper, cayenne and black pepper, salt, and yogurt. Chill well before serving.

YIELD: 6 servings

Marinated Mushrooms

4 cups water
2 tablespoons salt
1 tablespoon vinegar
1 pound fresh mushrooms
¼ cup chopped onion
2 tablespoons chopped parsley
2 tablespoons lemon juice

1 tablespoon vinegar
2 teaspoons sugar
¼ teaspoon leaf thyme
¼ teaspoon salt
⅛ teaspoon white pepper
¾ cup plain yogurt

1. In a 2-quart saucepan bring water, 2 tablespoons salt, and 1 tablespoon vinegar to a boil; add mushrooms; cover. Reduce heat and simmer about 10 minutes. Drain and cool slightly.

2. Meanwhile in a bowl combine onion, parsley, lemon juice, 1 tablespoon vinegar, sugar, thyme, ¼ teaspoon salt, and pepper; fold in yogurt, then mushrooms. Cover and chill about 12 hours or overnight.

YIELD: approximately 2 cups

Fancy Cocktail Tomatoes

¼ cup plain yogurt
1 tablespoon minced onion
½ teaspoon dried dill weed
Dash of salt

12 ripe cherry tomatoes, centers scooped out
24 tiny cooked canned shrimp

Combine the yogurt, onion, dill, and salt. Fill the center of each tomato with the mixture and top with two shrimp each.

YIELD: 12 hors d'oeuvres

Stuffed Tiny Onions

12 small white onions, with centers scooped out
1 egg yolk
¼ cup plain yogurt

2 teaspoons minced parsley
½ teaspoon salt
Dash of pepper
½ teaspoon garlic powder

1. Preheat the oven to 375 degrees.
2. Parboil onions in water for 5 minutes. Mix together egg yolk, yogurt, parsley, salt, pepper, and garlic powder. Fill centers of onions.
3. Bake on a buttered cookie sheet 15 minutes. Serve hot as an hors d'oeuvre.

YIELD: 12 hors d'oeuvres

Cheesy Stuffed Celery

½ cup mashed blue cheese
1 cup plain yogurt
¼ cup finely chopped chives

1 tablespoon brandy
1 bunch celery, washed and cut into 2-inch pieces

Combine cheese, yogurt, chives, and brandy. Chill until hardened to spreading consistency. Fill celery pieces and serve cold.

YIELD: 24-30 hors d'oeuvres

Cheese Ball

3 cups (12 oz.) shredded
   Cheddar cheese
⅓ cup crumbled blue cheese
½ cup plain yogurt

½ teaspoon Worcestershire
   sauce
¼ cup minced ripe olives
½ cup chopped nuts
¼ cup chopped parsley

1. In a small mixing bowl beat together Cheddar and blue cheeses until smooth. Add yogurt and Worcestershire sauce and beat until creamy. Stir in olives. Cover and chill.

2. Shape into a ball and roll in nuts and parsley. Return to refrigerator. Allow to come to room temperature before serving.

YIELD: 3 cups

Stuffed Grape Leaves

1 pound grape leaves
1 onion finely chopped
3 tablespoons olive oil
6 tablespoons rice, uncooked
¼ cup pine nuts
¾ pound minced lamb or beef
   Pinch of mint

2 tablespoons chopped dill
   Dash of cinnamon
   Salt and pepper to taste
1½ cups meat stock
½ cup white wine
1 cup plain yogurt
1 clove garlic, minced

1. Clean and wash grape leaves; drop into boiling salted water and cook 3 minutes; drain well, pressing out all water. Cut large leaves in half down the center vein.

2. Saute onion in oil until limp; add rice and cook until golden. Add pine nuts and toast for 1 minute; remove from heat and add meat, mint, dill, cinnamon, salt, and pepper.

3. Put 1 tablespoon of mixture on each leaf half and roll into finger shape, tucking in the edges. Put the rolls in a casserole, cover with meat stock and wine. Cook for 45 minutes over medium heat. Add more stock if needed.

4. Serve on hot platter, topped with blend of yogurt, mint, and minced garlic.

YIELD: 4 servings

Fresh Cucumbers in Yogurt

6 medium-size cucumbers
1 tablespoon cooking salt
1½ cups plain yogurt

Salt and pepper to taste
1 tablespoon chives, finely
chopped

1. Peel cucumbers, split lengthwise, scoop out seeds with small spoon, slice as thin as possible. Place in chilled bowl, sprinkle with salt, and blend well. Stand in refrigerator 1 hour.

2. Place cucumbers between dry towels and press firmly until free of water. Return to chilled bowl; add yogurt along with salt and pepper to taste. Blend well. Sprinkle with chives.

YIELD: 6 servings

Cucumber Borani

1 large cucumber, peeled,
  pitted, sliced
Salt to taste
1 cup plain yogurt
1 small onion, sliced

1 clove garlic, mashed
½ teaspoon fresh mint, chopped
Juice of ½ lemon
Lettuce leaves
Walnuts for garnish

1. Season sliced cucumber with salt. Allow to stand for 10-15 minutes. Drain off any liquid residue.

2. To cucumbers, add yogurt, sliced onion, garlic, mint, and lemon juice. Toss well.

3. Arrange on lettuce leaves and garnish with walnuts.

YIELD: 2 servings

Yogurt Seafood Cocktail

½ bunch watercress
1 cup plain yogurt
¼ cup catsup
2 teaspoons lemon juice

2 teaspoons horseradish
½ teaspoon salt
2 cups flaked cooked fish or
  shellfish

1. Chop watercress stems fine. Combine yogurt, catsup, lemon juice, horseradish, salt. Stir in seafood and watercress stems.

2. Chill thoroughly in glass jar with cover. When ready to serve, combine with coarsely cut watercress leaves.

YIELD: 4-6 servings

Stuffed Mussels (Midia Yemista I)

2 quarts fresh mussels
  (approximately 48)
½ cup cold water
½ cup dry white wine
½ teaspoon salt
1 large onion, chopped

2 tablespoons olive oil
½ cup uncooked rice
¼ cup pine nuts or slivered
  blanched almonds
¼ cup plain yogurt
  Freshly ground black pepper

1. Wash mussels under cold running water and scrub thoroughly with stiff brush. Remove beards. Place in kettle or large pot, add cold water, wine, and salt. Bring to a boil, cook until shells open. (Discard any that do not open.)

2. Let cool. Remove, saving broth. Take mussels from shells, chop the meat. Cook chopped onion in the olive oil, add rice and 1 cup of the strained liquid in which mussels cooked.

3. Cook rice, covered, until all liquid is absorbed. Stir in chopped mussels, pine nuts, yogurt, and pepper. Add salt to taste if needed. Use mixture to stuff the half shells. Serve as an hors d'oeuvre.

YIELD: approximately 40 stuffed mussels

Soups

Cool Cucumber Soup

2 large cucumbers
½ teaspoon salt
2 cups plain yogurt

½ cup milk
2 teaspoons minced onion
½ teaspoon dill weed

1. Pare cucumbers and split lengthwise. Remove seeds. Grate cucumbers. Combine grated cucumber and salt in bowl; let it stand 15 minutes. Drain.

2. Combine yogurt, milk, onion, and dill weed; mix well. Add drained cucumber and stir to combine. Cover bowl and chill 3-4 hours before serving.

YIELD: 6 servings

Chilled Cucumber-Yogurt Soup

2 large cucumbers
¼ cup chopped green onions
1 crushed small garlic clove
2 chicken bouillon cubes
½ teaspoon salt

¼ teaspoon dill weed
⅛ teaspoon white pepper
1 cup water
2 cups plain yogurt

1. Peel cucumbers. Cut lengthwise and remove seeds (pulp) with spoon. Discard seeds. Cut cucumbers into ¼-inch slices. (Makes about 4 cups cucumber slices.)

2. Combine cucumbers, onion, garlic, bouillon cubes, salt, dill weed, pepper, and water in medium saucepan; cover. Cook over medium heat 8 minutes; stir occasionally.

(cont'd)

155

3. Remove from heat. Pour mixture into blender. Puree at medium speed until smooth. Return to saucepan. Cool to room temperature. Gradually add yogurt to mixture. Chill at least 4 hours. Garnish with dill weed or mint leaves.

YIELD: 4 cups

Cucumber and Yogurt Cold Soup (Tzatziki)

1 large cucumber	2 tablespoons olive oil
4 cups plain yogurt	1 tablespoon vinegar
2 medium garlic cloves, crushed	½ teaspoon salt or to taste
	1 tablespoon minced dill

1. The cucumber should be thinly peeled, then coarsely grated; or crush cucumber (in big chunks) in an electric blender at low speed.

2. Add yogurt, garlic, oil, vinegar, salt, and dill. Blend thoroughly. Serve chilled.

YIELD: 6 servings

Chilled Yogurt Soup with Walnuts (Taratori)

4 walnuts, shelled	½ cup cold water
1 teaspoon salt	2 small cucumbers, finely chopped
1 clove garlic	
¼ cup olive oil	Additional salt and pepper to taste
1 tablespoon vinegar	
4 cups plain yogurt	

Mash walnut meats with the 1 teaspoon salt (using mortar and pestle). Add garlic and olive oil. Continue to mash to a smooth paste. Blend in vinegar and gradually stir in yogurt and water. Stir in chopped cucumber and correct seasoning. Serve very cold.

YIELD: 6 servings

Hot Weather Garden Soup

1 cup cucumber pulp
1½ cups plain yogurt
¼ cup minced onion
¼ cup chili sauce
¾ teaspoon salt
1 cup chicken bouillon, chilled
¼ teaspoon pepper

1 tablespoon olive oil
½ cup finely chopped green pepper
¼ cup finely chopped cucumber, seeded
½ cup finely chopped fresh tomatoes, peeled

1. Prepare the cucumber pulp by blending 1 large cut-up seeded cucumber, with peel, in an electric blender.

2. Blend yogurt, cucumber pulp, onion, chili sauce, and salt in a glass or plastic storage container. Chill.

3. Stir in the bouillon, pepper, and olive oil. Add the chopped green pepper, cucumber, and tomatoes. Chill thoroughly before serving.

YIELD: 4 servings

Creamy Russian Borscht

1 can (16 oz.) sliced beets, with liquid
1 teaspoon sugar or equivalent sugar substitute
¼ cup lemon juice

4 tablespoons minced onions
½ teaspoon salt
¼ teaspoon pepper
¼ teaspoon dill weed
1 cup plain yogurt

1. Place beets, sugar, lemon juice, onion, salt, pepper, and dill in a blender and blend until smooth. Stir in yogurt until well mixed and chill thoroughly.

2. Serve cold. Garnish each portion with a dollop of yogurt.

YIELD: approximately 6 cups

Russian Beet Borscht

4 cups stock
1 cup beet juice
1 cup beets, cooked and cubed
Juice and rind of 1 lemon
1 cup plain yogurt

1 teaspoon soy flour
3 tablespoons nutritional yeast
½ teaspoon salt
1 sprig parsley
½ teaspoon tarragon

In blender, blend stock, beet juice, beets, lemon, yogurt, flour, yeast, salt, parsley, and tarragon until smooth. Chill. Serve garnished with minced chives.

Yɪᴇʟᴅ: 6 servings

Yogurt Borscht Soup

2 onions
1–2 carrots
3–4 beets
2 tablespoons flour
½ small head of green cabbage, shredded

1 cup tomato puree
1 quart soup stock
1 teaspoon salt
½ cup or more of plain yogurt

1. Chop onions; cut carrots and raw beets into fingers like shoestring potatoes. Sauté lightly without browning for 10 minutes or until almost tender.

2. Add flour and stir well. Add shredded cabbage, cover pot and steam 8 minutes. Add tomato puree, soup stock, and salt.

3. Heat quickly to simmering. As soon as heated through serve with 2 tablespoons yogurt in center of each soup bowl.

Yɪᴇʟᴅ: 4 servings

Hot Tomato and Yogurt Soup

1 large ripe tomato
1 small onion, peeled
1 teaspoon butter
¼ cup chicken stock
½ teaspoon honey

½ cup milk
2 tablespoons plain yogurt
¼ teaspoon basil leaves
Sea salt and pepper to taste

1. Chop the tomato and onion and sauté in butter until the onion is transparent. Add a tablespoon or two of stock if necessary to keep the vegetables from browning.

2. Add the stock and honey. Simmer for 5 minutes. Stir in milk, yogurt, basil, sea salt, and pepper. Continue simmering for 3 minutes more. Serve hot.

Yɪᴇʟᴅ: approximately 2 servings

158

Hot Asparagus Soup

12 spears fresh asparagus
2 cups hot asparagus water
1 can (10½ oz.) condensed
  chicken broth
1 tablespoon flour
1 teaspoon onion salt
  Small pinch of basil
½ cup plain yogurt

1. Boil the asparagus in enough water to cover. Remove them and cut off tough ends. Retain 2 cups of asparagus water and pour into a 2-quart saucepan. Mash asparagus (or mix in a blender) and add to water in saucepan.

2. Add chicken broth, flour, onion salt, and basil. Bring to boiling point and remove from heat. Add yogurt slowly to avoid curdling. Serve hot with crisp crackers.

YIELD: 4 servings

Chilled Cream of Asparagus Soup

2 cans (14½ oz. each) cut-up
  asparagus with liquid
2 packets chicken broth crystals
1 teaspoon seasoned salt
½ teaspoon pepper
1 teaspoon onion powder
1 teaspoon sugar
1½ cups plain yogurt
  Dash of paprika

1. Drain asparagus liquid into a small saucepan and bring to a boil. Add chicken broth crystals and stir until dissolved.

2. Place the asparagus, liquid, salt, pepper, onion powder, and sugar in a blender. Blend until smooth.

3. Add yogurt and blend slowly. Chill thoroughly and serve cold with a dash of paprika.

YIELD: 6 cups

Mediterranean Gazpacho Soup

1 cucumber
2 cups plain yogurt
2 tablespoons white vinegar
1 teaspoon salt
1 small clove garlic, chopped
3 medium tomatoes
½ small onion, finely chopped

1. Pare cucumber and cut lengthwise into halves. Discard seeds. Cut into chunks.

(cont'd)

2. In electric blender combine cucumber, yogurt, vinegar, salt, garlic, tomatoes, and onion.

3. Chill several hours or overnight for best flavor. Garnish with additional chopped cucumber and tomato if desired.

YIELD: 5 cups

Yogurt Gazpacho

4 tomatoes, skinned and coarsely chopped
1 tablespoon chopped hot green seeded chilies, fresh or canned, or to taste
1 onion, finely chopped

¼ cup chopped parsley
Sea salt to taste
3 cups plain yogurt
Radish or cucumber slices
Watercress sprigs

1. Combine the tomatoes, chilies, onion, parsley, and salt. Chill in the refrigerator at least 2 hours.

2. Stir in the yogurt. Garnish each serving with radish or cucumber slices and a sprig of watercress.

YIELD: 4 servings

Vichyssoise

3 tablespoons oil
3 leeks, chopped
1 onion, chopped
3 potatoes, cubed
4 cups chicken stock
1 teaspoon salt

2 cups milk
½ cup milk powder
1 tablespoon soy flour
3 tablespoons nutritional yeast
1 cup plain yogurt
¼ cup chives, minced

1. Heat oil in pot and in it sauté leeks and onion. Add potatoes, stock, and salt. Cover. Simmer for 30 minutes.

2. Puree mixture. Return to pot. Add mixture of milk, milk powder, soy flour, and yeast.

3. Cover and heat just until soup comes to a boil. Remove from heat. Chill. Blend in yogurt. Serve garnished with chives.

YIELD: 6 servings

Cold Yogurt and Eggplant Soup (Tarata)

2 medium eggplants, peeled, seeded, diced
2 green peppers, seeded, chopped
2–3 crushed garlic cloves
6 tablespoons olive oil
4 cups plain yogurt
½ teaspoon salt
¼ teaspoon black pepper
   Pinch of cayenne
¼ teaspoon onion salt
¼ teaspoon powdered mint
   Sesame seeds
   Minced parsley or watercress

1. Cook diced eggplant, peppers, and crushed garlic in olive oil over moderate heat until tender; do not brown. Puree, blend with yogurt and seasonings. Marinate 12-24 hours.

2. Toast sesame seeds: spread them out in a shallow pan, place in 350-degree oven until seeds are golden.

3. Serve ice cold topped with toasted sesame seeds and minced parsley or watercress.

YIELD: 10-12 servings

Turkish Chicken Soup (Tavuk Corbasi)

5 cups rich chicken stock
2 tablespoons uncooked rice
2 tablespoons butter, melted
2 tablespoons flour
1 cup plain yogurt
   Salt and pepper to taste
2 tablespoons chopped chives
1 cup diced cooked chicken meat
1 tablespoon lemon juice
1 teaspoon grated lemon rind

1. Add the uncooked rice to the chicken stock and simmer over a low heat for 20 minutes or until the rice is tender.

2. Melt the butter in another saucepan and blend in the flour.

3. Add the yogurt to flour mixture and cook over a low heat until the sauce is thick and smooth.

4. Add the sauce to the chicken stock and cook over low heat until thickened.

5. Add salt and pepper to taste, chopped chives, diced cooked chicken meat, lemon juice, and lemon rind. Heat through and serve at once.

YIELD: 4 servings

Turkish Yogurt Soup (Yala Chorbashi)

½ cup pearl barley
4 cups chicken broth
2 large onions, chopped
2 tablespoons butter
½ cup chopped fresh mint, or
   1 teaspoon mint flakes

A few sprigs of parsley
1 teaspoon salt
White pepper to taste
2 cups plain yogurt, at room
   temperature

1. Soak barley overnight in water to cover. Next day, drain and simmer in the chicken broth for about 15 minutes, or until tender.

2. Sauté onion in butter until transparent. Add to the broth. Add mint, parsley, salt, and pepper to taste and simmer for 30 minutes.

3. Five minutes before serving remove from heat, let stand 3 minutes, and stir in yogurt mixed with a little of the hot broth. Serve in heated bowls.

YIELD: 4 servings

Russian Yogurt Soup (Okrochka)

1 cup plain yogurt
2 cups milk
1 cup chicken, cooked, diced
2 cucumbers, peeled, diced
1 can (4½ oz.) shrimp or
   lobster, minced
1 teaspoon instant chopped
   onion, softened in water, or
   1 tablespoon minced chives

1 tablespoon minced dill
1 teaspoon fennel weed or ¼
   teaspoon powdered fennel
1 cup chicken broth, preferably
   homemade
2 hard-boiled eggs, minced

1. Beat yogurt and milk together; add chicken, cucumbers, shrimp or lobster, onion or chives, dill, fennel, and chicken broth. Place in refrigerator to chill for at least 8 hours or overnight.

2. Add minced cooked eggs as garnish. Note: Instead of chicken broth, the liquid from a jar of dill pickles can be used. In this case, omit minced dill.

YIELD: 8 servings (suitable as a luncheon entrée)

Summertime Soup

2 cups plain yogurt
1 can chilled condensed tomato
  soup

Celery and onion salt to taste
Chopped olives and parsley

Mix yogurt with tomato soup. If soup is too heavy, thin with milk. Season lightly with celery salt and onion salt. Sprinkle with freshly chopped olives and parsley. A refreshing cold soup for hot summer days.

YIELD: approximately 3-4 servings

Refreshing Cold Fruit Soup

1 cup sour pitted cherries with
  juice
16 apricot halves
½ cup apricot liquid

2 teaspoons lemon juice
6 drops artificial sweetener
1 cup plain yogurt

Blend on puree setting cherries with juice, apricot halves and liquid, lemon juice, and artificial sweetener. When mixture is smooth, fold in yogurt and chill. Serve with a dollop of yogurt.

YIELD: 4 servings

Watercress Soup

4 cups stock
2 bunches watercress
1 teaspoon salt

3 tablespoons nutritional yeast
1 teaspoon soy flour
1 cup plain yogurt

Mix stock, watercress, salt, yeast, flour, and yogurt in blender until smooth. Chill.

YIELD: 6 servings

Meat

Orange-Ginger Pork Chops

8 lean pork chops
1 tablespoon salad oil
½ cup orange juice
½ teaspoon salt

1 teaspoon ground ginger
8 orange slices (1 large
  orange)
¾ cup plain yogurt

1. In skillet, brown chops in oil until well done (about 10 minutes per side). Drain excess fat.

2. Add orange juice, cover, and simmer about 30 minutes. Uncover, sprinkle chops with salt and ginger; top each with an orange slice.

3. Cover and cook 10-15 minutes more or until chops are fork-tender. Remove chops to ovenproof platter and top each with yogurt. Place under broiler about 1 minute; serve immediately.

YIELD: 8 servings

Persian-Style Pork Chops

1 cup plain yogurt
3 scallions, chopped
½ teaspoon salt
¼ teaspoon white pepper
4 thick center-cut pork chops

1 teaspoon butter
¼ cup dry white wine
1½ tablespoons cornstarch
1 cup chicken broth (make
  with bouillon cubes)

1. Combine yogurt, scallions, salt, and pepper in a large bowl. Add the pork chops, covering them completely, and marinate for 3 hours at room temperature.

2. Remove the chops, scraping back into the bowl as much of the yogurt mixture as possible. Sauté the chops in a skillet in the butter until browned.

3. Add the wine and simmer, covered, until tender. Move to a warm platter.

4. To the pan juices add the yogurt mixture. Dissolve the cornstarch in the chicken broth and stir in over very low heat until thickened. Pour the sauce over the pork chops and serve.

YIELD: 4 servings

Pork Chops in Yogurt

This is good with a sliced tomato-and-cucumber salad.

1 can condensed cream of mushroom soup	4 pork chops, trimmed of fat
½ cup plain yogurt	2 cups thinly sliced peeled potatoes
2 tablespoons chopped parsley	Salt and pepper to taste
½ cup water	

1. Preheat oven to 375 degrees.

2. Blend soup, yogurt, and parsley with ½ cup water. Lightly brown the chops in a frying pan.

3. In a 2-quart casserole, alternate layers of potatoes and the sauce, sprinkling each layer with a dash of salt and pepper. Save some sauce.

4. Arrange the chops on top and pour the rest of the sauce over them. Bake for 1¼ hours, turning chops after 1 hour.

YIELD: 4 servings

Veal with Tangy Mushroom Sauce

1½ pounds boneless veal, cubed	⅓ cup dry white wine
2½ tablespoons butter	¾ cup plain yogurt
1 tablespoon chopped onion	½ teaspoon salt
½ pound fresh sliced mushrooms	⅛ teaspoon pepper
	1 chicken bouillon cube
2 tablespoons flour	Water

1. Preheat the oven to 300 degrees.

(cont'd)

2. Brown veal lightly in 1½ tablespoons butter. Remove meat to lightly greased ovenproof baking dish. Add 1 tablespoon of butter to same skillet.

3. Stir and sauté lightly the chopped onion and mushrooms. Remove skillet from heat. Stir flour in slowly.

4. Add wine, yogurt, salt, and pepper to the onion and mushroom mixture. Blend until smooth.

5. Dissolve bouillon cube in ⅓ cup boiling water. Stir into onion and mushroom mixture until smooth and well blended. Pour over veal.

6. Cover the baking dish. Bake for about 1 hour. Can be served over noodles, if desired.

YIELD: 4 servings

Veal Paprika with Yogurt

1 tablespoon butter	Flour
2 onions, sliced	Salt and pepper to taste
Paprika	1 cup plain yogurt
1 pound veal steak, cut in cubes	

1. Melt butter in skillet. Add sliced onions and sauté lightly without browning. Season onion with paprika.

2. Roll veal cubes in flour; add salt and pepper. Place in skillet with onions and brown. Add yogurt gradually. Cover and cook slowly for 20 minutes.

YIELD: 2-3 servings

Veal Paprika

3 slices bacon, diced	½ cup tomato sauce
¼ cup chopped onion	1 tablespoon flour
1½ pounds veal steak, cut in serving portions	1 teaspoon paprika
	½ teaspoon salt
1 cup plain yogurt	

1. In large skillet (with cover) fry bacon and onion until bacon is crisp; remove and set aside. Brown veal on both sides.

2. Meanwhile in a small bowl combine yogurt, tomato sauce, flour, paprika, salt, bacon and onion. Pour over veal. Cover.

166

3. Reduce heat to simmer and cook 25-35 minutes or until meat is tender. Stir sauce to combine.

YIELD: 4-6 servings

Veal Steaks with Yogurt

6 small veal steaks
4 cups diced potatoes
3 tablespoons butter

Salt, pepper, sage, or mushrooms to taste
2 cups plain yogurt

1. Preheat the oven to 375 degrees.
2. Brown the veal steaks in butter, place in casserole, and cover with potatoes. Add seasoning to suit taste and pour yogurt over all. Bake for 45 minutes.

YIELD: 4-6 servings

Swedish Meatballs

2 pounds lean ground beef
1 cup soft bread crumbs, packed
¾ cup milk
1 egg
¼ cup minced onion
2 teaspoons instant vegetable soup greens

2 tablespoons oil
1 teaspoon flour
¼ cup boiling water
1 teaspoon beef bouillon
1 teaspoon Worcestershire sauce
1 cup plain yogurt

1. Mix beef, bread crumbs soaked in milk, egg, onion, and vegetable soup greens. Shape into small balls. Brown slowly on all sides in oil. Remove to serving bowl.
2. Skim excess fat from pan juices, add flour, stirring constantly.
3. Gradually add boiling water, beef bouillon, and Worcestershire sauce. Cook, stirring until sauce is smooth and thickened.
4. Add yogurt, and heat; return meatballs to pan. Simmer very gently for 20 minutes.
5. Serve over buttered noodles or rice; can be served alone as an hors d'oeuvre.

YIELD: 8 servings

Meatballs with Yogurt

1 pound ground round or chuck	1 teaspoon salt
¼ cup bread crumbs	Pinch of black pepper
½ cup black coffee	1 tablespoon butter
½ cup minced onion	1 tablespoon flour
1 egg, beaten	1 cup beef stock
1 tablespoon grated lemon rind	1 cup plain yogurt

1. Preheat the oven to 350 degrees.

2. Combine ground beef, bread crumbs, coffee, onion, egg, lemon rind, salt, and pepper and mix thoroughly. Make into small balls.

3. Sauté meatballs in butter in a large skillet until browned on all sides. Remove them to a 2-quart baking dish or casserole.

4. Place flour and beef stock in skillet in which meat was browned and simmer over low flame, stirring until sauce is smooth and thick. Pour over meatballs and bake for 40 minutes.

5. When ready to serve, remove meatballs with a perforated spoon and place in serving bowl. Stir yogurt into sauce slowly to avoid curdling. Pour over meatballs and serve immediately.

YIELD: 4 servings

Meatballs with Yogurt Sauce
(Keftaides Me Yaorti)

1 pound ground lean lamb (or use 4 prepared lamb patties)	1 egg, beaten
	½ cup crushed cracker crumbs or fine bread crumbs
1 teaspoon salt	2 tablespoons olive oil
¼ teaspoon black pepper	1 cup plain yogurt
¼ teaspoon oregano	¼ teaspoon dried mint, crushed
¼ teaspoon thyme	¼ teaspoon black pepper

1. If lamb patties are used, a larger proportion of fat will be in the meat than if lamb is ground to order; this means more fat will be drawn out when the meatballs are sautéed.

2. Add salt, pepper, oregano, and thyme to meat; work in egg and crumbs.

3. Form into 1-inch balls. Sauté the meatballs in olive oil until well browned. Pour off excess fat.

4. Add the mint and pepper to yogurt, add the yogurt to the skillet, turning off heat. Enough heat will be left to warm the yogurt. Serve meatballs in this sauce, accompanied by rice or potatoes.

YIELD: 4 servings

Corned Beef Hash Pie

1 can prepared refrigerator biscuits
¼ cup sliced green olives
1 cup plain yogurt
4 tablespoons chopped chives
2 teaspoons prepared mustard
½ teaspoon salt
Dash of pepper
2 cans (15 oz.) prepared corned beef hash
2 tablespoons minced parsley

1. Preheat the oven to 375 degrees.
2. Line a 10x6-inch casserole dish with refrigerator biscuits to form a crust.
3. Combine the olives, yogurt, chives, mustard, salt, and pepper.
4. Stir half of the yogurt mixture into the hash and turn it into the crust, spreading evenly.
5. Spread the remaining yogurt mixture evenly over the top of the hash. Sprinkle with parsley and bake 30 to 35 minutes until crust is brown.

YIELD: 6 servings

Armenian Hash

3 medium potatoes, boiled in jackets
1 pound ground meat
1 onion, finely chopped
1 teaspoon cumin oil
½ cup plain yogurt
1 egg, beaten

1. Peel boiled potatoes and chop in small cubes. Mix meat, potatoes, onion, and cumin.
2. Blend together yogurt and egg; add to meat mixture. Toss lightly until well mixed.
3. Shape into patties and sauté in oil until done.

YIELD: 4 servings

Cheese Lasagna

1 package (1 lb.) lasagna
noodles
3 cans (8 oz. each) tomato
sauce with onion
2 teaspoons Angostura bitters

1 cup plain yogurt
1 pound cottage cheese
1 pound mozzarella cheese,
sliced
½ cup grated Parmesan cheese

1. Preheat the oven to 350 degrees.

2. Cook lasagna noodles according to package directions. Drain and separate noodles into a single layer placed on wax paper.

3. Mix tomato sauce and bitters. Mix yogurt and cottage cheese. Spoon some of the sauce into a well-greased 9x13x2-inch baking pan.

4. Add a layer of noodles, some sauce, some of the yogurt mixture, slices of mozzarella cheese, and a sprinkle of Parmesan cheese.

5. Continue layering, ending with noodles, sauce, sliced mozzarella cheese, and grated Parmesan cheese.

6. Bake uncovered for 45 minutes or until lightly browned and bubbly. Remove from oven and let stand for 10 minutes before cutting into servings.

YIELD: One 9x13-inch pan

Baked Lasagna

1 package (8 oz.) lasagna
noodles, cooked according to
package directions
½ pound lean ground beef
¼ cup finely chopped onion
1 can (6. oz.) tomato paste
1 can (8 oz.) tomato sauce
½ cup canned mushroom pieces,
drained
1 garlic clove, crushed
1 teaspoon dried basil leaves
1 teaspoon dried parsley flakes

1 teaspoon salt
½ teaspoon oregano
¼ teaspoon pepper
1½ cups plain yogurt
2 cups creamed cottage cheese
1 cup chopped frozen spinach,
drained thoroughly
¼ cup diced salami
1 egg
1 cup shredded mozzarella
cheese

1. Preheat the oven to 350 degrees.

2. Brown beef and onion in a large skillet, adding the tomato paste, sauce, and mushrooms.

170

3. Stir in the garlic, basil, parsley, ½ teaspoon salt, oregano, ⅛ teaspoon pepper, and yogurt. Heat thoroughly, but do not boil.

4. In a bowl combine the cottage cheese, spinach, salami, egg, ½ teaspoon salt, and ⅛ teaspoon pepper.

5. In a 12x8-inch baking dish alternate layers of two thicknesses of noodles, cottage cheese mixture, beef mixture, and mozzarella cheese, ending with a cheese layer.

6. Place in the oven and bake 30 minutes. Remove from oven and let stand 15 minutes before serving.

YIELD: 6-8 servings

Easy Beef Stroganoff

1 cup onions, finely chopped	¼ teaspoon pepper
1 pound fresh mushrooms, sliced	1 teaspoon Worcestershire sauce
½ cup butter or margarine	2 cups plain yogurt
2 pounds lean ground beef	1 box (16 oz.) wide noodles, cooked according to package directions
1 cup beef bouillon	
1 can (6 oz.) tomato paste	
1 teaspoon paprika	2 tablespoons butter or margarine
½ teaspoon salt	

1. In a large skillet or saucepan sauté the onions and mushrooms in ½ cup butter. When tender, add the beef and simmer until browned.

2. Add the bouillon, tomato paste, paprika, salt, pepper, and Worcestershire sauce.

3. Stir in the yogurt and heat thoroughly, but do not boil. Serve over hot buttered noodles.

YIELD: 6 servings

Frank-Mac Skillet

2 tablespoons butter	1 can (1 lb.) tomatoes
1 pound frankfurters, cut in 1-inch pieces	¾ cup water
½ cup chopped onion	1 teaspoon chili powder
½ cup chopped green pepper	1 teaspoon salt
1 package (7 or 8 oz.) uncooked elbow macaroni	1 cup plain yogurt
	2 teaspoons flour

1. In a large skillet melt butter; sauté frankfurters, onion, and green pepper 5 minutes. Add macaroni, tomatoes, water, chili powder, and salt.

2. Cover and simmer 20 minutes, stirring occasionally. Meanwhile combine yogurt and flour.

3. Stir into macaroni mixture; heat over low heat 5 additional minutes.

YIELD: 6-8 servings

Ham and Noodle Bake

1 package (8 oz.) medium noodles
1 pound cooked ham, cubed (about 3 cups)
1 cup plain yogurt
1 cup cottage cheese
1 cup (4 oz.) shredded Cheddar cheese

2 tablespoons pimiento strips
1 teaspoon caraway seed
1 teaspoon instant minced onion
¾ teaspoon salt
¼ teaspoon garlic powder

1. Preheat the oven to 350 degrees.
2. Cook noodles according to package directions; drain.
3. In a large bowl combine noodles, ham, yogurt, cottage cheese, cheese, pimiento, caraway seed, onion, salt, and garlic powder.
4. Turn into buttered 2-quart casserole and bake 35-45 minutes.

YIELD: 6-8 servings

Ham and Noodle Casserole

1 package (16 oz.) wide noodles, cooked according to package directions
2 cups chopped leftover ham or smoked shoulder
2 cups plain yogurt

1 package (10 oz.) frozen mixed vegetables, cooked and drained
Salt and pepper to taste
1½ cups fine bread crumbs
½ cup grated Parmesan cheese
2 tablespoons butter or margarine

1. Preheat the oven to 350 degrees.
2. Mix cooked, drained noodles with ham and yogurt in a large buttered casserole dish. Add salt and pepper and vegetables.

3. Cover with bread crumbs and Parmesan cheese. Dot with butter and bake 30 minutes, or until top is nicely browned.

YIELD: 4-6 servings

Chili Casserole

1 tablespoon butter
1½ pounds ground beef
¾ cup chopped onion
1 clove garlic, minced
1½ cups (6 oz.) shredded
   Cheddar cheese
1 can (15 oz.) enchilada sauce

1 can (1 lb.) kidney beans,
   drained
¾ teaspoon salt
½ teaspoon chili powder
1 package (6 oz.) corn chips
1 cup plain yogurt

1. Preheat the oven to 350 degrees.
2. In a large skillet melt butter; add beef, onion, and garlic. Cook until beef is browned.
3. Add cheese, enchilada sauce, beans, salt, and chili powder. Note: If using hot enchilada sauce, chili powder may be omitted.
4. Place 2 cups corn chips in bottom of shallow baking dish (2-quart); set aside remaining corn chips. Spoon meat mixture on top of chips; bake 20 minutes.
5. Place dollops of yogurt over meat, then remaining corn chips. Bake an additional 5-8 minutes.

YIELD: 6-8 servings

Yogurt Burgers

1 pound ground beef
1 teaspoon salt
   Pepper to taste
1 onion, finely chopped

½ cup wheat germ
1 cup plain yogurt
¾ cup fine dry bread crumbs

1. Preheat the oven to 375 degrees.
2. Mix beef, salt, pepper, onion, and wheat germ together in a large bowl. Add yogurt gradually, beating constantly. Add bread crumbs and mix thoroughly.
3. Shape into patties and place in shallow baking pan. Bake until done.

YIELD: 6 patties

Herbed Yogurt Burgers

2 pounds extra-lean hamburger
1 egg
1 cup wheat germ
¼ cup finely chopped scallions
¼ cup finely chopped parsley
¾ teaspoon savory
¾ teaspoon thyme leaves
1 cup plain yogurt

1. Combine hamburger, egg, wheat germ, scallions, parsley, savory, thyme, and yogurt in a large bowl.

2. Shape into 8 hamburgers and broil until desired degree of doneness. Serve on toasted buns.

YIELD: 8 servings

Eggplant Casserole

1 medium-size eggplant, about 1½ pounds
½ cup chopped onion
1 tablespoon safflower oil
1 pound round or chuck steak, ground
1 teaspoon salt
½ teaspoon paprika
⅛ teaspoon coarse black pepper
½ cup flour
2 medium-size tomatoes
½ cup plain yogurt
2 egg yolks
¼ cup flour

1. Preheat the oven to 350 degrees.

2. Peel eggplant and cut into finger-size pieces. Sauté onion in oil until glossy.

3. Add meat, salt, paprika, and pepper and simmer over medium heat, separating the meat with a fork as it cooks. Pour excess fat into another skillet as it accumulates.

4. Dredge eggplant in ½ cup flour and sauté in the excess fat until nicely browned.

5. In a 2-quart casserole, arrange layers of meat and eggplant. Slice the tomatoes and place them on top of the meat-eggplant layers. Combine yogurt, egg yolks, and ¼ cup of flour and pour over top.

6. Bake for 20 minutes or until brown and bubbly on top. Serve with salad as a complete dinner.

YIELD: 4 servings

Sweetbreads and Yogurt

1 pair sweetbreads, parboiled and trimmed
2 tablespoons butter
½ cup minced onion
12 mushrooms with stems, sliced
1 cup plain yogurt

2 egg yolks, beaten
1 teaspoon garlic powder
½ teaspoon salt
¼ teaspoon coarse black pepper
1 teaspoon capers

1. Cut up sweetbreads into bite-size pieces. Melt butter in a skillet and sauté onion and mushrooms until tender.

2. Heat yogurt in a double boiler and add egg yolks, garlic, salt, and pepper. (To avoid cooking the eggs, pour some of the warm yogurt on the eggs first, then return to rest of yogurt.)

3. Place sweetbreads on a warm platter; pour yogurt sauce over sweetbreads. Garnish with capers. You may also use this as a filling for a plain omelet.

YIELD: 4 servings

Musaka with Potatoes (Orient)

This mixture of ground meat and vegetables originated in Turkey but can be found today throughout the countries once dominated by Turks—especially Yugoslavia, Greece, and Bulgaria. Generally, lamb or mutton is used. This recipe uses a mixture of ground beef and pork along with eggplant. The custardlike sauce is called saliwka.

3 medium potatoes
Salt to taste
½ cup oil
4 small eggplants
2 onions, finely chopped
1 pound beef and pork, ground
Pepper, paprika, thyme, rosemary, sage to taste

2 tablespoons tomato puree
½ cup broth or bouillon

Sauce (Saliwka):

1 cup plain yogurt
3 eggs
⅛ teaspoon baking powder
2 tablespoons flour
Salt to taste

1. Preheat the oven to 350 degrees.

2. Pare and slice (or dice) potatoes; salt lightly and brown in heated oil in a large heavy skillet and set aside.

(cont'd)

3. Pare and slice eggplants lengthwise; sprinkle with salt and set aside for 30 minutes. Fry them in 3-4 tablespoons of the hot oil till eggplant meat is tender.

4. Heat a little oil in a skillet; add onions and ground meat and cook about 5 minutes. Add eggplant; season to taste and let simmer for a few minutes, stirring occasionally. Add tomato puree and broth; bring to boil.

5. Arrange alternate layers of potatoes and the ground meat mixture in a greased baking dish. Cover and bake for 40 minutes.

6. Mix yogurt with other sauce ingredients. Pour over the musaka, cover, and return to oven for another 10 minutes. Place under broiler and heat a few minutes to brown well on top. Serve immediately.

YIELD: approximately 6 servings

Moussaka (Bulgaria)

1 teaspoon salt	1½ pounds ground lamb (or beef)
2 large eggplants	beef)
2 onions, finely chopped	Salt, pepper, paprika to taste
1 green pepper, chopped	Flour
3 garlic cloves, minced	2 cups plain yogurt
2 tablespoons oil	3 egg yolks
	½ cup flour, sifted

1. Preheat the oven to 375 degrees.

2. Sprinkle 1 teaspoon salt over slices of 2 large eggplants, ¼ inch thick.

3. In a large skillet, fry onion, green pepper, and garlic in oil; add ground meat, separating into particles with fork.

4. Season with salt, pepper, paprika, and brown well. Remove from skillet and set aside.

5. Dip eggplant slices in flour and brown on both sides in same pan. In a casserole arrange alternate layers of eggplant slices and meat mixture; bake for about 1 hour.

6. In a bowl, mix yogurt, egg yolks, and sifted flour. Spoon over contents of the casserole. Pass it briefly under the flames of the broiler for a custardlike topping.

YIELD: 6-8 servings

Liver Kebabs

1½ pounds thickly sliced calves liver
2 teaspoons ground coriander
½ teaspoon grated ginger
1 clove garlic, crushed
¼ teaspoon ground cinnamon
¼ teaspoon black pepper
¼ teaspoon ground cloves
½ cup plain yogurt
Melted clarified butter
Salt

1. Wash liver. Pat dry with paper towels and cut into 1½-inch squares.
2. Combine liver with the coriander, ginger, garlic, cinnamon, black pepper, cloves, and yogurt.
3. Set aside to marinate at least 1 hour.
4. Thread on skewers. Brush with melted butter and broil to desired doneness. Sprinkle with salt.

YIELD: 2-3 servings

Beef Kabobs

1 cup plain yogurt
2 tablespoons grated onion
½ teaspoon salt
¼ teaspoon crushed chilies
¼ teaspoon Worcestershire sauce
4 drops Tabasco sauce
1½ pounds boneless beef sirloin or chuck (if using beef chuck, use high quality) cut in 1½-inch cubes
¾ pound fresh whole mushrooms

1. In a shallow dish combine yogurt, onion, salt, chilies, Worcestershire and Tabasco sauces.
2. Alternate meat and mushrooms on skewers. Place in marinade 3 or more hours.
3. Broil 3-4 inches from heat, turning occasionally, for 10 minutes or until meat is desired degree of doneness.

YIELD: 6-8 servings

Elegant Lamb Shanks

6 lamb shanks
1 clove garlic, thinly sliced
1 teaspoon salt
¼ teaspoon pepper
2 tablespoons salad oil
1 can (4 oz.) mushroom pieces, with liquid

½ cup finely chopped onion
1 cup dry white wine
2 tablespoons flour, diluted with a little water
1 cup plain yogurt
½ teaspoon dill weed
1 teaspoon paprika

1. Make a slit next to the bone in each shank and insert a sliver of garlic. Sprinkle with salt and pepper and brown in a skillet on all sides in the oil.

2. Add mushrooms, onions, and wine and simmer 1½ hours or until the meat is tender. Remove shanks to a heated platter.

3. Combine flour mixture with the pan drippings, stirring until thickened. Reduce heat and stir in the yogurt, dill, and paprika. Heat thoroughly and serve sauce over lamb shanks.

YIELD: 6 servings

Lamb and Eggplant Casserole

1 2½-pound eggplant
1 small onion, chopped
3 tablespoons soy oil
2 pounds ground lean lamb
2 teaspoons salt
1 teaspoon cracked pepper

½ teaspoon garlic powder
½ teaspoon rosemary
3–4 tomatoes, sliced
1 cup plain yogurt
4 egg yolks
½ cup flour

1. Preheat the oven to 350 degrees.

2. Peel and slice an eggplant in ½-inch slices. Sprinkle slices with salt and let stand 1 hour. Chop onion and sauté in a little soy oil until transparent.

3. Add lamb, salt, pepper, garlic, and rosemary. Sauté till meat is browned slightly. Remove everything from frying pan, add remainder of the soy oil, dip eggplant slices in flour, and brown on both sides.

4. In a 3-quart casserole arrange alternate layers of eggplant and meat. Top with sliced tomatoes.

5. Bake 1 hour. Blend yogurt, egg yolks, and flour and mix well. Pour over casserole. Bake 15 minutes longer or until brown.

YIELD: 6-8 servings

Punjab Lamb Roast

1 5-pound leg of lamb
2 cups plain yogurt
½ teaspoon powdered ginger
½ teaspoon chili powder
4 garlic cloves, minced

⅓ cup ground almonds
¼ teaspoon salt
½ teaspoon saffron
4 tablespoons (½ stick) butter

1. Prick surface of lamb with a fork.
2. Mix together yogurt, ginger, chili powder, garlic, almonds, salt, and saffron. Rub the mixture well into the meat.
3. Cover loosely and let seasoned meat stand overnight or for at least 12 hours at room temperature. Turn the lamb at least once.
4. When ready to cook, preheat oven to 450 degrees. Rub lamb once more with marinade and place in a shallow roasting pan.
5. Dot with butter. Roast lamb, uncovered, 15 minutes. Reduce heat to 300 degrees and cook for 2-2½ hours, basting occasionally. Serve with pan juices.

YIELD: 4-6 servings

Mild Lamb Curry

2 pounds lamb, cubed
6 cloves garlic, crushed
4 tablespoons vegetable oil
3 medium onions, thinly sliced
2 teaspoons ground coriander
1 teaspoon cumin
½ teaspoon paprika

½ teaspoon ginger, finely chopped
¼ teaspoon cayenne pepper
Pinch of ground cardamom
1½ cups water
1½ teaspoons salt
½ teaspoon sugar
½ cup plain yogurt

1. Mix together the lamb cubes and crushed garlic. Set aside 1 hour.
2. Heat vegetable oil and fry onions until golden. Add coriander, cumin, paprika, ginger, cayenne pepper, and ground cardamom. Fry for 2 minutes. Put in lamb and fry for 5 minutes.
3. Add water and bring to a simmer. Add salt and sugar. Cover and simmer until meat is tender. Just before serving, stir in the yogurt.

YIELD: 6 servings

Lamb in Gourmet Sauce

2 pounds lamb shoulder, cut into 1-inch strips
2 tablespoons salad oil
¼ cup finely chopped onion
¼ cup chopped green pepper
¼ cup flour, diluted in a little water
½ cup dry white wine
2 teaspoons salt
Dash of pepper
1 teaspoon tarragon leaves
1 teaspoon thyme leaves
1 cup plain yogurt
1 package (8 oz.) medium-width flat noodles, cooked according to package directions

1. Brown meat on all sides in oil in a large skillet. Add onions and green pepper and brown for 5 minutes.

2. Add flour and wine and pour over meat. Stir until thickened.

3. Add seasonings and cook over very low heat for approximately 30-60 minutes or until meat is tender.

4. Blend in yogurt and heat thoroughly. Serve over hot buttered noodles.

YIELD: 6 servings

Lamb with Yogurt Sauce (Laban Immo)

1 pound leg of lamb, cut into 1-inch cubes
2½ cups water
1 teaspoon salt
12 tiny white onions
1 cup plain yogurt
1 tablespoon olive oil
1 clove garlic, minced
1 teaspoon crushed coriander seeds

1. Put lamb in a heavy saucepan with the water and salt. Bring to a boil and simmer for 1 hour. Add onions, cover, and cook for 30 minutes longer or until liquid is reduced to ½ cup. Cool to lukewarm.

2. Stir in yogurt and cook, stirring, over moderate heat until sauce is smooth and thick.

3. In small skillet heat oil and in it sauté the garlic and coriander for 30 seconds.

4. Add to lamb and serve with cooked rice.

YIELD: 3-4 servings

Dilly Lamb Stew

1 tablespoon butter
1½ pounds lamb stew meat
1 teaspoon salt
¾ teaspoon dill weed
2 cups water
4–5 medium potatoes, peeled and quartered
4–5 carrots, peeled and cut in 2-inch pieces
3–4 stalks celery, cut in 2-inch pieces
1 cup plain yogurt
2 tablespoons flour

1. In a large skillet melt butter; brown meat on all sides. Add salt, dill weed, and water. Cover and simmer 1 hour or until meat is almost tender.

2. Add potatoes, carrots, and celery; simmer 30 additional minutes or until vegetables are tender.

3. Meanwhile in a small bowl combine yogurt and flour. Remove meat and vegetables to warmed serving dish.

4. Add yogurt mixture to liquid in skillet. Cook over low heat, stirring constantly, until thickened. Cook 2 additional minutes. Pour gravy over lamb and vegetables.

YIELD: 4-6 servings

Lamb and Yogurt (Hyderabadi Goshth)

4 pounds boneless leg of lamb, fat trimmed
1 teaspoon ground turmeric
1 cup plain yogurt
2 teaspoons salt
2 teaspoons ground coriander
3 tablespoons vegetable shortening
3 half-inch cinnamon sticks
½ teaspoon ground cardamom
8 cloves
8 peppercorns
1 medium onion, finely sliced
8 garlic cloves, sliced
¾ teaspoon ground ginger

1. Place meat, turmeric, yogurt, salt, and coriander in large bowl. Mix well. Set aside for 2 hours.

2. Heat vegetable shortening in Dutch oven or casserole. Add cinnamon, cardamom, cloves, and peppercorns. Fry 2 minutes.

3. Add meat and yogurt. Simmer for 10 minutes. Add onion, garlic, and ginger. Cover.

4. Simmer until meat is tender, approximately 2 hours. Serve.

YIELD: 6-8 servings

Lamb Chops and Yogurt (Dahi Chop)

1½ cups plain yogurt
4 garlic cloves, crushed
1½ teaspoons ground ginger
¼ teaspoon ground coriander
Crushed red pepper to taste
½ teaspoon ground turmeric

10 peppercorns, ground
Salt to taste
8 lamb chops, fat trimmed
5 tablespoons vegetable shortening, divided
2 medium onions, thinly sliced

1. Place yogurt and spices in large mixing bowl. Mix well. Add chops and mix. Set aside for 1 hour.

2. Heat 4 tablespoons vegetable shortening in large skillet. Fry chops and yogurt until brown and tender.

3. Heat 1 tablespoon vegetable shortening in separate skillet. Fry onions until crisp. Garnish chops with crisp onions.

YIELD: 4-5 servings

Yogurt Pot Roast Continental

2 tablespoons bacon fat
2 onions, chopped
2 cloves garlic, chopped
5 pounds pot roast
8 carrots, quartered

8 medium potatoes
Salt and pepper to taste
2 tablespoons flour, moistened
with water
1 cup yogurt

1. Melt bacon fat in deep saucepan. Add onions and garlic and sauté till brown. Add pot roast and brown on all sides.

2. Add carrots and potatoes and sprinkle with salt and pepper. Add 1 inch of water and cook slowly for 4 hours, adding water as it becomes necessary.

3. Remove meat and vegetables to platter. Add flour moistened with water and yogurt. Stir thoroughly and cook 5 minutes. Serve gravy in separate dish.

YIELD: 6 servings

Cabbage and Hamburger

1 medium-size head cabbage,
sliced
1 pound ground beef
2 tablespoons salad oil or
shortening

1 cup plain yogurt
½ cup grated American cheese
1 teaspoon salt
Pepper to taste
Buttered bread crumbs

1. Preheat the oven to 350 degrees.

2. In a small amount of salted water, steam coarsely sliced cabbage until tender but still crisp; drain.

3. Brown meat in oil or shortening, stirring as it cooks to break it into coarse crumbles. Mix with cabbage.

4. Combine yogurt, cheese, salt, and pepper. Stir into cabbage and meat. Spread in a large shallow pan, cover with buttered crumbs mixed with additional cheese, if desired, and bake 30 minutes or until lightly browned.

YIELD: 6 generous servings

Macaroni and Cheese

2 cups (8 oz.) uncooked small elbow macaroni
¼ cup butter
¼ cup dry bread crumbs
⅓ cup chopped onion
3 tablespoons flour
¼ teaspoon salt
⅛ teaspoon pepper
1 cup milk
2 cups (8 oz.) shredded process American cheese
1 cup plain yogurt
1 sliced small tomato

1. Preheat the oven to 350 degrees.

2. Cook macaroni according to label directions. Drain and rinse.

3. Melt 1 tablespoon butter in small saucepan. Add bread crumbs. Stir until crumbs are golden in color.

4. Sauté onion in remaining 3 tablespoons butter in medium saucepan. Stir in flour, salt, and pepper. Gradually stir in milk. Cook over medium heat. Stir constantly until mixture just comes to boil.

5. Add cheese and yogurt. Stir until cheese melts. Remove from heat. Combine cooked macaroni and cheese sauce. Mix lightly but thoroughly.

6. Spoon into 1½-quart casserole. Arrange sliced tomato on casserole. Top with buttered bread crumbs. Bake 20-30 minutes or until bubbly.

YIELD: 6 cups

Beef Stroganoff

1 pound thin-cut round steak
½ cup chopped onion
1 clove garlic, minced
2 tablespoons flour
½ teaspoon salt
¼ teaspoon pepper

1 can (10½ oz.) condensed
  cream of mushroom soup
1 can (4 oz.) mushroom stems
  and pieces, undrained
1 cup plain yogurt

1. Cut steak into thin strips, 3 inches long. Brown steak strips, onion, and garlic in skillet over medium heat, about 5 minutes.

2. In small bowl combine flour, salt, pepper, soup, and mushrooms and liquid. Stir into meat mixture; mix well. Cover, reduce heat to low, and simmer 10 minutes. Stir in yogurt just before serving. Serve over cooked noodles.

YIELD: 4 servings

Mock Stroganoff

1½ pounds ground chuck
¾ cup chopped onion
1 teaspoon paprika
1½ teaspoons seasoned salt
¼ teaspoon garlic salt
2 tablespoons flour
1¼ cups (10½-oz. can) cream of
  mushroom soup

½ cup water
⅔ cup (4-oz. can) sliced mushrooms, drained
¼ cup fresh parsley, chopped
1 cup plain yogurt
  Hot cooked noodles

1. Combine chuck, onion, paprika, seasoned salt, and garlic salt in medium skillet. Cook over medium heat until chuck is browned. Gradually stir in flour.

2. Add soup, water, mushrooms, and parsley. Stir until blended. Heat to boiling. Reduce heat; simmer uncovered for 10 minutes. Stir occasionally.

3. Add yogurt. Heat to serving temperature. Serve over hot noodles.

YIELD: 6 servings

Yogurt Quiche

1½ cups shredded Swiss cheese
6 bacon slices, cooked and crumbled
1 scallion, thinly sliced
1 9-inch unbaked pie shell
4 eggs, slightly beaten
1 cup plain yogurt

1 tablespoon cornstarch
¾ cup milk
½ teaspoon salt
Dash of pepper
2 tablespoons grated Parmesan cheese

1. Preheat the oven to 350 degrees.

2. Sprinkle Swiss cheese, bacon, and scallion over bottom of pastry shell.

3. In mixing bowl combine eggs, yogurt, cornstarch, milk, salt, and pepper. Beat with electric mixer at medium speed until smooth.

4. Pour egg mixture into pastry shell. Sprinkle with Parmesan cheese.

5. Bake 45-50 minutes or until knife inserted in center of quiche comes out clean. Let stand 10 minutes before cutting. Cut into wedges for serving.

YIELD: 6 servings

Poultry

Chicken with Wine

1 tablespoon butter
1 tablespoon safflower oil
1 frying chicken (3 to 3½ pounds), cut into serving pieces
⅛ teaspoon cayenne pepper
½ cup chicken broth or water
½ cup dry white wine or chicken broth
2 tablespoons chopped chives
Sea salt to taste
1 tablespoon unbleached white flour
½ cup yogurt

1. Heat the butter and oil in a heavy skillet and fry the chicken pieces in it, a few at a time, until golden brown. Return all chicken to the skillet.

2. Add cayenne, cover skillet, and cook over moderate heat 10 minutes, turning chicken once.

3. Add broth or water and wine or more broth. Sprinkle with chives and salt, cover, and cook over low heat for 20 minutes or until chicken is done. Remove chicken to warm platter.

4. Remove surface fat from broth. Mix flour and yogurt and add to skillet. Cook until thickened but do not boil. Pour over chicken.

YIELD: 4 servings

Chicken with Yogurt (Kotopoulo Me Yoarti)

1 chicken (2½ pounds), cut up
4 cups boiling water
1 teaspoon salt
3 tablespoons butter
1 cup chicken stock
1 medium onion, chopped
¼ cup raisins
2 tablespoons flour
1 cup plain yogurt

186

1. Blanch chicken by scalding with boiling water; drain, pat dry, sprinkle with salt. Let stand 15 minutes. Separate giblets, neck, and wing tips; use these to make stock by cooking in salted water ½ hour.

2. Melt butter, add remaining chicken pieces, brown quickly on all sides; remove.

3. Add onion, lower heat, cook until onion is soft and yellow. Replace chicken, add strained stock and raisins, cook covered about 20 minutes.

4. To thicken sauce, first make a thin paste of flour and a little water; add this paste to chicken stock, cook until sauce is smooth and thickened. Turn off heat, stir in yogurt. Serve at once.

YIELD: 4 servings

Chicken Pilaf (Kotopoulo Pilafi)

1 frying chicken (3 pounds), cut up	2 tablespoons olive oil
2 cups salted water	2 medium onions, chopped
1 cup plain yogurt	1 cup converted rice
2 tablespoons flour	1 tablespoon tomato paste
½ teaspoon salt	¼ teaspoon cinnamon
¼ teaspoon pepper	2 cups chicken broth
¼ pound (1 stick) butter	2–3 tablespoons minced parsley

1. Separate the chicken neck, giblets, wing tips, and back sections from the other chicken pieces. Make broth of these pieces by simmering in the salted water for 30 minutes. Strain; measure 2 cups of broth (adding water if necessary).

2. As broth simmers marinate remaining chicken pieces in yogurt. Remove chicken, dust the pieces in the flour seasoned with the salt and pepper.

3. Melt half the butter in a heavy skillet with the olive oil. Add some of the chicken pieces to the skillet, taking care not to crowd the pan. Remove pieces as they are browned; add remaining chicken until all pieces are cooked. Set aside.

4. Add the onion to the pan, lower heat, cook until soft. Pour off excess fat. Add the rice, stir to glaze. Blend tomato paste, cinnamon, and chicken broth; add this to the skillet.

(cont'd)

5. Replace chicken pieces over the rice. Bring to a boil, lower heat, cover skillet. Cook 20-25 minutes or until all liquid is absorbed. Serve with parsley sprinkled over the top.

YIELD: 4 servings

Chicken Tandoori

1 cup plain yogurt	½ teaspoon cayenne pepper
3 tablespoons lime juice	1 clove garlic, finely chopped
1½ teaspoons grated fresh gingerroot	1 chicken (2½ to 3 pounds), cut into serving pieces
1½ teaspoons ground coriander	⅓ cup melted butter
1 teaspoon ground cumin	Lime wedges
½ teaspoon ground anise seeds	

1. Combine all ingredients except the chicken, butter, and lime wedges and mix well. Set the chicken in a bowl and pour the yogurt mixture over all. Marinate in the refrigerator 24 hours, turning often.

2. Preheat the oven to 375 degrees.

3. Place the chicken pieces on a rack in a shallow roasting pan and bake 45-60 minutes or until done, basting three times with the melted butter during the cooking. Serve with lime wedges.

YIELD: 4 servings

Chicken Baked with Spiced Yogurt

¼ cup almonds	Generous pinch of saffron
½ cup grated unsweetened coconut	1 fryer (2 to 3 pounds), disjointed
2 cloves garlic	¼ cup clarified butter
1-inch piece of ginger	2 onions, thinly sliced
1 teaspoon chili powder	1 teaspoon salt
1 cup plain yogurt	Coriander or mint leaves, optional
Juice of one lemon	
1 cup chopped tomatoes	

1. Preheat the oven to 325 degrees.

2. Grind together the almonds, coconut, garlic, ginger, and chili powder in a food mill or electric blender.

3. Add this mixture to the yogurt, along with the lemon juice, chopped tomatoes, and saffron. Add the chicken parts to this mixture. Be sure that each piece is coated. Let marinate 1 or 2 hours.

4. In a heavy casserole, melt the butter and sauté the onions until brown. Put in the chicken and its marinade. Add salt. Cover, bring to a simmer, and seal edges of casserole with aluminum foil.

5. Bake about 1½ hours. Serve garnished with coriander or mint leaves, if desired.

YIELD: 4 servings

Spicy Chicken

1 cup plain yogurt	¼ teaspoon cinnamon
1½ teaspoons salt	¼ teaspoon ginger
1 small clove garlic, crushed	1 broiler-fryer chicken (2½ to
½ teaspoon ground cardamom	3 pounds), quartered
½ teaspoon chili powder	2 teaspoons flour

1. In a small bowl combine yogurt, salt, garlic, cardamom, chili powder, cinnamon, and ginger. In a shallow dish marinate chicken in yogurt mixture at least 4 hours or overnight.

2. Preheat the oven to 350 degrees.

3. Place chicken skin side up in a shallow baking pan. Combine flour with marinade; spoon on chicken.

4. Bake 1¼-1½ hours or until tender, occasionally basting with marinade.

YIELD: 4 servings

Chicken Breasts de Valaille

4 large chicken breasts, boned	1½ cups sliced fresh mushrooms
Salt and white pepper to taste	¼ cup chicken broth
¼ cup lemon juice	¼ cup dry white wine
¼ cup margarine	2 teaspoons flour
2 tablespoons finely chopped onion	1½ cups plain yogurt

1. Sprinkle chicken breasts with salt and pepper to taste and 1 tablespoon of the lemon juice. Sauté the chicken in the margarine until soft but springy. Remove from heat and keep warm.

(cont'd)

2. Add the onions and mushrooms to the pan drippings and sauté until tender. Add the chicken broth and wine and cook over high heat until syrupy.

3. Stir in the flour and yogurt and cook over low heat, stirring constantly until thickened. Correct seasoning and add remaining lemon juice. Pour over chicken and serve.

YIELD: 4 servings

Chicken Bombay

1 chicken (3 lb.), quartered	1 clove garlic, crushed
1 brown-in-the-oven bag (6-lb. capacity)	1 medium-size onion, chopped
4 cups plain yogurt	1 cup converted long-grain rice (not instant)
1 tablespoon curry powder	Salt and pepper to taste
Pinch of ginger	¼ cup golden raisins
4 tablespoons apricot preserves	1 scallion, finely chopped

1. Preheat the oven to 350 degrees.

2. Place the chicken parts in the bag, skin side down.

3. In a mixing bowl, blend together yogurt, curry powder, ginger, preserves, garlic, onion, rice, salt, pepper, and raisins.

4. Pour into the bag containing the chicken and close with a bag tie. Work the bag with your hands until the chicken is covered with the yogurt and rice mixture.

5. Place in a baking pan, with the chicken skin side up. Pierce the bag to let steam escape.

6. Bake for 1 hour. Pour the cooked chicken and rice onto a platter and garnish with chopped scallions.

YIELD: 4 generous servings

Yogurt Chicken-Zucchini

This is a delicately flavored, one-dish meal that's easy to prepare if you remember to marinate the chicken before you cook it. The curry flavor is just a whisper.

1 frying chicken, cut in serving
  pieces
1 cup plain yogurt
1 teaspoon salt
1 teaspoon turmeric
1 teaspoon curry powder
1 clove crushed garlic
1 tablespoon lemon juice

2 tablespoons cooking oil
1 large onion, thinly sliced
2 large carrots, sliced
5 small (red-skinned) potatoes,
  scrubbed but unpeeled and
  cut into chunks
2 small zucchini, sliced

1. Wash chicken and slit skin in several places. In a large bowl mix the yogurt, salt, turmeric, curry powder, garlic, and lemon juice. Add the chicken, turn to make sure all pieces are coated, and marinate in the refrigerator, covered, overnight or for 24 hours. Turn once or twice.

2. In a Dutch oven or large frying pan, heat the oil and sauté the onion until soft. Add chicken and marinade. Add carrots and potatoes. Simmer, covered, for about an hour. Add the zucchini and cook a half hour more or until chicken and vegetables are fork-tender.

YIELD: 3-4 servings

Turkey Tetrazzini

2 cups sliced fresh mushrooms
1 package (8 oz.) spaghetti,
  cooked according to package
  directions
¼ cup butter or margarine
2 tablespoons flour
2 cups chicken broth or
  bouillon
1 cup plain yogurt

1 teaspoon sugar
3 tablespoons sherry
1 teaspoon salt
  Dash of pepper
⅛ teaspoon nutmeg
3 cups cooked leftover turkey,
  cubed
¼ cup grated Parmesan cheese

1. Preheat the oven to 375 degrees.

2. Sauté the mushrooms in the butter until tender. Combine with the cooked spaghetti in a large buttered casserole dish.

3. Melt 2 tablespoons butter in a saucepan and blend in flour. Add chicken broth and cook, stirring until thickened. Remove from heat and add yogurt, sugar, sherry, salt, pepper, and nutmeg.

(cont'd)

4. Add half of the sauce to the turkey and half to the spaghetti-mushroom mixture in casserole. Make a well in the center of the spaghetti and spoon in the turkey.

5. Sprinkle the top with Parmesan cheese and bake 20-25 minutes, until lightly browned.

YIELD: 8 servings

Chicken with Sherry

1 cup sliced mushrooms	Salt to taste
2 tablespoons chopped green pepper or red sweet pepper	1½ cups chicken stock
½ cup butter	1 cup plain yogurt
4 tablespoons flour	1 cup cooked chicken, chopped
Dash of cayenne	1 cup green peas, cooked
	¼ cup sherry

1. Sauté mushrooms and peppers in 4 tablespoons butter until lightly browned. Set aside.

2. In another pan, blend flour and 4 tablespoons butter. Add seasonings and cook over low heat until bubbling. Remove from heat; add stock. Stir well.

3. Beat yogurt and blend in gradually. Bring to boiling point, stirring constantly, about 1 minute. Add chicken, peas, mushrooms, and peppers.

4. Reheat, then add sherry just before serving. Spoon over toast or rice.

YIELD: 4 servings

Chicken Polynesian

1 ripe pineapple	¾ cup plain yogurt
4 cooked chicken breasts, boned and cubed	1 tablespoon chopped chutney
1 cup water chestnuts, sliced	Lemon juice
1 cup chopped celery	Salt to taste
2 tablespoons chopped candied ginger	Nutmeg

1. Slice pineapple lengthwise through green top. Scoop out pineapple, discard the core, cube, and reserve pineapple shells as "boats" for serving.

192

2. In a large bowl, combine cubed pineapple, chicken, water chestnuts, celery, ginger, yogurt, chutney, lemon juice, and salt. Mound mixture in pineapple "boats" and sprinkle lightly with nutmeg. Serve garnished with seasonal fruits.

YIELD: 2 servings

Chicken and Onion Stew

3 tablespoons butter or margarine
1½ teaspoons salt
¾ teaspoon pepper
1 broiler-fryer chicken, cut in serving pieces
1 tablespoon paprika
12 small onions, about ½ pound

2 tablespoons chopped celery leaves
½ pound mushrooms, sliced
1 cup sliced celery
1½ cups chicken broth
1½ cups dry white wine
½ teaspoon thyme leaves
½ cup plain yogurt
½ teaspoon cornstarch

1. Melt 2 tablespoons butter in Dutch oven or large skillet. Sprinkle 1 teaspoon salt and ¼ teaspoon pepper over chicken. Brown chicken in butter; remove.
2. Stir paprika into butter in skillet, adding remaining tablespoon butter. Add onions, celery leaves, and mushrooms, cover, and cook over low heat 5 minutes.
3. Return chicken, add sliced celery, chicken broth, white wine, remaining salt and pepper, and thyme. Cover and simmer 25 minutes until chicken is tender.
4. Mix together 1 teaspoon cornstarch and yogurt, stir into chicken mixture. Heat.

YIELD: 4-6 servings

Yogurt Chicken Casserole

1 chicken
Salt and pepper to taste
2 tablespoons butter
2 large onions, sliced

4 tablespoons flour
2 cups water
2 cups plain yogurt
Paprika to taste

1. Cut chicken into 6 pieces. Sprinkle with salt and pepper. Melt butter in frying pan. Add chicken and brown on both sides.

(cont'd)

2. Place chicken in casserole with sliced onions scattered between and over. Sprinkle with flour and cover with water.

3. Bake for 2 hours or until chicken is tender. Ten minutes before serving, add yogurt and paprika. Mix thoroughly and serve hot.

YIELD: 4 servings

Fish

Fish with Yogurt (Dahimachi)

1 pound halibut
2 tablespoons vegetable oil
2 medium onions, thinly sliced
1 teaspoon cumin
¼ teaspoon ground cloves
¼ teaspoon ground cinnamon
¼ teaspoon ground cardamom
¼ teaspoon turmeric
2 slices ginger, minced
1½ teaspoons salt
1½ cups plain yogurt

1. Cut fish into serving pieces. Heat oil and brown the onions. Add cumin, cloves, cinnamon, cardamom, turmeric, and ginger. Fry for 2 or 3 minutes.

2. Put in fish, salt, and yogurt. Mix well and simmer until fish is cooked, watching carefully and stirring occasionally.

YIELD: approximately 3-4 servings

Fish with Tomato Yogurt Sauce

1 pound fillets, halibut or flounder
3 tablespoons vegetable oil
1 small onion, finely chopped
1 clove garlic, crushed
1 tablespoon coriander leaves, optional
1 fresh or pickled green chili, finely chopped
1 teaspoon ground coriander
⅛ teaspoon turmeric
¼ cup grated unsweetened coconut
¼ cup tomato sauce
1 cup yogurt
1 teaspoon salt or to taste

1. Lightly brown fish fillets in hot oil; remove from skillet and set aside. Put in onion and fry until golden. Add garlic, coriander leaves, green chili, coriander, turmeric, and coconut.

(cont'd)

2. Fry for 2 or 3 minutes, stirring constantly. Add tomato sauce, yogurt, and salt. Simmer for 5 minutes.

3. Put in fish, cover, and simmer for 5 minutes, watching carefully.

YIELD: approximately 3-4 servings

Shrimp Stroganoff

3 tablespoons butter
½ cup chopped onion
1 small clove garlic, minced
¼ cup regular all-purpose flour
1 teaspoon salt
½ teaspoon dill weed

1 can (10½ oz.) condensed beef broth
1 can (2 oz.) sliced mushrooms
2 cups cooked shrimp
1 cup plain yogurt at room temperature
Hot buttered noodles or rice

1. In a large skillet melt butter; sauté onion and garlic until onion is tender. Stir in flour, salt, and dill weed.

2. Remove from heat; gradually stir in beef broth and mushrooms with liquid. Cook over medium heat, stirring constantly, until thickened.

3. Add shrimp; heat over low heat 5-10 minutes. Stir in yogurt; heat to serving temperature (do not boil). Serve over noodles or rice.

YIELD: 4-6 servings

Shrimp and Asparagus

1 package (10 oz.) asparagus, cooked according to directions
2 cans (4½ oz.) large shrimp, drained

1 cup plain yogurt
½ cup blue cheese, crumbled
4 English muffins, toasted

1. Place asparagus in a buttered baking dish. Top with the shrimp.

2. Blend the yogurt and blue cheese in a bowl and spoon over the shrimp. Broil for 3-5 minutes until lightly browned. Serve hot over English muffins.

YIELD: 4 servings

196

Indian Shrimp Curry

¼ cup butter or margarine
2 large onions, finely chopped
1 pound fresh mushroms, sliced
2 garlic cloves, crushed
1 tablespoon curry powder
1 teaspoon chili powder
Salt and pepper to taste

2 pounds small raw shrimp,
peeled and deveined
4 medium tomatoes, peeled and
chopped
1 cup plain yogurt
2 tablespoons cornstarch

1. In a large skillet sauté the onions, mushrooms, and garlic in the butter. Stir in all of the spices and add the shrimp, stirring until the shrimp turns pink.

2. Add the tomatoes and cook slowly for 5 minutes. Stir in the yogurt and heat, but do not boil.

3. Add the cornstarch, stirring until thickened. Serve over hot steamed rice.

YIELD: 6 servings

Yogurt Fillet of Sole

2 pounds fillet of sole
1 tablespoon butter
¼ cup capers
½ lemon, sliced very, very thin
1 teaspoon dill seed

½ cup minced onion
1 teaspoon paprika
1 cup plain yogurt
1 teaspoon salt
Large pinch of white pepper

1. Preheat oven to 325 degrees.

2. Place raw fillets on a baking sheet that has been greased with 1 tablespoon butter. Scatter capers over fish, then cover with the thin slices of lemon.

3. Combine dill seed, onion, paprika, yogurt, salt, and pepper in a bowl. Spread half the yogurt mixture over the fish.

4. Bake about 20 minutes. Remove from oven, cover with remaining yogurt, and place under hot broiler for 3 minutes, or until brown.

YIELD: 4-6 servings

Stuffed Fillets of Sole

1½ cups soft wheat bread crumbs
¼ cup finely chopped celery
2 tablespoons finely chopped onion
3 tablespoons toasted chopped almonds
½ teaspoon salt
⅛ teaspoon pepper
⅓ cup plain yogurt
1 pound (4-6) fresh or thawed frozen fillets of sole
½ cup milk
Salt and pepper to taste

1. Preheat the oven to 350 degrees.

2. Combine bread, celery, onion, almonds, salt, and pepper in medium bowl. Mix thoroughly. Gently stir in yogurt.

3. Place about ¼ cup stuffing on each fish fillet. Roll each fillet and secure with toothpick.

4. Place seam side down in 10x6x2-inch baking dish. Pour milk over fish. Sprinkle with salt and pepper to taste.

5. Bake 25-30 minutes or until fish flakes easily with fork. Drain and reserve fish liquid for *Parsleyed Cream Sauce*. Keep fish warm.

YIELD: 4 servings

Parsleyed Cream Sauce

2 tablespoons butter
2 tablespoons flour
¼ teaspoon salt
1 tablespoon chopped parsley
Reserved fish liquid
½ cup yogurt

1. Melt butter in small saucepan. Stir in flour, salt, and parsley. Gradually stir in reserved fish liquid (should measure ⅔ cup; if necessary, add water).

2. Cook over medium heat, stirring constantly, until mixture comes to boil. Stir in yogurt. Heat to serving temperature. Do not boil. Serve over *Stuffed Fillets of Sole*.

Scalloped Oysters

1½ cups coarse Ritz cracker crumbs
½ cup grated Parmesan cheese
¼ cup butter or margarine, melted
½ teaspoon salt
Dash of pepper
Dash of mace
1 pint (2 cups) fresh oysters, drained
¼ cup sherry
½ cup plain yogurt
1 tablespoon butter or margarine

1. Preheat the oven to 375 degrees.

2. Combine crumbs, cheese, ¼ cup butter, salt, pepper, and mace in a skillet. Stir until well mixed and slightly browned.

3. Spread half of the crumb mixture in a buttered 10x6-inch baking dish. Spoon oysters over crumbs.

4. Combine the sherry and yogurt and spoon on top of the oysters. Top with remaining crumbs, dot with 1 tablespoon butter, and bake 20 minutes, until crumbs are golden brown.

YIELD: 6 servings

Lobster Thermidor

2 packages (9 oz. each) frozen lobster tails	½ cup plain yogurt at room temperature
2 tablespoons butter	1 can (2 oz.) sliced mushrooms, drained
¼ cup finely chopped celery	
1½ tablespoons flour	½ teaspoon grated lemon rind
¼ teaspoon salt	½ teaspoon prepared mustard
1 cup milk	2 tablespoons grated Parmesan cheese
1 egg, beaten	Buttered toast

1. Cook lobster according to package directions; cut into ½-inch pieces. In 2-quart saucepan melt butter; add celery and sauté 2-3 minutes. Add flour and salt. Remove from heat; gradually add milk.

2. Return to heat and cook, stirring constantly, until thickened. Cook 2 additional minutes. Add small amount of hot mixture to egg; return all to saucepan. Cook 1 minute.

3. Stir in yogurt, then lobster, mushrooms, lemon rind, mustard, and cheese. Heat to serving temperature (do not boil). Serve about ½-¾ cup mixture over toast.

YIELD: 4-6 servings

Halibut Parmesan

1 cup plain yogurt	1 teaspoon grated lemon rind
2 tablespoons flour	
1 can (10¾ oz.) condensed tomato soup	½ teaspoon salt
½ cup grated Parmesan cheese	2–2½ pounds North Pacific halibut steaks
	Chopped parsley

1. Preheat the oven to 350 degrees.

2. In a bowl combine ¼ cup yogurt with flour; fold in remaining yogurt, soup, cheese, lemon rind, and salt. (Yield: approximately 2½ cups sauce.)

3. Place halibut in shallow 2-quart baking dish; pour sauce over. Bake 30-40 minutes or until fish flakes when tested with a fork. Sprinkle top with parsley.

YIELD: 6 servings

Crab Casserole

1 cup uncooked regular rice
2 packages (6 oz. each) frozen king crabmeat, thawed
2 tablespoons butter
½ cup sliced celery
¼ cup chopped green pepper
¼ cup chopped onion
1 can (10½ oz.) condensed cream of mushroom soup

1 cup (4 oz.) shredded Cheddar cheese
1 cup plain yogurt
¼ cup chopped pimiento
½ teaspoon salt
⅛ teaspoon Worcestershire sauce

1. Preheat the oven to 350 degrees.

2. Cook rice according to package directions. Drain crabmeat well; flake. In a large skillet melt butter; sauté celery, green pepper, and onion for 5 minutes.

3. Remove from heat; stir in soup, cheese, yogurt, pimiento, salt, and Worcestershire sauce.

4. Layer rice and crabmeat in shallow buttered baking dish (2-quart); pour sauce over all and bake 30 minutes.

YIELD: 6-8 servings

Saucy Salmon Steaks

1 cup plain yogurt
1½ tablespoons flour
1 tablespoon grated onion
2 teaspoons grated lemon rind

1 teaspoon salt
⅛ teaspoon paprika
4 drops Tabasco sauce
1½ pounds salmon steaks

1. Preheat the oven to 350 degrees.

2. In a small bowl blend together yogurt, flour, onion, lemon rind, salt, paprika, and Tabasco sauce.

3. Place salmon steaks in a shallow 2-quart baking dish; pour sauce over.

4. Bake 20-30 minutes or until fish flakes easily with a fork.

YIELD: 4-6 servings

Baked Macaroni and Tuna

1½ cups uncooked elbow macaroni	2 cups plain yogurt
¼ cup butter or margarine	2 cans (6½ oz. each) tuna, drained and flaked
1 large onion, chopped	1 can (10¾ oz.) condensed cream of celery soup
1 green pepper, chopped	
1 teaspoon salt	1 package (8 oz.) sharp Cheddar cheese, shredded
¼ teaspoon pepper	

1. Preheat the oven to 350 degrees.

2. In a saucepan, cook macaroni according to package directions until tender. Drain.

3. In a small skillet, heat butter and sauté onion and green pepper until golden.

4. In a large bowl, mix macaroni, sautéed vegetables, and their drippings. Add salt, pepper, yogurt, tuna, celery soup, and Cheddar cheese. Mix well.

5. Pour into a well-buttered 2-quart casserole and bake 45 minutes.

YIELD: 6 servings

Baked Stuffed Haddock

¼ cup flour	1 whole (4-lb.) haddock, cleaned, scaled, with head and tail removed
½ teaspoon salt	
¼ teaspoon pepper	

(cont'd)

Stuffing:

3 tablespoons margarine
1 can (4 oz.) small shrimp, drained
1 can (6 oz.) crabmeat, drained
1 egg, slightly beaten
½ teaspoon salt

Dash of pepper
¼ teaspoon dried, crushed thyme
2 teaspoons finely chopped celery

Topping:

1 tablespoon margarine
½ cup finely chopped onion
½ cup minced parsley
1 cup plain yogurt

½ cup shredded American cheese
¼ cup bread crumbs

1. Preheat the oven to 375 degrees.

2. Combine the flour, salt, and pepper. Coat the haddock. Place in a buttered baking dish.

To Prepare Stuffing:

1. Combine margarine, shrimp, crabmeat, egg, salt, pepper, thyme, and celery in a skillet. Sauté until celery is barely tender.

2. Stuff the fish and secure the edges with toothpicks to hold the stuffing in during baking.

To Prepare Topping:

1. Melt margarine in a skillet and sauté the onion until tender. Remove from heat and add the parsley, yogurt, and cheese.

2. Spoon over the fish, top with bread crumbs and bake 30-40 minutes.

Yield: 4-6 servings

Shrimp or Lobster Tail Newburg

2 pounds frozen cooked shrimp or tiny lobster tails (langostinos)
1 can (10½ oz.) Cheddar cheese soup
1 can (10½ oz.) cream of shrimp soup

1 can (8 oz.) sliced mushrooms, drained
½ cup plain yogurt
Dash of salt
Dash of pepper
Rice, cooked

Combine shrimp or lobster tails, cheese and shrimp soups, mushrooms, yogurt, salt, and pepper in a saucepan. Heat thoroughly and serve over rice.

YIELD: 6 servings

Tuna Bake

1 package (8 oz.) egg noodles	1 cup shredded Cheddar cheese
1 can (12½ oz.) tuna, drained and flaked	1 cup plain yogurt
	2 tablespoons minced onion
1 can (10½ oz.) condensed cream of mushroom soup	2 tablespoons chopped pimiento

1. Preheat the oven to 350 degrees.
2. Cook noodles according to package directions.
3. Combine cooked noodles, tuna, soup, cheese, yogurt, onion, and pimiento in large bowl; mix well.
4. Turn tuna mixture into a 2-quart buttered casserole and bake, uncovered, 30-40 minutes or until bubbly.

YIELD: 6-8 servings

Eggs

Sunday Brunch Eggs

1 medium-size onion, minced	Salt and pepper to taste
¼ teaspoon garlic powder	6 slices cooked ham or
2 tablespoons vegetable oil	Canadian bacon
2 tablespoons tomato paste	6 thin slices Swiss cheese
½ teaspoon oregano	6 large eggs
1½ cups plain yogurt	Dash paprika
⅓ cup sliced black olives	6 slices toast

1. Preheat the oven to 350 degrees.

2. Sauté the onions and garlic powder in the oil in a saucepan. Add the tomato paste and oregano, stirring well.

3. Mix in the yogurt and olives and season to taste. Cook over low heat for several minutes, stirring constantly until well blended.

4. Arrange the ham slices in the bottom of a shallow baking dish. Place a slice of cheese over each. Carefully break an egg over each cheese slice and spoon the yogurt sauce over each.

5. Sprinkle with paprika and bake for about 10 minutes, or until eggs are set. Serve over toast.

YIELD: 6 servings

Scrambled Eggs

6 eggs	½ teaspoon salt
½ cup plain yogurt	2 tablespoons butter

1. In a bowl beat eggs, yogurt, and salt just until blended. In a large skillet, over low heat, melt butter; add egg mixture.

2. Turn portions of egg mixture with spatula as it begins to thicken; do not stir and do not overcook.

Yield: 4 servings

Variation: Substitute orange or mandarin orange yogurt for plain yogurt.

Mushrooms and Eggs

2 tablespoons melted butter or margarine
1 cup diced mushrooms
1 cup yogurt

¼ cup minced onion
½ teaspoon lemon juice
Pinch of salt and white pepper
4 eggs

1. Preheat the oven to 350 degrees.
2. Brush melted butter or margarine on a shallow Pyrex baking dish. Scatter mushrooms over the surface.
3. In a bowl combine yogurt, onion, lemon juice, salt, and pepper and spoon over the mushrooms.
4. With a spoon, make 4 shallow impressions in the yogurt and carefully break an egg into each one.
5. Bake in oven until eggs are done, about 10 minutes. If desired, grated Parmesan cheese may be sprinkled over the eggs for added flavor. You won't believe how good this is until you've tried it.

Yield: 2-4 servings

Yogurt Omelet

6 eggs
½ cup cottage cheese, drained well
½ cup yogurt
12 pearl onions

1 tablespoon chopped pimiento
Salt and pepper to taste
2 tablespoons butter or margarine

1. Beat eggs thoroughly. Add cottage cheese, yogurt, onions, pimiento, salt, and pepper. Place heavy skillet over moderate heat and melt butter or margarine. Pour in eggs and turn heat low. Cover.
2. Stir the omelet occasionally with a fork. Remove lid when eggs are almost done. To serve, cut into wedges.

Yield: 3-4 servings

Omar Omelet

3 eggs, lightly beaten	1 tablespoon minced chives
Salt and pepper to taste	2 tablespoons flour
⅓ cup plain yogurt	1 tablespoon butter

1. Add salt and pepper to lightly beaten eggs; whisk in the yogurt and chives.

2. Sprinkle flour over egg mixture and blend lightly but thoroughly.

3. Heat a frying pan; add butter and pour in half the omelet mixture. Cook over low heat, moving the omelet around in the pan to avoid burning.

4. When brown underneath, turn it, as you would a pancake. Cook the other side. Serve at once. Repeat with the remaining batter.

YIELD: 2 servings

Vegetables

Broccoli with Mornay Sauce

1 chicken bouillon cube
¾ cup boiling water
¼ cup butter or margarine
¼ cup flour
1½ cups plain yogurt

½ cup grated Parmesan or
  Romano cheese
½ cup shredded Swiss cheese
1 large bunch broccoli, cooked

1. Dissolve bouillon cube in water. Melt butter or margarine in a small saucepan and blend in the flour.

2. Stir in yogurt and blend until thickened. Add bouillon and cheeses and stir over low heat until cheeses melt. Serve over hot, cooked broccoli.

YIELD: 3 cups sauce

Fried Eggplant (Melitzanes Tiyanites)

1 medium eggplant, unpeeled,
  cut in ¼-inch-thick slices
½ cup flour, blended with ½
  teaspoon salt

½–¾ cup olive oil
½ cup plain yogurt
1 garlic clove, crushed
  Salt and pepper to taste

1. Dust eggplant slices with flour-salt mixture. Fry in olive oil until lightly browned on each side.

2. Serve with sauce made of yogurt blended with garlic, salt, and pepper to taste.

YIELD: 4-6 servings

207

Stuffed Eggplant

1 large eggplant
1 tablespoon salad oil
½ pound lean ground beef
1 can (6 oz.) tomato paste
1 egg slightly beaten
2 tablespoons finely chopped onion
2 tablespoons finely chopped green pepper

1 garlic clove, minced
½ teaspoon salt
¼ teaspoon pepper
½ cup dry red wine
½ cup plain yogurt
1 can (8 oz.) tomato sauce
½ cup shredded mozzarella cheese

1. Preheat the oven to 350 degrees.

2. Cut eggplant in half, scoop out pulp, leaving shell intact. Finely dice eggplant.

3. In a skillet, brown the diced eggplant in the oil, and add the beef, turning until browned.

4. Add the tomato paste, egg, onion, green pepper, garlic, salt, pepper, red wine, and yogurt. Heat thoroughly, but do not boil.

5. Spoon mixture into eggplant halves, top with tomato sauce and mozzarella cheese. Place in baking dish and bake for 45 minutes.

YIELD: 4 servings

Eggplant with Yogurt

1 large eggplant
4 tablespoons vegetable oil
3 large onions, chopped
2 cloves garlic, crushed
1 tablespoon freshly grated ginger
1 teaspoon ground coriander

¼ teaspoon cayenne pepper
½ teaspoon turmeric
1 teaspoon cumin
1 teaspoon salt
1 cup plain yogurt
½ teaspoon sugar

1. Roast eggplant for 1 hour in a 350-degree oven or until tender. When cool, peel and cut into cubes.

2. Brown onions in 2 tablespoons of the vegetable oil. Add garlic, ginger, coriander, cayenne, turmeric, cumin, and salt. Fry for several minutes.

3. Add other 2 tablespoons of the oil and the eggplant cubes. Cook about 5 minutes.

4. Just before serving, stir in the yogurt and sugar. This is usually served with rice.

YIELD: approximately 4-6 servings

Hot Stuffed Cabbage Leaves

12 large cabbage leaves
2 medium onions, chopped
2 tablespoons oil
½ pound minced lamb
1 tablespoon minced parsley
⅛ teaspoon sage
1½ teaspoons salt

½ cup uncooked rice
½ cup water
2 tablespoons raisins
1½ cups tomato juice
Juice ½ lemon
1 cup plain yogurt

1. Select large perfect outer cabbage leaves. Blanch with scalding water, leaving cabbage in water 2 minutes. Drain.
2. *To Prepare Filling:* Cook onions in oil until soft; add meat, herbs, and salt. Cook until meat loses pink color, then add rice.
3. Stir until rice is glazed. Add the water and the raisins. Simmer, covered, 10 minutes. All liquid should be absorbed.
4. Spoon mixture into cabbage leaves, roll up loosely (rice will swell). Place with overlapped sides down in Dutch oven in layers, with additional cabbage leaves between layers.
5. Combine tomato and lemon juices and pour over cabbage. Place overturned plate on top to hold cabbage leaves in place while cooking.
6. Cover pot, cook at low heat for 1½ hours. Remove cabbage from pan. Strain remaining sauce, stir in yogurt. Season to taste. Serve sauce over hot stuffed cabbage leaves.

YIELD: 6 entrée servings

Easy Rice Pilaf

1 cup long-grain rice
3 tablespoons butter
1 small onion, diced

2 cups stock, chicken or beef
Salt and pepper to taste
Plain yogurt

1. Preheat oven to 375 degrees.
2. Braise rice in 2 tablespoons of melted butter, stirring frequently until butter bubbles and rice is light brown.

(cont'd)

3. In separate pan, fry onion (in remaining butter) until brown. Add to rice; add stock.

4. Blend well, bake for 30 minutes. Stir. Bake for about 10 minutes longer. Top with plain yogurt.

YIELD: approximately 2-3 servings

Rice Pilaf

2 tablespoons butter or margarine
⅔ cup minced onion
2 cups long-grain rice
1 bay leaf
3 cups water and 2 teaspoons chicken base or 3 cups chicken broth

½ teaspoon salt
Dash of pepper
2 cups plain yogurt
1–1½ cups shredded Cheddar cheese (about 6 oz.)
Buttered Bread Crumbs (recipe below)

1. Preheat oven to 375 degrees.

2. In a large ovenproof saucepan, melt butter. Add onion and sauté until tender, about 3 to 5 minutes. Stir in rice and bay leaf and cook until rice is well coated. Add water and chicken base or chicken broth, salt, and pepper. If using chicken base dissolve in boiling water before adding to rice. Heat to boiling.

3. Cover and bake for 18-20 minutes. Remove from oven and stir in 1 cup yogurt and 1 cup shredded cheese. Remove bay leaf. Mix well.

4. Spoon into a 2-quart baking dish. Spread with remaining yogurt and sprinkle on remaining cheese. Top with Buttered Bread Crumbs. Return to oven and bake until top is golden brown, about 15 minutes.

Buttered Bread Crumbs

1 tablespoon butter or margarine

1 cup fresh bread crumbs (2 slices)

1. In a small skillet, melt butter or margarine. Add bread crumbs and stir until well coated. Note: A dash of cayenne pepper or Tabasco sauce may be added with Cheddar cheese.

2. May be stored in refrigerator and heated up later.

YIELD: 6-8 servings

Yogurt Rice

In India, this dish is prepared the last thing at night and eaten at noon the next day. It is especially refreshing during hot weather.

1½ cups plain yogurt
1 cup buttermilk
1 teaspoon salt
1 tablespoon minced green pepper
½ teaspoon grated ginger

¼ teaspoon cayenne pepper
4 cups cooked rice, at room temperature
2 teaspoons vegetable oil
1 teaspoon mustard seeds
1 bay leaf, crumbled

1. Combine yogurt, buttermilk, salt, green pepper, grated ginger, and cayenne pepper. Mix thoroughly. Combine with rice.

2. Heat vegetable oil and fry mustard seeds and crumbled bay leaf until seeds pop. Stir into rice. Serve cold with pickles.

YIELD: 5 servings

Saucy Green Beans

1½ pounds fresh green beans
1 medium-size onion, chopped
1 teaspoon salt
1 cup boiling water

⅔ cup plain yogurt
2 tablespoons flour
1 tablespoon minced parsley
Dash of pepper

1. Snap off ends of green beans and slice diagonally into 1-inch slices. Cook beans and onion with ½ teaspoon salt in boiling water in a saucepan until tender. Drain and reserve ½ cup liquid.

2. In the saucepan over low heat, combine the liquid, yogurt, and flour, stirring until smooth. Add parsley, ½ teaspoon salt, and pepper.

3. Pour over cooked beans and serve immediately.

YIELD: 4-6 servings

Brussels Sprouts in Yogurt

1 package (10 oz.) frozen brussels sprouts
1 teaspoon vinegar
2 cups plain yogurt

½ cup minced scallions, including tops
1 teaspoon cider vinegar
A pinch of tarragon
A pinch of dill

1. Cook sprouts according to directions on package, but add 1 teaspoon vinegar to the water. Drain.

2. Combine yogurt, scallions, cider vinegar, tarragon, and dill in saucepan and heat (do not boil). Add sprouts and serve hot.

YIELD: 3 servings

Pumpkin and Yogurt (Erisheri)

2 cups pumpkin, cut into ¾-inch squares
1½ teaspoons salt
2 tablespoons vegetable oil
1½ teaspoons yellow split peas, soaked for 1 hour and drained
1 bay leaf, crumbled
¾ cup plain yogurt
1 teaspoon ground dry mustard
2 tablespoons grated unsweetened coconut

1. Combine pumpkin and salt. Add enough water to cook. Simmer until tender and drain.

2. Heat vegetable oil and dry split peas until browned, sprinkling in the bay leaf during last minute of cooking.

3. Add to yogurt. Combine mustard and coconut and add to the yogurt mixture, along with the drained pumpkin. Mix well. Add more salt if necessary.

YIELD: 4 servings

Tuna Scalloped Potatoes

3 cups peeled thinly sliced baking potatoes
¾ cup sliced onions
1 can (7 oz.) tuna, drained and flaked
1 can (10½ oz.) condensed cream of celery soup
1 cup plain yogurt
1½ tablespoons flour
½ teaspoon salt
1 cup (4 oz.) shredded Cheddar cheese

1. Preheat the oven to 350 degrees.

2. In buttered shallow baking dish (1½-quart) alternate layers of potatoes, onions, and tuna.

3. In a bowl combine soup, yogurt, flour, and salt; pour over all.

4. Bake 1 hour and 15-30 minutes or until potatoes are tender. Sprinkle cheese over top; return to oven 5-10 minutes.

YIELD: 4-6 servings

Curried Potato Balls

Potato Balls:

2 cups hot mashed potatoes
2 tablespoons onion, finely minced
⅛ teaspoon chili powder

½ teaspoon salt
2 eggs
1 tablespoon flour
Deep fat

Sauce:

1 tablespoon vegetable oil
1 small onion, finely chopped
2 teaspoons ground coriander
½ teaspoon chili powder or to taste
⅛ teaspoon turmeric

¼ teaspoon cumin
3 large tomatoes, chopped
1 cup water
1 teaspoon salt
¼ cup plain yogurt

1. *To Prepare Potato Balls*: Combine hot mashed potatoes, onion, chili powder, salt, eggs, and flour. Mix well and drop by the spoonful into hot fat. When browned, drain well and keep warm.

2. *To Prepare Sauce*: Heat vegetable oil and fry onion, coriander, chili powder, turmeric, and cumin for 2 or 3 minutes. Put in tomatoes, water, and salt.

3. Simmer about 15 minutes. Stir in yogurt. Add potato balls and serve very hot.

YIELD: 3-4 servings

Potatoes and Onions in Yogurt

2 tablespoons vegetable oil
2 medium onions, chopped
½ teaspoon cumin
¼ teaspoon turmeric
2 teaspoons ground coriander

⅔ cup plain yogurt
½ teaspoon chili powder
1 teaspoon salt
3 medium potatoes, cooked and diced

1. Heat the vegetable oil and brown the onions. Add the cumin, turmeric, and coriander; fry for another minute.

2. Combine the yogurt, chili powder, and salt; add to the fried onions. Put in potatoes and simmer slowly for 10 minutes.

YIELD: 3-4 servings

Potatoes with Yogurt

2 tablespoons oil
1 pound small red-skinned new potatoes, boiled until tender and peeled
¼ teaspoon ground cloves
½ teaspoon cinnamon
½ teaspoon ground cardamom
2 bay leaves, crumbled
¼ cup water
½ teaspoon grated fresh ginger
¾ cup plain yogurt
Sea salt to taste

1. Heat the oil in a skillet and add the potatoes. Cook quickly until lightly browned. Remove potatoes and drain on paper towels; keep warm.

2. Add the cloves, cinnamon, cardamom, bay leaves, and water to skillet and bring to a boil. Stir in the ginger and yogurt.

3. Reheat but do not boil. Add potatoes and salt.

YIELD: 6 servings

Baked Potato Topping

½ cup shredded Cheddar cheese
½ cup plain yogurt
1 tablespoon snipped chives or scallion greens

Combine cheese, yogurt, and chives or scallion greens in mixing bowl; mix well. Serve over baked potatoes.

YIELD: 1 cup

Yogurt Baked Potatoes

4 baked potatoes
1 cup plain yogurt
2 teaspoons grated onion
Salt and pepper to taste
8 tablespoons grated Cheddar cheese
Paprika

1. Cut hot baked potatoes in half lengthwise and scoop out centers.

2. Mix yogurt, onion, salt, pepper, and grated cheese with potato.

3. Put potato back in skin and sprinkle with paprika or grated cheese. Cover and refrigerate or freeze until ready to reheat. Blue cheese may be varied with Cheddar cheese.

YIELD: 4 servings

214

Tangy Creamed Mushrooms

2 tablespoons flour
½ cup water
3 tablespoons butter
1 cup plain yogurt
½ teaspoon salt

1½ teaspoons prepared mustard
1 pound fresh mushroom caps, whole, with sliced stems
1 teaspoon fresh or dried dill weed

1. Blend flour and water in top of double boiler, stirring until it boils and thickens. Remove from heat and blend in 1 tablespoon butter. Cool.

2. Stir in yogurt, salt, and mustard. Place over simmering water in the double boiler to warm.

3. Meanwhile, melt remaining butter in a large skillet over low heat. Sauté mushroom caps and stems until tender

4. Turn mushrooms into the yogurt sauce and mix. Serve sprinkled with dill.

YIELD: 4 servings

Mushrooms with Curry Cream

1 pound fresh mushrooms
½ cup plain yogurt

3 tablespoons mayonnaise
1 teaspoon curry powder

1. Wipe mushrooms gently with a damp paper towel (choose mushrooms that are reasonably unblemished). Trim off any hard, discolored stems. Mix yogurt, mayonnaise, and curry powder well.

2. Mix the mushrooms with the curry powder and chill in the refrigerator for 1 hour before serving. You can serve these as a side dish on a bed of lettuce or serve alone as an hors d'oeuvre.

YIELD: 4 servings

Mushooom Starter

1 pound fresh mushrooms, sliced
1 onion, minced
1½ tablespoons butter
1½ tablespoons olive oil
½ teaspoon salt

Dash of pepper
½ teaspoon dried mint, crumbled fine between the fingers
¾ cup plain yogurt

Sauté the mushrooms and onion in butter and oil until lightly cooked, about 3 minutes. Add the salt, pepper, and mint. Off heat, stir in yogurt. Mix well. Serve cold.

YIELD: 3-4 servings

Cauliflower with Yogurt

1 teaspoon vegetable oil	½ teaspoon chili powder
¼ teaspoon cumin	¼ teaspoon turmeric
¼ teaspoon mustard seeds	1 teaspoon salt
1 medium cauliflower, divided into flowerets	¼ cup water
	¼ cup plain yogurt

Heat oil and add cumin and mustard seeds. When seeds pop, add cauliflower, chili powder, turmeric, salt, and water. Cover and cook until tender. Add yogurt just before removing from fire.

YIELD: approximately 2-3 servings

Spinach Starter

1 package frozen chopped spinach	1½ tablespoons olive oil
½ onion, minced	½ teaspoon salt
1 clove garlic, minced	½ teaspoon pepper
1½ tablespoons butter	Scant ½ teaspoon cinnamon
	1 cup plain yogurt

1. Cook spinach according to package directions; drain well, squeeze out excess water.

2. Sauté onion and garlic in the butter-oil mixture until soft, about 3 minutes. Add spinach, salt, pepper, and cinnamon and cook a few minutes longer.

3. Off heat, stir in yogurt. Mix well. Refrigerate. Serve cold as a first course or salad substitute.

YIELD: 3-4 servings

216

Spinach with Yogurt

2 bunches spinach
2 tablespoons vegetable oil
1 medium onion, chopped
1 clove garlic, crushed
¼ teaspoon turmeric
½ teaspoon cumin

¼ teaspoon sugar
¼ teaspoon chili powder
½ teaspoon salt
1 cup plain yogurt
1 hard-cooked egg, chopped

1. Wash and clean spinach. Cook until tender and drain well. Cut up with 2 knives or chop very fine. Fry onion in oil until lightly browned.

2. Add garlic, turmeric, cumin, sugar, chili powder, and salt. Continue frying for several minutes.

3. Add spinach and yogurt. Stir well. Heat through. Serve garnished with chopped hard-cooked egg.

YIELD: 5-6 servings

Super Spinach with Curry Cream

2 pounds fresh spinach
½ cup plain yogurt

3 tablespoons mayonnaise
1 teaspoon curry powder

1. Break the stems off spinach and wash the leaves very carefully. Simmer, covered, for 5 minutes (the water clinging to the leaves will provide enough moisture).

2. Meanwhile mix yogurt, mayonnaise, and curry powder well. When spinach is just tender, boil rapidly for a minute, uncovered, to evaporate excess liquid, and add the curry cream.

3. Toss quickly to coat the spinach and warm the sauce. Serve right away.

YIELD: 4 servings

Yogurt Stuffed Tomato

4 large unpeeled tomatoes
1 sliced cucumber
1 small grated onion

4 tablespoons plain yogurt
½ teaspoon salt
Pepper to taste

Cut ½-inch slice from stem end of each tomato. Remove pulp and combine with cucumber, onion, yogurt, salt, and pepper. Fill tomato shells with mixture. Serve on bed of lettuce or other greens.

Yield: 4 servings

Salads

Yogurt-Cucumber Salad

1 teaspoon dried mint
½ teaspoon garlic powder
1 cup plain yogurt

1 large cucumber, peeled and
  sliced thin
Lettuce
4 radishes, chopped

Mix the mint and garlic powder into the yogurt. Distribute the cucumber slices on four beds of lettuce. Pour the yogurt over the cucumbers. Garnish with chopped radishes.

YIELD: 4 servings

Cukes 'n' Gurt

Dressing:

2 tablespoons chopped parsley
¾ teaspoon dill weed

⅛ teaspoon garlic salt
1 cup plain yogurt

Salad:

2 unpeeled cucumbers, scored
  and thinly sliced (about 6
  cups)

1½ teaspoons salt
   Chopped parsley

To Prepare Dressing:

In a small bowl combine 2 tablespoons parsley, dill weed, and garlic salt; fold in yogurt. Cover and chill.

To Prepare Salad:

In a bowl sprinkle salt over cucumbers and toss. Chill 30-45 minutes, tossing occasionally.

(cont'd)

219

To Serve:

Drain cucumbers well; stir in yogurt dressing. Garnish with additional chopped parsley.

Yield: 6-8 servings

Stuffed Tomatoes

Dressing:

½ teaspoon salt   1 cup plain yogurt
¼ teaspoon leaf tarragon

Salad:

1 can (8½ oz.) crushed pine-   ½ cup toasted slivered almonds
  apple, drained   ½ cup chopped celery
1½ cups diced cooked chicken   6 tomatoes

To Prepare Dressing:

In a small bowl combine salt and tarragon; stir in yogurt. Cover and chill.

To Prepare Salad:

In a bowl combine pineapple, chicken, almonds, and celery; chill. Add dressing and toss lightly. Fill tomatoes that have been partially cut into sections.

Yield: 6 servings

Variation: Use pineapple yogurt in place of plain yogurt. Omit crushed pineapple.

Potato Salad

Dressing:

1 tablespoon prepared horse-   ½ teaspoon prepared mustard
  radish   1 cup plain yogurt
1 teaspoon salt

Salad:

4 cups diced cooked potatoes   ¼ cup chopped onion
½ cup chopped celery   1 tablespoon chopped pimiento
¼ cup chopped green pepper

To Prepare Dressing:

In a small bowl combine horseradish, salt, and mustard; fold in yogurt.

To Prepare Salad:

In a medium bowl combine potatoes, celery, green pepper, onion, and pimiento. Add dressing to salad and toss only until blended. Cover and chill.

YIELD: 6 servings

VARIATIONS: Reduce potatoes to 3 cups and add to salad mixture one can (7 oz.) tuna, drained and broken into pieces, *or* 1 cup chopped cooked chicken.

Dilly Potato Salad

4 tablespoons grated onion	¼ teaspoon garlic powder
1 teaspoon salt	4 cups plain yogurt
Dash of pepper	7 cups warm boiled potatoes,
½ cup diced peeled cucumber	cubed (about 10 medium-
½ cup finely chopped celery	size)
1 teaspoon dried dill weed	

Combine onion, salt, pepper, cucumber, celery, dill, garlic powder, and yogurt in a large bowl. Fold in the warm potatoes and chill thoroughly before serving.

YIELD: 8 servings

Potato Salade Supreme

7 cups warm boiled potatoes, diced (about 10 medium-size)	3 tablespoons sugar
	2 tablespoons tarragon vinegar
4 tablespoons grated onion	2 scant tablespoons English dried mustard
1 teaspoon salt	
Dash of pepper	6 tablespoons crumbled fried bacon
1 cup finely chopped celery	
4 tablespoons finely chopped parsley	4 cups plain yogurt

Combine potatoes, onion, salt, pepper, celery, parsley, sugar, vinegar, mustard, bacon, and yogurt in a large bowl and chill.

YIELD: 6-8 generous servings

Potato Salad with Yogurt Dressing

6 diced potatoes, steamed in skins
2 diced hard-cooked eggs
1 cup sliced celery
6 chopped scallions

2 chopped pickles
Salt, pepper, paprika to taste
1 cup Yogurt Mayonnaise (page 236) or Yogurt French Dressing (page 241)

Combine potatoes, eggs, celery, scallions, pickles, salt, pepper, and paprika with Yogurt Mayonnaise or Yogurt French Dressing.

YIELD: approximately 5-6 servings

Apple and Roquefort Potato Salad

6 medium-size boiling potatoes
1 cup diced celery
4 tablespoons vinegar
3 tablespoons vegetable oil
2 teaspoons salt
¾ cup plain yogurt

1 large red apple, cored and thinly sliced
½ cup crumbled Roquefort cheese
Iceburg lettuce

1. Cook potatoes until tender. Peel potatoes and cut into thin slices; place in large bowl with celery.
2. Combine vinegar, oil, and salt in jar with screw top. Cover jar and shake well. Pour over potato slices and celery. Toss to coat.
3. Add yogurt and toss well. Add apple slices and cheese, toss lightly. Line a salad bowl with iceberg lettuce; spoon salad into bowl; garnish with apple slices if you wish. Chill.

YIELD: 6 servings

VARIATION: Place above in a casserole dish and bake for 30 minutes in a 375-degree oven.

Yogurt-Beet Salad

2½ cups sliced cooked beets
½ cup French dressing
½ cup plain yogurt

2 teaspoons sugar
Lettuce or other greens

Combine beets and French dressing and let stand 1 hour. Add yogurt and sugar; mix well with beets. Serve on lettuce or other greens.

YIELD: 6 servings

Onion and Yogurt Salad

3 large onions, finely sliced
1 teaspoon salt
1 large tomato, chopped
2 fresh or pickled green chilies, finely chopped
1 tablespoon chopped coriander leaves, optional
1 cup plain yogurt

Mix salt with onion rings and set aside for 20 minutes. Drain. Combine with tomato, chilies, coriander, and yogurt. Mix well. Serve ice cold.

YIELD: 4 servings

Carrot Salad

4–5 large carrots, grated
¼ cup plain yogurt
½ teaspoon salt
Pinch of black pepper
2 teaspoons clarified butter
¼ teaspoon mustard seeds
1 small fresh or pickled green chili, finely chopped

1. Combine carrots, yogurt, salt, and black pepper. Refrigerate.
2. Heat butter and fry mustard seeds until they crackle. Add chopped green chili and fry for 2 minutes. Remove from heat and cool. Add to carrots. Mix well and serve.

YIELD: approximately 3-4 servings

Spinach Salad

4–5 ounces fresh spinach, washed, stems removed
2 fresh mushrooms, sliced
1 green onion, sliced
Juice of ½ lemon
1 cup plain yogurt
½ teaspoon fresh mint, chopped
Salt and pepper to taste

Combine spinach, mushrooms, onion, lemon juice, yogurt, mint, salt, and pepper. Toss well.

YIELD: as entrée, 1 serving; as appetizer, 2-3 servings

VARIATIONS: Half of a hard-cooked egg, chopped, and 4 strips of cooked bacon, diced, can be added.

Cabbage Salad

1 head (1½ lb.) cabbage
1 cup plain yogurt
⅓ cup lemon juice
1 tablespoon sugar
1 teaspoon dill
½ teaspoon salt
Large pinch of coarse black pepper

Grate the cabbage and combine with yogurt, lemon juice, sugar, dill, salt, and pepper in a large bowl. Press down with a saucer and chill overnight, covered.

YIELD: 4-6 servings

Coleslaw

¼ cup mayonnaise
1 cup plain yogurt
½ teaspoon dry mustard
1 teaspoon seasoned salt
½ teaspoon celery salt
½ teaspoon salt
⅛ teaspoon pepper
¼ cup finely chopped onion
2 tablespoons sugar
8 cups (2-lb. head) shredded cabbage
1 cup (2 medium) grated carrots
1 cup (8-oz. can) crushed pineapple, drained

1. Combine mayonnaise, yogurt, dry mustard, seasoned salt, celery salt, salt, pepper, onion, and sugar in medium bowl. Stir until well blended. Cover and chill for at least 2 hours.

2. Combine cabbage, carrots, and pineapple in large bowl. Pour chilled dressing over vegetables. Toss lightly to blend dressing. Serve immediately.

YIELD: 7-8 cups

Apple Caraway Slaw

Dressing:

1 tablespoon vinegar
1 teaspoon caraway seeds
1 teaspoon prepared mustard

½ teaspoon salt
⅛ teaspoon garlic salt
1 cup plain yogurt

Salad:

1½ cups chopped unpeeled apple
(1 medium)
Lemon juice

4 cups shredded cabbage
½ cup chopped celery

To Prepare Dressing:

In a small bowl combine vinegar, caraway seeds, mustard, salt, and garlic salt; fold in yogurt. Cover and chill.

To Prepare Salad:

Dip apple in lemon juice. Before serving, lightly toss apple, cabbage, and celery with dressing. Note: For added color use 2 cups shredded red cabbage and 2 cups shredded green cabbage.

YIELD: 6-8 servings

Waldorf Salad

Dressing:

1 teaspoon sugar
½ teaspoon salt
½ teaspoon grated lemon rind

⅛–¼ teaspoon cinnamon
1 cup plain yogurt

Salad:

3½ cups chopped unpeeled red
apples (2-3 apples)
Lemon juice

1 cup chopped celery
½ cup chopped walnuts
½ cup seedless raisins

To Prepare Dressing:

In a small bowl mix together sugar, salt, lemon rind, and cinnamon; fold in yogurt.

To Prepare Salad:

Dip apples in lemon juice. In a medium bowl toss apples, celery, walnuts, and raisins with dressing. Cover and chill.

YIELD: 6-8 servings

Avocado Mold

1 package (3 oz.) lime flavor gelatin
1 cup boiling water
1 avocado, halved and peeled
1 tablespoon lemon juice
½ teaspoon salt

1 cup plain yogurt
¾ cup cottage cheese
1 large orange, sectioned and diced (about ¾ cup)
⅓ cup chopped pecans

1. In a bowl pour boiling water over gelatin; stir until dissolved. Chill until partially set.

2. Meanwhile, in a shallow dish mash avocado with lemon juice and salt. Fold avocado, yogurt, cottage cheese, orange, and pecans into gelatin.

3. Turn into salad mold (4-cup). Chill until firm.

YIELD: 6 servings

VARIATION: For an Avocado-Pineapple Mold substitute pineapple yogurt for plain yogurt.

Lobster Salad Bowl

Dressing:

⅓ cup chili sauce
1 tablespoon chopped green onion
2 teaspoons tarragon vinegar

2 teaspoons lemon juice
½ teaspoon salt
1½ cups plain yogurt

Salad:

1 small head lettuce, torn
6 ounces Swiss cheese, cut in strips
2 cups cut-up cooked lobster
¼ cup chopped parsley

2 tablespoons sliced green onions
Hard-cooked egg slices
Tomato wedges

To Prepare Dressing:

In a small bowl combine chili sauce, 1 tablespoon onion, vinegar, lemon juice, and salt; fold in yogurt. Cover and chill.

226

To Prepare Salad:

In a salad bowl toss together lettuce, cheese, lobster, parsley, and 2 tablespoons onions. Garnish with egg slices and tomato wedges. Serve dressing separately.

YIELD: 6 servings

Crabmeat Salad

1 cup plain yogurt
¼ cup chili sauce

1 tablespoon lemon juice
Canned or cooked crabmeat

Mix yogurt, chili sauce, and lemon juice well. Add crabmeat (shredded if canned) broken up into small pieces. Either fold in yogurt dressing or serve crabmeat on crisp lettuce leaves and serve dressing separately.

YIELD: 2 servings

Shrimp Stuffed Avocados

Dressing:

¾ teaspoon dill weed
½ teaspoon seasoned salt

¾ cup plain yogurt

Salad:

1 cup chopped cooked shrimp
½ cup chopped unpeeled cucumber
½ cup grated carrots
¼ cup chopped celery

2 tablespoons sliced green onions
3 avocados, halved
Lemon juice

To Prepare Dressing:

In a small bowl combine dill weed and seasoned salt; stir in yogurt. Cover and chill.

To Prepare Salad:

In a bowl combine shrimp, cucumber, carrots, celery, and green onions; add dressing and toss lightly. Dip cut surface of avocado halves in lemon juice. Spoon salad into avocado halves.

YIELD: 6 servings

Salmon Toss Salad

1 can (16 oz.) salmon, drained
½ cup diced celery
1 can (17 oz.) small early peas, drained
2 tablespoons lemon juice
1 teaspoon minced onion
½ teaspoon salt
⅛ teaspoon pepper
1 cup plain yogurt
Boston lettuce

1. Break salmon into bite-size pieces with a fork in a medium-size bowl. Add celery and peas.
2. Mix lemon juice, onion, salt, pepper, and yogurt. Pour over salmon mixture. Toss lightly with a fork and chill. Serve on Boston lettuce.

YIELD: 4-5 servings

Langostino Salad

Frozen langostinos (24 oz.) thawed and drained
3 cups diced cooked potatoes
3 cups cooked cut green beans
3 hard-cooked eggs, chopped
1 cup sliced celery
½ cup sliced black olives
½ cup chopped red onion
1¼ cup plain yogurt
1 teaspoon curry powder
¾ cup V-8 juice
Salt and pepper to taste
1 head iceberg lettuce

In a bowl, mix langostinos, potatoes, green beans, eggs, celery, olives, red onion, yogurt, curry powder, and V-8 juice. Add salt and pepper to taste. Chill. Serve over shredded lettuce.

YIELD: 4 servings

Mango Salad

3 large mangoes, diced
½ cup grated unsweetened coconut
1 fresh or pickled green chili, finely chopped
1 tablespoon sugar
¼ teaspoon salt
¾ cup plain yogurt
2 teaspoons clarified butter
¼ teaspoon mustard seeds

1. Combine diced mangoes, coconut, chopped green chili, sugar, salt, and yogurt.

2. Heat butter and fry mustard seeds until they crackle. Cool a few minutes and add to mangoes. Mix well.

YIELD: 4-5 servings

Tropical Dream Salad

Salad:

2 pounds (about 3 cups) bone-less cooked turkey, cubed
½ cup sliced canned water chestnuts
½ cup diced celery

¼ cup sliced scallions
½ cup canned mandarin orange sections
6–12 lettuce leaves
½ cup roasted slivered almonds

Dressing:

½ cup plain yogurt
¼ cup mayonnaise

½ teaspoon frozen orange juice concentrate
¼ teaspoon salt

1. In a large bowl, combine turkey, water chestnuts, celery, and scallions.
2. In a small bowl, combine the yogurt, mayonnaise, frozen orange juice concentrate, and salt.
3. Stir the dressing gently into turkey salad. Now add the mandarin orange sections, being careful not to mash them.
4. Line six individual salad bowls with lettuce leaves. Divide salad evenly among the bowls. Sprinkle with almonds.

YIELD: 6 servings

Year-Round Salad

Dressing:

½ teaspoon celery salt
½ teaspoon onion salt

1 cup plain yogurt

Salad:

6 strips bacon, cooked and crumbled
1 medium head lettuce, torn
2 grapefruits, peeled and sectioned

2 oranges, peeled and sectioned
¾ cup sliced radishes (about 12)

To Prepare Dressing:

In a small bowl combine celery and onion salts; stir in yogurt. Cover and chill.

To Prepare Salad:

In a salad bowl toss together bacon, lettuce, grapefruit and orange sections, and radishes. Top with dressing.

YIELD: 8-10 servings

Peachy Frozen Salad

1 can (1 lb.) cling peach slices	¼ cup sugar
½ cup peach syrup	¼ teaspoon salt
1 cup miniature marshmallows	1 cup plain yogurt
1 package (8 oz.) cream cheese, softened	1 can (1 lb.) dark sweet pitted cherries, drained

1. Drain peaches reserving ½ cup syrup. In a small saucepan combine peach syrup and marshmallows; heat over low heat, stirring occasionally, until marshmallows are melted; cool slightly.

2. In a small mixing bowl beat cream cheese until smooth; gradually add sugar and salt and beat until light and fluffy.

3. Add cooled marshmallow mixture to cream cheese and beat until combined. Fold in yogurt, then peaches and cherries.

4. Turn into two refrigerator trays or square pan (8-inch). Freeze. Remove from freezer; allow to stand at room temperature about 1-1½ hours before serving.

YIELD: 8 servings

Two-Tone Salad Mold

Orange Layer:

1 can (11 oz.) mandarin orange segments	½ cup orange syrup
	½ cup chopped celery
1 package (3 oz.) orange flavor gelatin	½ cup cottage cheese
	½ cup plain yogurt
1 cup boiling water	

230

Raspberry Layer:

1 package (10 oz.) frozen
  raspberries, thawed
1 package (3 oz.) raspberry
  flavor gelatin

1 cup boiling water
½ cup raspberry syrup
½ cup plain yogurt

To Prepare Orange Layer:

Drain oranges reserving ½ cup syrup; set aside. In a bowl pour
boiling water over gelatin; stir until dissolved. Add reserved orange
syrup. Chill until partially set. Add orange segments, celery, cottage
cheese, and yogurt. Turn into salad mold (7-cup). Chill until set but
not firm.

To Prepare Raspberry Layer:

Drain raspberries reserving ½ cup syrup; set aside. In a bowl
pour boiling water over gelatin; stir until dissolved. Add reserved
raspberry syrup. Chill until partially set. Add raspberries and yogurt.
Pour over Orange Layer. Chill until firm.

YIELD: 8-10 servings

California Salad

3 jars (6 oz. each) marinated
  artichoke hearts
⅔ cup plain yogurt
1 teaspoon salt
  Dash of pepper
2 teaspoons sugar

1 medium-size head of iceberg
  lettuce broken into pieces
3 tomatoes, cut into wedges
½ medium-size cantaloupe,
  pared and diced

1. Drain liquid from the artichokes into a small bowl. Stir
yogurt, salt, pepper, and sugar into the liquid.

2. In a salad bowl place the lettuce, tomatoes, and artichoke
hearts, along with the cantaloupe.

3. Dribble the dressing over the salad and toss just before serving.

YIELD: 6-8 servings

Fruit Salad with Yogurt-Honey Dressing

1–2 cups fresh or canned fruit
1 cup plain yogurt

3 tablespoons honey

Use favorite mixture of fresh or canned fruits. Sweeten yogurt with honey. Arrange chilled fruit on salad greens. Add generous amount of yogurt-honey dressing.

YIELD: 2-3 servings

Frozen Fruit Salad

Salad:

1 cup plain yogurt
1 cup mayonnaise
½ teaspoon rum flavoring
1 can (1 lb.) fruit cocktail, drained

½ cup chopped walnuts
3 bananas, sliced
1 package (9 oz.) frozen whipped topping, thawed
Lettuce leaves

Dressing:

1 cup plain yogurt
¼ cup frozen concentrated pineapple juice

2 teaspoons sugar

To Prepare Salad:

In a bowl, mix yogurt, mayonnaise, and rum flavoring. Fold in fruit cocktail, nuts, bananas, and whipped topping. Spread mixture evenly into a 9-inch square pan. Cover and freeze until hard.

To Prepare Dressing:

In a small bowl, combine yogurt, pineapple juice, and sugar; chill. Cut salad into squares, place on lettuce leaves, and top with dressing.

YIELD: one 9-inch square

Curried Macaroni Salad

1 medium-size onion, finely chopped
3 teaspoons curry powder
¼ teaspoon chili powder
1 teaspoon sugar
1 teaspoon seasoned salt
½ teaspoon garlic powder

2 packages (10 oz.) frozen mixed vegetables, cooked but still crisp
1 can (8 oz.) sliced mushrooms, drained
4 cups plain yogurt
8 cups elbow macaroni, cooked
Dash of paprika

232

Mix together onion, curry, chili powder, sugar, salt, garlic powder, vegetables, mushrooms, and yogurt in a large bowl. Fold in the macaroni and sprinkle the top with paprika. Chill well before serving.

YIELD: 8 servings

Cool Tropical Salad

1 small fresh pineapple
1 cup mango chunks or melon balls
1 cup diced papaya or fresh peaches
2 cups plain yogurt
2 tablespoons honey
1 cup sliced strawberries
4 whole strawberries
4 sprigs fresh mint

1. Cut pineapple into quarters, lengthwise. Remove core; slice pineapple from shell and cut in cubes. Refrigerate empty shell to chill until serving time. Toss 1 cup of cubed pineapple with mango and papaya. Chill.

2. To serve, put ⅓ cup yogurt on each pineapple shell and cover with mixed fruit. Top with layer of remaining yogurt that has been sweetened with honey and cover with sliced strawberries.

3. Garnish each serving with one whole strawberry and a sprig of fresh mint.

YIELD: 4 servings

Cheesy Meat Salad

8 ounces elbow macaroni, cooked
1½ cups plain yogurt
¼ cup sweet pickle relish, drained
½ teaspoon Dijon mustard
¼ cup chopped green onion
¼ cup diced green pepper
1½ cups Cheddar cheese, diced
½ pound cooked salami or ham, sliced and diced
Parsley

In large bowl, toss macaroni with yogurt, pickle relish, and mustard. Add onion and green pepper, mix well. Fold in cheese and salami or ham. Chill to blend flavors. Garnish with parsley.

YIELD: 6 servings

Yogurt-Filled Pears

Pear halves
Shredded lettuce or romaine

Cream cheese or cottage
cheese
Fresh mint

For each serving, place 2 pear halves on lettuce or romaine. Fill cavity with mashed cream cheese or cottage cheese. Garnish with sprig of mint and serve with favorite yogurt dressing.

Lettuce Hearts with Yogurt

Pour generous portion of Yogurt Thousand Island Dressing (page 243) over chilled hearts of lettuce. Sprinkle with paprika and serve.

Salad Dressings and Sauces

Yogurt Dressing

1 cup plain yogurt
3 tablespoons vinegar
1 thin slice of onion (cut in half)
¼ teaspoon salt
2 teaspoons honey
¼ pimiento

Put yogurt, vinegar, onion, salt, honey, and pimiento in blender until onion is finely chopped.

YIELD: approximately 1¼ cups

Yogurt and Chives Dressing

1 cup plain yogurt
2 teaspoons chopped chives
¼ teaspoon onion powder
¼ teaspoon curry powder
½ teaspoon salt

In a small bowl, mix yogurt, chives, onion powder, curry powder, and salt. Cover and chill. Serve over fresh sliced tomatoes, baked potatoes, or as a dip for raw fresh vegetables.

YIELD: 1 cup

Yogurt Salad Dressing

1 cup plain yogurt
½ teaspoon dry mustard
½ teaspoon paprika
¼ teaspoon garlic salt

In a small mixing bowl combine yogurt, mustard, paprika, and garlic salt. Stir gently until smooth. May be used for tossed salads or as dressing for coleslaw.

YIELD: 1 cup

Yogurt Mayonnaise Dressing

1 cup plain yogurt
¼–½ cup mayonnaise

½ teaspoon salt
1–4 teaspoons sugar

Mix yogurt, mayonnaise, salt, and sugar together thoroughly. Use for seafood, vegetable, or fruit salads. Vary by adding 3 tablespoons tomato catsup.

YIELD: approximately 1½ cups

Avocado Dressing

2 small or 1 medium avocado
1 cup plain yogurt
½ teaspoon garlic powder
1 small onion, chopped
1 tablespoon chopped parsley

1 teaspoon salt
¼ teaspoon pepper
3 tablespoons vinegar
Dash of tarragon
1 tablespoon water

Peel and seed avocado. Blend avocado, yogurt, garlic powder, onion, parsley, salt, pepper, vinegar, tarragon, and water in a blender. Refrigerate in a covered dish. Approximately 13 calories per tablespoon.

YIELD: 2½ cups

Easy Avocado Dressing

1 avocado
½ cup yogurt
½ clove garlic, mashed fine

1 teaspoon lemon juice or to taste

Mash avocado in small bowl. Add yogurt, garlic, and lemon juice. Beat until thick consistency; serve over crisp lettuce.

YIELD: approximately 1 cup

Curry Dressing

1 cup plain yogurt
2 tablespoons minced parsley
1 tablespoon lemon juice
½ teaspoon seasoned salt
1 teaspoon curry powder

Blend yogurt, parsley, lemon juice, salt, and curry powder. Splendid over shrimp and roast beef. Approximately 10 calories per tablespoon.

YIELD: 1 cup

Olive Dressing

⅓ cup mayonnaise
2 tablespoons finely chopped pimiento-stuffed olives
2 tablespoons chopped onion
1 tablespoon chopped pimiento
⅛ teaspoon garlic powder
½ teaspoon sugar
1 cup plain yogurt

In a small bowl, mix mayonnaise with olives, onion, pimiento, garlic powder, and sugar. Fold in yogurt. Cover and chill until serving time. Serve with salad greens.

YIELD: approximately 1⅓ cups

Herb Garlic Dressing

⅓ cup mayonnaise
1 teaspoon sugar
¾ teaspoon chopped chives
½ teaspoon basil leaves
½ teaspoon garlic powder
½ teaspoon onion salt
¼ teaspoon oregano leaves
1 cup plain yogurt

In small bowl, mix mayonnaise with sugar, chives, and seasonings. Fold in yogurt. Cover and chill until serving time. Serve as a dressing for salad greens or cold cooked vegetables; spoon over sliced tomatoes just before serving.

YIELD: approximately 1⅓ cups

Green Onion Dressing

1 cup plain yogurt
2½ cups mayonnaise
2 tablespoons lemon juice
½ teaspoon salt
¾ cup thinly sliced green onions, including tops

Combine yogurt and mayonnaise with wire whisk. Add lemon juice, salt, and onions. Store in glass quart container in refrigerator, covered.

YIELD: approximately 3½ cups

Green Goddess Dressing

1 cup plain yogurt
1 hard-boiled egg, peeled
1 teaspoon Worcestershire sauce
1 tablespoon lemon juice

1 teaspoon celery salt
1 teaspoon Dijon mustard
1 bunch parsley, chopped
¼ cup chives or green onions, chopped

Blend yogurt, egg, Worcestershire sauce, lemon juice, celery salt, mustard, parsley, and chives together in a covered blender. Chill in a covered dish. Approximately 12 calories per tablespoon.

YIELD: approximately 1½ cups

Sesame Citrus Dressing

2 tablespoons toasted sesame seeds
2 tablespoons honey
1 teaspoon grated orange rind

1 teaspoon grated lemon rind
⅛ teaspoon salt
1 cup plain yogurt

In a small bowl blend together sesame seeds, honey, orange and lemon rinds, and salt; fold in yogurt. Cover and chill. Use as a dressing for fruit salads.

YIELD: approximately 1 cup

VARIATION: For a Sesame Orange Dressing substitute orange or mandarin orange yogurt for plain yogurt.

Fresh Fruit Salade Dressing

2 tablespoons sugar
2 tablespoons grenadine
1 cup plain yogurt

1 teaspoon salt
Juice of ½ lemon

Combine sugar, grenadine, yogurt, salt, and lemon. Mix well and refrigerate to thicken. Serve over any canned or fresh fruits, espe-

238

cially strawberries, blueberries, peaches, nectarines, grapes, plums, melon, or apples.

YIELD: 1½ cups

Waldorf Dressing

1 cup plain yogurt
1 teaspoon salt
½ teaspoon grated lemon rind

¼ teaspoon cinnamon
2 tablespoons golden raisins

Stir yogurt, salt, lemon rind, cinnamon, and raisins together. Serve over diced apples and celery.

YIELD: 1 cup

Roquefort-Garlic Dressing

1 cup plain yogurt
3 tablespoons crumbled Roquefort cheese

¼ teaspoon garlic powder
1 tablespoon minced onion
Dash of pepper

Combine yogurt, Roquefort cheese, garlic powder, onion, and pepper. Chill in a covered container. Approximately 16 calories per tablespoon.

YIELD: 1 cup

Easy Blue Cheese Dressing

⅓ cup mayonnaise
⅓ cup crumbled blue cheese

1 cup plain yogurt

In a small bowl, mix mayonnaise and blue cheese. Fold in yogurt. Cover and chill until serving time. Serve with salad greens.

YIELD: approximately 1½ cups

Blue Cheese Dressing

¼ cup crumbled blue cheese
1 teaspoon vinegar
½ teaspoon sugar

¼ teaspoon salt
1 cup plain yogurt

In a small bowl mash cheese with a fork. Mix in vinegar, sugar, and salt; fold in yogurt. Cover and chill. Use as a dressing for tossed salads.

YIELD: approximately 1 cup

Tangy Blue Cheese Dressing

½ cup mayonnaise
⅓ cup crumbled blue cheese
2 tablespoons milk
⅛ teaspoon ground thyme

½ clove garlic, minced
Dash white pepper
1 cup plain yogurt

Stir together mayonnaise, blue cheese, milk, thyme, garlic, and pepper. Fold in yogurt. Chill.

YIELD: 1½ cups

Diet Gourmet Dressing

1 cup cottage cheese
2 teaspoons tarragon vinegar
1 teaspoon salt
½ teaspoon salad herbs, crushed

Dash of garlic powder
Dash of onion powder
1 cup plain yogurt

In a small mixing bowl beat cottage cheese until fairly smooth. Add vinegar, salt, salad herbs, garlic and onion powders. Mix thoroughly. Fold in yogurt. Cover and chill to blend flavors. Use as a dressing for tossed salads. Keeps well in covered container in refrigerator for several days.

YIELD: approximately 2 cups

Russian Dressing

1 cup plain yogurt
1 hard-boiled egg, peeled
4 tablespoons chopped onion
½ teaspoon garlic salt

Dash of pepper
4 teaspoons catsup
2 tablespoons chopped sweet pepper

Blend yogurt, egg, onion, garlic salt, pepper, and catsup in a blender until smooth. Stir in the chopped pepper and chill. Approximately 12 calories per tablespoon.

YIELD: approximately 1¼ cups

240

Italian Dressing

1 cup plain yogurt
½ teaspoon garlic powder
1 tablespoon vinegar
Dash of tarragon
½ teaspoon Tabasco sauce

1 tablespoon Worcestershire
sauce
½ teaspoon prepared horseradish
1 tablespoon minced parsley
Dash of salt and pepper

Blend yogurt, garlic powder, vinegar, tarragon, Tabasco sauce, Worcestershire sauce, horseradish, parsley, salt and pepper. Chill in a covered dish. Approximately 10 calories per tablespoon.

YIELD: 1 cup

French Dressing

1 cup plain yogurt
¾ cup catsup
1 tablespoon vinegar

Dash of tarragon
¼ teaspoon salt
Dash of pepper

Stir yogurt, catsup, vinegar, tarragon, salt, and pepper together and chill in a covered container. Approximately 12 calories per tablespoon.

YIELD: approximately 1½ cups

Yogurt French Dressing

1 cup plain yogurt
½ cup French dressing

Salt and pepper to taste

Mix yogurt, French dressing, salt, and pepper together thoroughly. Use for vegetable salads.

YIELD: approximately 1½ cups

Tangy Vegetable Dressing

1 tablespoon vinegar
1 teaspoon prepared mustard
½ teaspoon seasoned salt

½ teaspoon sugar
1 cup plain yogurt

In a small bowl combine vinegar, mustard, seasoned salt, and sugar; fold in yogurt. Cover and chill. Use as a dressing for chilled, cooked vegetable salad.

YIELD: approximately 1 cup

Maple Nut Dressing

1 cup plain yogurt
3 tablespoons maple-blended
  syrup

¼ cup chopped walnuts

In a small bowl combine yogurt and syrup; fold in nuts. Cover and chill. Use as a dressing for fruit salads.

YIELD: approximately 1¼ cups

Thousand Island Dressing

2 tablespoons chili sauce
2 tablespoons pickle relish
1 tablespoon finely chopped
  onion

1 teaspoon vinegar
1 teaspoon prepared mustard
½ teaspoon salt
1 cup plain yogurt

In a bowl blend together chili sauce, relish, onion, vinegar, mustard, and salt; fold in yogurt. Cover and chill. Use as a dressing for tossed salads.

YIELD: approximately 1¼ cups

Tangy Thousand Island Dressing

⅓ cup mayonnaise
¼ cup chili sauce
2 tablespoons chopped
  pimiento-stuffed olives
1 tablespoon chopped onion

1 tablespoon chopped green
  pepper
2 teaspoons chopped parsley
1 cup plain yogurt

In a small bowl, mix mayonnaise with chili sauce, olives, onion, green pepper, and parsley. Fold in yogurt. Cover and chill until serving time. Serve as a dressing for salad greens.

YIELD: approximately 1⅔ cups

Yogurt Thousand Island Dressing

1 cup plain yogurt
½ cup mayonnaise

½ cup well-drained India relish
Salt to taste

Mix yogurt, mayonnaise, relish, and salt together thoroughly. Use on head lettuce or watercress salads or mixed greens.

Yield: approximately 1½ cups

Gourmet Salad Dressing

1 cup plain yogurt
1 cup mayonnaise
1½ cups salad oil
Juice of 1 lemon
1 tablespoon chopped parsley
1½ teaspoons chopped chives

1 teaspoon Dijon-style mustard
1 clove garlic, mashed
½ cup minced onion
½ cup minced green pepper
1 hard-cooked egg, chopped
Salt and pepper to taste

Mix yogurt and mayonnaise in a bowl, using wire whip. Slowly add salad oil, in a slow stream, beating constantly. Stir in lemon juice, parsley, chives, mustard, garlic, onion, green pepper, egg, salt and pepper.

Yield: 4½ cups

Caesar Dressing

1 cup plain yogurt
2 raw eggs
2 tablespoons lemon juice
4 tablespoons grated Parmesan cheese

1 heaping teaspoon garlic powder
½ teaspoon salt
¼ teaspoon pepper
1 tablespoon finely minced fresh parsley

Stir yogurt, eggs, lemon juice, cheese, garlic powder, salt, pepper, and parsley together and serve on romaine lettuce. Garnish with red onion rings and croutons. Approximately 17 calories per tablespoon.

Yield: approximately 1 cup

Mustard-Yogurt Dressing

½ cup yogurt   Dash of white vinegar
1 tablespoon dry mustard

Combine yogurt, mustard, vinegar, and chill. Serve with most meats, hot or cold. You can make it hot in a copper butter pan. (Don't let the yogurt boil.)

YIELD: 4 servings

Yogurt Peanut Dressing

½ cup peach yogurt   ⅛ teaspoon ground ginger
¼ cup peanut butter (smooth,   ⅛ teaspoon nutmeg
    not chunky)

Combine yogurt, peanut butter, ginger, and nutmeg. Blend well. Cover and chill. Spoon dressing over fresh fruit salad.

YIELD: approximately ½ cup

Cucumber Parsley Dressing

1 cup mayonnaise   1 clove garlic, minced
1 cup pared, seeded, chopped   ½ teaspoon salt
    cucumber   ⅛ teaspoon ground black
2 tablespoons finely chopped   pepper
    parsley   1 cup plain yogurt

Stir together mayonnaise, cucumber, parsley, garlic, salt, and pepper. Fold in yogurt. Chill.

YIELD: 2⅔ cups

Pecan Dressing

⅓ cup mayonnaise   ¼ cup light corn syrup
⅓ cup chopped pecans   1 cup plain yogurt

Stir together mayonnaise, pecans, and corn syrup. Fold in yogurt. Chill. Serve over fruit.

YIELD: 1½ cups

Sea Sauce

1 cup plain yogurt
½ teaspoon lemon juice
  A large pinch of garlic
  powder
1 cucumber, peeled and
  chopped fine

2 finely chopped scallions,
  including tops
1 stalk celery, chopped fine
  Pinch of dill
  Salt and pepper to taste

Combine yogurt, lemon juice, garlic powder, cucumber, scallions, celery, dill, salt, and pepper with a fork. Heat in a double boiler until warm, not hot. Serve over fish.

YIELD: 2 servings

Yogurt Sour Cream Sauce

¼ cup yogurt
¼ cup sour cream
½ teaspoon each caraway and
  poppy seeds
1 teaspoon butter

1 scallion with 3 inches green
  top, minced
¼ medium-size tomato, minced
½ clove garlic, crushed
⅛ teaspoon cayenne

1. Mix yogurt and sour cream. Brown the caraway and poppy seeds in butter.

2. Mix yogurt and sour cream with scallion, tomato, caraway and poppy seeds, garlic, and cayenne. Refrigerate and serve cold.

YIELD: approximately ½ cup

Horseradish Sauce

1 cup plain yogurt
2 teaspoons salt

2 teaspoons mustard

Combine yogurt, salt, and mustard together thoroughly. Serve with cold roast beef or stir into potato salad.

YIELD: 1 cup

Breads, Muffins, Pancakes

Yogurt Pancakes (Iranian)

4 cups plain yogurt
2 tablespoons sugar
1 teaspoon salt
2 teaspoons baking powder

1 teaspoon baking soda
2 eggs
4 tablespoons butter, melted, cool
1–1½ cups flour

Blend yogurt, sugar, salt, baking powder, baking soda, eggs, butter, adding flour until batter is light and falls in folds. Cook on skillet or griddle till browned—turn and brown other side. Keep warm until all are cooked. A delicate, light pancake; good with warm syrup, honey, or currant jelly.

YIELD: 6-8 servings

Sunday Brunch Pancakes

6 eggs, separated
5 tablespoons raw sugar
1 cup plain yogurt
1 cup milk

1 cup flour
½ cup cornstarch
4 teaspoons baking powder
½ teaspoon salt

1. Whip together egg yolks and sugar. Add yogurt and milk and blend until smooth.

2. Sift flour, measure; sift again with cornstarch, baking powder, and salt.

3. Combine flour mixture with yogurt mixture; mix well.

246

4. Beat egg whites until stiff and fold in. Bake on a medium hot griddle. Serve with melted butter and Yogurt Topping or your favorite syrup.

YIELD: 6 servings

Yogurt Topping
Mix 1-2 tablespoons honey to 1 cup blueberry or boysenberry flavored yogurt. Other fruit flavors may be used.

Apple-Yogurt Pancakes

1 cup flour
1 tablespoon sugar
1 teaspoon baking powder
½ teaspoon salt
1 egg, slightly beaten

1 cup milk
2 tablespoons butter, melted
½ cup plain yogurt
1 medium apple, cored and
    grated

1. Preheat the griddle to 375 degrees.
2. In mixing bowl combine flour, sugar, baking powder, and salt.
3. In separate bowl combine egg, milk, and melted butter. Pour into dry ingredients, stirring until just moist. Add yogurt and grated apple; stir until smooth.
4. Grill pancakes on lightly greased griddle, about 1 minute per side.

YIELD: 12-16 four-inch pancakes

Yogurt-Honey Bread

2 cups plain yogurt
3 eggs
Juice of 1 lemon
½ cup honey

2½ cups whole wheat flour
2½ teaspoons baking powder
½ teaspoon salt
1 cup brown sugar

1. Preheat the oven to 350 degrees.
2. Combine yogurt, eggs, lemon juice, and honey just enough to mix. Add flour, baking powder, salt, and sugar. Do not overmix.
3. Pour into a 9x9-inch pan greased with butter. Bake 1 hour. Cool and slice thinly. Serve with your favorite jellies, jams, or preserves.

Boston Brown Bread

1 cup sifted all-purpose flour	1 cup dark raisins
1 cup whole wheat flour	2 cups plain yogurt
2 teaspoons baking soda	¾ cup dark molasses
1 teaspoon salt	2 tablespoons salad oil
1 cup cornmeal	

1. Preheat the oven to 450 degrees.

2. Sift flours with soda and salt in a large mixing bowl. Add the cornmeal and raisins. Stir in the yogurt, molasses, and salad oil and mix well.

3. Grease three 1-pound fruit or vegetable cans with shortening and fill ⅔ with batter. Cover each can with foil and place on a rack in a large steamer or pot.

4. Add water to a depth of 2 inches in the steamer and cover. Steam for 3 hours. Cool 15 minutes and remove from can. Note: Bread can be reheated nicely in aluminum foil.

YIELD: 3 loaves

Wheat Germ Honey Loaves

4½–5 cups flour	1 cup plain yogurt
2½ teaspoons salt	2 tablespoons honey
2 packages (¼ oz. each) active dry yeast	1 tablespoon margarine
	1 beaten egg
1 cup milk	½ cup wheat germ

1. Combine 2 cups flour, salt, and yeast in large mixer bowl.

2. Combine milk, yogurt, honey, and margarine in medium saucepan. Cook over low heat until milk mixture is warm (120-130 degrees F.). Gradually add milk mixture to dry ingredients; beat at medium speed until well blended. Add egg.

3. Continue beating 2 minutes, scraping sides and bottom of bowl. Gradually add remaining 2½ cups flour and wheat germ. Beat mixture until it makes soft dough.

4. Knead on lightly floured pastry cloth or board 8-10 minutes, adding additional flour as necessary to make smooth dough. Place in lightly buttered large bowl. Brush top with melted butter.

5. Cover with towel. Let rise in warm place until doubled in bulk, about 1½ hours. Punch dough down; divide in half. Roll each half into 12x8-inch rectangle. Roll up, beginning at short side.

6. Press ends to seal; fold under and place seam side down in buttered 9¼x5¼x2¾-inch loaf pans. Cover with towel. Let rise until double in bulk, about 1 hour.

7. Bake in hot oven (400 degrees) 30-35 minutes. Remove loaves from pans. Cool on rack.

YIELD: 2 loaves

Nut Bread

This rich nut bread keeps well for several days if wrapped in aluminum foil and stored in refrigerator. Bake it before the holiday season and serve with creamy eggnog in demitasse cups when guests drop in.

Mix:

1 egg
½ cup yogurt
5 packets granulated sugar
   substitute

1 teaspoon vanilla extract
1 teaspoon nut extract

Toss Together:

½ cup self-rising cake flour
½ cup bread crumbs

½ cup ground walnuts
1 teaspoon baking powder

1. Preheat the oven to 350 degrees.
2. In separate bowls, make both mixtures.
3. Add the second mixture to the first and stir until well blended. Pour into lightly greased, lightly floured loaf pan. Bake about 40 minutes. Calories per slice: 74.

YIELD: 10 servings

Yogurt Muffins

2 eggs, lightly beaten
1 cup plain yogurt
2 tablespoons oil
¼ cup molasses
1½ cups whole wheat flour

2 tablespoons soy flour
1 teaspoon sea salt
¼ cup raisins
¼ cup chopped nuts

1. Preheat the oven to 375 degrees.
2. Combine the eggs and yogurt. Beat in the oil and molasses.
3. Sift together the whole wheat flour, soy flour, and salt.
4. Add the egg mixture to the dry ingredients and stir until just moistened. Stir in the raisins and nuts.
5. Fill oiled muffin tins two-thirds full. Bake 20 minutes or until done. Note: These muffins have no raising agent and will be compact in texture.

YIELD: 12 muffins

Banana Cream Tarts

1½ cups plain yogurt
1 package (3¾ oz.) instant banana cream pudding mix
⅓ cup toasted flaked coconut
5 individual 4-inch tart shells

Whipped topping
Mandarin orange segments
Toasted coconut
Chocolate curls

1. Combine yogurt and pudding mix in small mixer bowl; beat at low speed 1 minute. Stir in coconut. Spoon into individual tart shells.
2. Chill 1-2 hours. Spread each tart with whipped topping. Garnish with mandarin orange segments, coconut, or chocolate curls.

YIELD: 5 tarts

Desserts

Cherry Crepes

Cherry Sauce:

1 can (1 lb.) dark cherries	⅛ teaspoon cinnamon
¼ cup sugar	1 cup cherry syrup
1 tablespoon cornstarch	1 teaspoon grated lemon rind
¼ teaspoon mace	1 tablespoon lemon juice

Crepes:

3 eggs, beaten	¼ teaspoon cinnamon
½ cup milk	Butter
½ cup buttermilk pancake mix	Plain yogurt
¼ teaspoon mace	

To Prepare Sauce:

Drain cherries. Add water to syrup to make 1 cup. Combine sugar, cornstarch, mace, and cinnamon; add syrup. Cook, stirring constantly, until thickened. Stir in rind and juice. Add cherries; heat.

To Prepare Crepes:

Combine eggs and milk; add pancake mix, mace, and cinnamon; beat with rotary beater until smooth. Heat heavy 6-inch skillet; add small amount of butter. Pour in 1 tablespoon batter; immediately tilt skillet to coat bottom evenly. Bake on each side. Repeat using additional butter when necessary. Fold crepes in quarters. Place in buttered shallow baking pan; heat in preheated 400-degree oven about 5 minutes. To serve: top 3 or 4 crepes with sauce, then yogurt.

YIELD: 6 servings

Cherry Parfait

1 package (3½ oz.) instant
  vanilla pudding
2 cups plain yogurt
1 package (8 oz.) cream cheese
¼ cup sugar

2 teaspoons almond extract
1 teaspoon vanilla extract
1 can (21 oz.) cherry pie filling
  Whipped cream or dessert
  topping

1. Combine pudding, yogurt, and cream cheese, slowly adding the sugar. Whip until smooth and add the extracts.

2. In parfait glasses layer the yogurt mixture and cherry filling to form stripes. Chill thoroughly. Just before serving top with whipped cream or topping.

YIELD: 8 servings

Cherry Yogurt Dessert

1 package (18.5 oz.) yellow
  cake mix
½ cup softened butter
½ cup flaked coconut
2½ cups (21-oz. can) cherry pie
  filling

½ teaspoon grated lemon rind
⅛ teaspoon nutmeg
2 cups plain yogurt
2 eggs
¼ teaspoon vanilla

1. Preheat the oven to 325 degrees.

2. Combine cake mix, butter, and coconut in medium bowl (mixture will be crumbly). Lightly pat mixture into 13x9x2-inch baking dish, building up sides about 1 inch. Bake 5 minutes.

3. Remove from oven. Cool 10 minutes. Increase oven temperature to 350 degrees.

4. Combine pie filling, rind, and nutmeg in medium bowl. Combine yogurt, eggs, and vanilla in small bowl; mix well.

5. Spoon cherry mixture evenly over crust. Pour yogurt over cherry mixture. Return to oven. Bake 30-35 minutes. (Custard will firm up while cooling.) Cool completely before cutting.

YIELD: 12 servings

Rhubarb-Peach Cobbler

1 can (1 lb. 14 oz.) sliced
   peaches
½ cup sugar
3 tablespoons cornstarch

1 cup peach syrup
3 cups fresh rhubarb, cut in
   ¾-inch pieces
Light cream or half and half

1. Preheat the oven to 400 degrees.

2. Drain peaches reserving 1 cup syrup. In a 2-quart saucepan combine sugar and cornstarch; gradually add syrup, then add rhubarb.

3. Cook over medium heat, stirring constantly, until mixture boils. Cook 2 additional minutes.

4. Add peaches and return to boil. Turn into shallow casserole (2-quart).

5. Prepare Yogurt Drop Biscuits: drop by spoonfuls over top of fruit. (For biscuit recipe see Strawberry Shortcake, page 272.) Bake 25-30 minutes. Serve warm with light cream.

YIELD: 8-10 servings

Frozen Peach Yogurt Mousse

2 cups (16-oz. can) drained
   sliced peaches
¼ cup sugar

1 tablespoon (1 envelope)
   unflavored gelatin
1 cup plain yogurt
½ cup whipping cream

1. Combine peaches and sugar in blender jar. Blend until smooth. Pour peach mixture into medium saucepan. Soften gelatin in peach mixture. Cook mixture over medium heat, stirring constantly, until gelatin is dissolved.

2. Place in freezer until mixture is the consistency of unbeaten egg whites, stirring occasionally. Stir yogurt into chilled peach mixture.

3. Whip cream until stiff in small mixer bowl. Fold whipped cream into peach-yogurt mixture. Return to freezer; chill 2 hours. Beat mixture with rotary beater occasionally. Serve immediately.

YIELD: approximately 3½ cups

Strawberries with Yogurt

Select fresh or frozen strawberries (or other berries); sweeten with powdered sugar. Alternate layers of berries with layers of sweetened plain yogurt in a cocktail glass. Serve thoroughly chilled. (Vary by flavoring fruit with dash of brandy, rum, cherry.)

Note: Many prefer the tart, refreshing taste of plain yogurt. Others like to sweeten or flavor their yogurt with sugar or honey.

Strawberry Yogurt Dessert

2 tablespoons unflavored gelatin	¼ cup honey
½ cup concentrated strawberry syrup (Hain's brand)	4 cups plain yogurt
1½ cups water	2 cups strawberries, sliced
	Wheat germ, optional

1. Soften the gelatin in the strawberry syrup and ½ cup of the water. Boil remaining water and add to gelatin mixture. Stir to dissolve gelatin.
2. Add the honey and yogurt to gelatin mixture and beat with a rotary beater until smooth. Cool until mixture starts to thicken slightly.
3. Fold in the fruit and pour into a large, well-buttered deep pie plate liberally sprinkled with wheat germ or into a serving dish. Chill.

YIELD: 6 servings

Raspberry Yogurt Smoothies

½ cup fresh raspberries	1–2 tablespoons honey, to taste
¾ cup plain yogurt	

Puree raspberries in blender; press through a wire strainer to remove seeds. Return puree to blender, adding yogurt and honey. Whirl. Chill.

YIELD: 2 servings

Nectarine Yogurt Mold

2 large fresh nectarines, peeled (or use canned, unsweetened peaches)

1 package (3 oz.) orange gelatin
1 cup plain yogurt
Lettuce

1. Finely dice 1 nectarine and set aside.

2. Puree the second nectarine in a blender, adding water to pureed fruit to measure 1¼ cups. Place in a saucepan and heat just to boiling. Remove from heat; add gelatin and stir until dissolved.

3. Cool to room temperature. Add the yogurt and stir until well blended. Chill until slightly thickened. Fold in diced nectarine.

4. Pour into oiled 3-cup mold. Chill until firm. Unmold onto a chilled serving plate lined with lettuce to serve. Add a hearty dollop of plain yogurt on top.

YIELD: 6 servings

Currant Walnut Dessert

1 cup plain yogurt
¼ cup currants
¼ cup chopped walnuts

1 teaspoon vanilla
1 pinch cinnamon
2 drops artificial sweetener

Mix yogurt, currants, walnuts, vanilla, cinnamon, and sweetener. Chill.

YIELD: 2 servings

Yogurt Pineapple Sherbet

1 cup plain yogurt

1 cup crushed pineapple with juice

1. Put yogurt in freezing tray and freeze slowly to a soft mush. Remove and stir in crushed pineapple with juice.

2. Return to freezing compartment and freeze to soft mush. Stir or beat well and freeze until solid.

YIELD: 2 servings

VARIATION: Instead of crushed pineapple, vary by using sweetened mashed strawberries, raspberries, finely diced peaches.

Pineapple-Orange Fluff

1 can (11 oz.) mandarin
orange segments, drained
(reserve liquid)
1 can (8 oz.) crushed pineapple, drained (reserve
liquid)

1 package (3 oz.) orange
gelatin
1 cup plain yogurt

1. Combine orange and pineapple juices. Add enough water to make 1¼ cups. Bring liquid to a boil and pour over gelatin. Stir until dissolved. Chill until firm.

2. Beat gelatin with electric mixer at high speed until frothy. Fold in orange segments, pineapple, and yogurt. Chill until mixture mounds, about 15 minutes. Spoon mixture into serving dishes and chill 10-15 minutes before serving.

YIELD: 6 servings

Orange Yogurt Mousse Dessert

2 cups orange juice, heated to
boiling
1 package (6 oz.) orange
gelatin

2 cups plain yogurt
3 egg whites, stiffly beaten

1. Pour hot juice over gelatin in large bowl, stirring until gelatin is completely dissolved. Chill until consistency of unbeaten egg white, about 1 hour.

2. Fold in yogurt and beaten egg whites. Chill until firm. To unmold mousse, dip mold into lukewarm water and tap to loosen.

YIELD: 3-4 servings

Spiced Bananas in Yogurt (Plantain Pachadi)

¼ cup grated coconut
1 cup plain yogurt
2 teaspoons powdered mustard
¼ teaspoon cayenne

1 teaspoon salt
2 cups sliced ripe bananas
1 tablespoon lime juice

1. Place coconut in food chopper. Use fine blade or high-speed blender. Grind to a paste.

2. Place yogurt, mustard, cayenne, salt, and coconut paste in bowl. Beat together until smooth.

3. Place bananas in serving bowl. Sprinkle with lime juice. Arrange bananas and yogurt mixture in layers, topping with yogurt mixture.

YIELD: 2-4 servings

Custard Pear Squares

Bottom Layer:

¼ cup (½ stick) butter	1 egg
¼ cup firmly packed light brown sugar	½ teaspoon vanilla
	1 cup regular all-purpose flour

Custard Layer:

2 eggs, beaten	¼ teaspoon ginger
1 cup plain yogurt	¼ cup chopped nuts
½ cup sugar	1 can (1 lb.) pear halves, drained and sliced
¼ teaspoon nutmeg	

To Prepare Bottom Layer:

In a small mixing bowl cream butter; add sugar and beat until light and fluffy. Beat in egg and vanilla. Gradually add flour and mix until blended. Spread evenly into square cake pan (8-inch). Bake 15 minutes.

To Prepare Custard Layer:

Meanwhile in a small mixing bowl thoroughly mix eggs, yogurt, sugar, nutmeg, and ginger; add nuts. Arrange pear slices on baked bottom layer; pour custard over pears. Bake in preheated 325-degree oven 45-50 minutes or until knife inserted near center in custard layer comes out clean. Serve warm.

YIELD: 8-9 servings

Grapes and Yogurt

This is a surprisingly sophisticated dessert, considering its simplicity of preparation. It's a nice touch after a rich meal. At a dinner party, serve with thin cookies.

4 cups seedless green grapes,　　½ cup brown sugar
　　halved if you wish　　　　　　1 cup plain yogurt

Combine grapes, sugar, and yogurt. Refrigerate for at least 2 hours. Serve chilled.

YIELD: 6-8 servings

Yogurt Ambrosia

2 tablespoons honey　　　　　　　1 banana, sliced
1 tablespoon lemon juice　　　　　1 pear, unpeeled and diced
2 oranges, peeled and sectioned　　1 can (3½ oz.) flaked coconut
1 red apple, unpeeled and　　　　　1 cup plain yogurt
　　diced

In a bowl combine honey and lemon juice. Add oranges, apple, banana, pear, and coconut. Toss gently to coat fruit. Chill. Just before serving add yogurt and toss. Serve immediately.

YIELD: 6-8 servings

VARIATION: Use your favorite fruit-flavored yogurt as a substitute for plain yogurt.

Ambrosia

2½ cups miniature marsh-　　　　　1¼ cups (11-oz. can) chilled,
　　mallows　　　　　　　　　　　　　drained mandarin orange
1 tablespoon water　　　　　　　　　sections
½ cup plain yogurt　　　　　　　　1½ cups chilled seedless grapes
1¼ cups (13½-oz. can) chilled,　　1 cup (2 small) sliced bananas
　　drained pineapple tidbits　　　　8 halved maraschino cherries
　　　　　　　　　　　　　　　　　　　1 cup flaked coconut

1. Combine 1½ cups marshmallows and water in small sauce-pan. Cook over low heat, stirring constantly, until marshmallows are melted. Cool thoroughly. Stir in yogurt; mix well.

2. Combine pineapple, mandarin oranges, grapes, bananas, cherries, coconut, and remaining 1 cup marshmallows in large bowl.

3. Fold in marshmallow-yogurt mixture. Chill 1 hour before serving.

YIELD: 6 cups

Creamy Fruit Mold

1 tablespoon unflavored gelatin
¼ cup sugar
1 cup pineapple juice
1 cup orange sections, cut-up

½ cup chopped maraschino
  cherries
½ cup toasted slivered almonds
¼ cup coconut
1 cup plain yogurt

Pineapple-Cherry Sauce:

1 tablespoon cornstarch
1 cup pineapple juice

¼ cup maraschino syrup
½ cup cut maraschino cherries

To Prepare Mold:

In a 1½-quart saucepan combine gelatin and sugar; add pineapple juice. Heat over low heat, stirring constantly, until gelatin is dissolved. Chill until partially set. Fold in oranges, cherries, almonds, and coconut, then yogurt. Turn into 4-cup mold. Chill until firm. Unmold and serve with sauce.

To Prepare Sauce:

In a 1-quart saucepan gradually add pineapple juice to cornstarch; add cherry syrup. Cook over medium heat, stirring constantly, until thickened. Cook 2 additional minutes. Add cherries. Cool.

YIELD: approximately 1⅓ cups

VARIATION: Use cherry yogurt in place of plain yogurt.

Rainbow Mold

Strawberry Layer:

¼ cup cold water
1 envelope unflavored gelatin
1½ cups medium strawberries

1 cup plain yogurt
3 tablespoons sugar

Lime Layer:

¼ cup cold water
1 envelope unflavored gelatin
½ cup lime juice

1 cup plain yogurt
¼ cup sugar
2–3 drops green food coloring

Peach Layer:

¼ cup cold water
1 envelope unflavored gelatin
3 large fresh peaches or 6
  canned peach halves

1 cup plain yogurt
2 tablespoon sugar, if using
  fresh peaches

Make the Strawberry Layer First:

1. Pour ¼ cup of cold water into a small saucepan. Sprinkle the unflavored gelatin over water; set aside. Cut strawberries in half; puree in blender until smooth. (You should have ¾ cup strawberry puree.) Combine yogurt, puree, and sugar.

2. Heat soaked gelatin over low heat, stirring constantly until dissolved. Add to yogurt mixture. Pour into a 6-cup glass mold or bowl. Place in freezer 15-20 minutes to set.

Meanwhile, Make Lime Layer:

Pour ¼ cup cold water into small saucepan. Sprinkle gelatin over water; set aside. Combine lime juice, yogurt, sugar. Add 2-3 drops of green food coloring. Heat soaked gelatin over low heat, stirring constantly until dissolved. Add to yogurt mixture. Pour over set strawberry layer. Replace in freezer for 15-20 minutes to set.

Now Make the Peach Layer:

Pour ¼ cup cold water into a small saucepan. Sprinkle gelatin over water; set aside. Cut peaches in chunks and blend until smooth. (You should have ¾ cup peach puree.) Combine yogurt and puree. If you use fresh peaches, add sugar. Heat soaked gelatin over low heat, stirring constantly until dissolved. Add to yogurt mixture. Pour over set lime layer. Place in refrigerator until peach layer has set. At serving time, garnish with a slice of lime and peach slices if you like.

YIELD: 8 servings

Dessert Cream

1 tablespoon (1 envelope) unflavored gelatin	½ cup sugar
	½ teaspoon vanilla
1¼ cups milk	1 cup plain yogurt

Cherry Sauce:

1 can (1 lb.) red sour pitted cherries in water pack	¼ cup sugar
	1 tablespoon butter
¼ cup sugar	¼ teaspoon Angostura bitters
1 tablespoon cornstarch	Red food color
½ cup cherry juice	

In a 1-quart saucepan soften gelatin in ½ cup milk. Over low heat, stir constantly until gelatin is dissolved. Add remaining ¾ cup milk, sugar, and vanilla; stir until sugar is dissolved. Chill until partially set. Fold in yogurt. Turn into molds (5 individual molds, 4-ounces each). Chill until firm.

To Prepare Sauce:

Drain cherries reserving ½ cup juice. Combine ¼ cup sugar and cornstarch; gradually stir in juice. Cook over medium heat, stirring constantly, until thickened. Cook 2 additional minutes. Remove from heat. Stir in ¼ cup sugar, butter, and bitters until sugar is dissolved and butter melted. Add cherries, then food color. Allow to stand at least 1 hour to blend flavors. Serve over Dessert Cream.

YIELD: 5 servings

Yogurt Sundae

1 apple, cored and quartered, unpeeled	1 cup plain yogurt
1 banana, cut lengthwise in half	¼ cup chopped nuts and seeds mixed
¼ cup wheat germ	

1. Place the cored, unpeeled, washed apple in a blender and blend until smooth. Divide the mixture between two sundae dishes. Top each with half a banana.

2. Sprinkle each dish with half of the wheat germ. Top each sundae with half a cup of yogurt and sprinkle with seeds and nuts.

YIELD: 2 servings

Berries 'n' Cream Yogurt

2 envelopes unflavored gelatin	2 cups raspberry, strawberry, or boysenberry yogurt
⅔ cup sugar	
3 eggs, separated	1 cup (½ pt.) heavy cream, whipped
1 cup milk	

1. In medium saucepan, mix unflavored gelatin and ⅓ cup sugar. Blend in egg yolks beaten with milk. Stir over low heat until gelatin dissolves, about 5 minutes.

2. With wire whisk or rotary beater, blend in yogurt. Chill, stirring occasionally, until mixture mounds slightly when dropped from spoon.

(cont'd)

3. In medium bowl, beat egg whites until soft peaks form; gradually add remaining ⅓ cup sugar and beat until stiff. Fold in gelatin mixture, then whipped cream.

4. Turn into individual dessert dishes or 8-cup bowl and chill until set.

YIELD: approximately 10 servings

Fruit 'n' Honey Yogurt

2 envelopes unflavored gelatin
1½ cups orange juice
2 cups plain, vanilla, or lemon yogurt
1 can (11 oz.) mandarin oranges, drained (reserve syrup)

2 tablespoons honey
½ cup raisins
½ cup chopped walnuts
2 bananas, cut into ½-inch slices

1. In medium saucepan, sprinkle unflavored gelatin over 1 cup orange juice. Stir over low heat until gelatin dissolves, about 3 minutes.

2. With wire whisk or rotary beater, blend in yogurt, remaining orange juice, reserved syrup, and honey. Chill, stirring occasionally, until mixture is consistency of unbeaten egg whites.

3. Fold in oranges, raisins, walnuts, and bananas. Turn into 6-cup mold or individual dessert dishes and chill until firm, about 3 hours.

YIELD: approximately 10 servings

Yogurt-Fruit Dessert

1 cup plain yogurt
¼ cup uncooked rolled oats
6 tablespoons honey
½ cup raw cashew nuts
1 tablespoon lemon juice

1 cup diced raw apple, pineapple, or banana
¼ cup orange juice
½ cup whipped cream

Mix yogurt with rolled oats and honey. Blend and place in refrigerator overnight. An hour before serving, mix in remaining ingredients.

YIELD: 4 servings

Yogurt Pudding

1 package pudding
1½ cups milk
1 cup plain yogurt

1 tablespoon sugar
Grated orange or lemon peel

Make pudding, using package of your favorite pudding powder, using only 1½ cups milk. When cooked, cool to lukewarm and mix in yogurt and sugar. Flavor, if desired, with grated orange or lemon peel. Pour into glasses or molds. Chill and serve when cold.

YIELD: approximately 4-6 servings

Jamaican Frost

2 cans (16 oz. each) fruit cocktail
4 cups plain yogurt

1 large package (6 oz.) lime gelatin
¼ teaspoon peppermint extract
Lime slices, for garnish

1. Drain fruit cocktail well. In saucepan combine 1 cup yogurt and gelatin. Cook over low heat, stirring constantly, until gelatin is dissolved.

2. Stir in remaining yogurt and peppermint. Chill until almost set.

3. Whip gelatin until smooth and frothy. Place ⅓ cup fruit in 8-cup mold; fold remainder into gelatin. Pour into mold. Chill until set.

4. Unmold gelatin onto platter. Garnish with lime slices. (Optional flavor: Strawberry gelatin and sliced strawberries may be used instead of lime gelatin and lime slices.)

YIELD: 10-12 servings

MOUSSE VARIATION: Follow same directions, ·except reserve ½ cup fruit for garnish; puree remainder and fold into whipped gelatin. Pour into stemmed glasses; chill. Garnish with reserved fruit and lime slices.

Nature Sweets

4 envelopes unflavored gelatin
½ cup apple juice
1 cup boiling water
2 cups Dutch apple yogurt

¼ cup honey
½ cup chopped walnuts or raisins

1. In a large bowl, sprinkle unflavored gelatin over apple juice; add boiling water and stir until gelatin is completely dissolved.

2. With wire whisk or rotary beater, blend in yogurt and honey.

3. Pour into 8- or 9-inch square pan and sprinkle with walnuts; chill until firm. Cut into squares to serve.

YIELD: 5-6 dozen squares

VARIATIONS: prune whip yogurt and orange juice; orange-pineapple yogurt and orange juice.

"Pour Topping" for Cereal or Fruit

Blend 2 cups plain or vanilla yogurt with ½ cup Domino Brownulated sugar until liquid or beat with electric or rotary beater. Pour over cereal or fruit. Add more or less sugar to suit taste.

Keep on hand in refrigerator for convenient use in place of cream or milk and sweetening. Stays homogenized and will keep for a couple of days.

"Spoon Topping" for Dessert

1 cup plain or vanilla yogurt
½ cup Domino Brownulated sugar

½ cup chopped walnuts or pecans
Dash of mace

Gently stir ingredients just enough to mix together. Store in refrigerator. Use as spoon-on topping for waffles, pancakes, cakes, fruit pies, crisps, puddings, raw, cooked, dried, or fresh fruits, sherbets, ice cream, etc.

This is thick and spoonable, rather than pourable, when stirred gently. It serves a different purpose from the Pour Topping.

Cakes, Pies, Cookies

Yogurt Cake (Yiaourtopeta)

½ cup butter (1 stick)
1 cup sugar
2½ cups self-rising cake flour
1 cup plain yogurt

4 eggs
Grated rind of ½ lemon
Confectioners' sugar

1. Use a Turk's head mold (gugelhopf pan) or a 9x13x2-inch pan for this cake. Grease the mold or pan; dust with flour, shake out excess. Turn on oven to 350 degrees.

2. Place butter and sugar in bowl of electric mixer, beat until creamy smooth. Slowly add self-rising cake flour and yogurt, beating to blend, then add eggs one at a time, beating until smooth. Add lemon rind, stir with spoon to blend. Pour into mold.

3. Bake 50 minutes, until toothpick or straw inserted in the center comes out clean. Let cake stand in pan 10 minutes, then turn out on rack. Dust with confectioners' sugar. Note: When baked in a 9x13x2-inch pan, a syrup like that for Baklava may be poured over the cake while hot instead of the sugar.

YIELD: one 9x13-inch cake

Mother's Cheesecake, Updated

1 8-ounce and 1 3-ounce
   package cream cheese
2 eggs
⅓ cup sugar (for filling)
   Prepared 8-inch graham
   cracker pie crust

1½ cups plain yogurt
¼ cup sugar (for topping)
½ teaspoon vanilla
   Grated rind of ½ lemon

1. Preheat the oven to 350 degrees.

2. Beat softened cream cheese in large bowl; add eggs and sugar and beat until smooth. Pour into the shell and bake for 20 minutes. Cool on wire rack for 15 minutes. Raise oven temperature to 475 degrees.

3. Combine yogurt, sugar, vanilla, and lemon rind. Spread over baked cheesecake. Bake for 5 minutes. The yogurt topping will still be liquid but will set later.

4. Cool cake on a wire rack, then chill for several hours, until topping has set.

YIELD: one 8-inch cheesecake

Lo-Cal Cheese Cake Squares

1 cup graham cracker crumbs	1 cup (8 oz.) drained yogurt*
3 tablespoons melted butter	2 eggs
1 package (8 oz.) softened imitation cream cheese	¾ cup sugar
	¼ teaspoon salt

1. Preheat the oven to 300 degrees.

2. Combine graham cracker crumbs and butter in small bowl. Reserve 3 tablespoons crumb mixture. Press remaining crumb mixture in bottom of 8x8-inch square baking dish.

3. Combine cream cheese and drained yogurt in small mixer bowl. Beat at medium speed until smooth.

4. Add eggs, sugar, and salt to cheese mixture. Continue beating until cheese-egg mixture is smooth and blended. Pour mixture over crust. Sprinkle reserved crumbs over mixture.

5. Bake 45-50 minutes or until center is set. Cool completely. Cut into squares. Serve plain or with your favorite fruit topping.

YIELD: 9 servings

* To drain yogurt: tie 3½-4 cups plain yogurt in several thicknesses of cheesecloth. Hang and drain for at least 8 hours or overnight. (Drained yogurt should be the consistency of softened cream cheese.)

Streusel Coffeecake

½ cup firmly packed light brown sugar
½ cup finely chopped walnuts
2 teaspoons cinnamon
3½ cups flour
2 teaspoons baking soda
1 tablespoon cardamom
¼ teaspoon salt
1 cup softened butter
2 cups sugar
2 eggs
1 teaspoon vanilla
1½ cups plain yogurt

1. Preheat the oven to 350 degrees.
2. Combine brown sugar, walnuts, and cinnamon in small bowl. Mix well.
3. Sift flour, baking soda, cardamom, and salt together.
4. Cream butter and sugar until fluffy in large mixer bowl. Add eggs and vanilla. Beat well.
5. Add flour mixture into creamed mixture alternately with yogurt, beginning and ending with flour mixture. Mix until well blended. Spread ⅓ batter (about 2 cups) in buttered 10-inch tube pan. Sprinkle ⅓ sugar mixture over batter. Repeat layers twice.
6. Bake 60-70 minutes or until toothpick inserted 2 inches from edge comes out clean.

YIELD: 14-16 servings

Breakfast Yogurt Cake

2 cups flour, sifted
1 tablespoon baking powder
1 teaspoon salt
½ cup butter, softened
¾ cup sugar
1 teaspoon vanilla extract
2 eggs
1 cup plain yogurt
½ cup chopped walnuts
1 pint (2 cups) strawberries, sliced

1. Preheat the oven to 350 degrees.
2. Stir together flour, baking powder, and salt.
3. Cream together butter and sugar until light and fluffy. Blend in vanilla. Beat in eggs, one at a time.
4. Thoroughly blend flour mixture into creamed mixture alternately with yogurt, beginning and ending with flour. Stir in chopped nuts.

(cont'd)

5. Pour batter into greased and floured 9x9x2-inch pan or 10-inch Bundt cake pan. Bake 45-50 minutes or until done. Cool 10 minutes before removing from pan. Garnish with strawberries.

YIELD: one 9x9-inch cake or one 10-inch Bundt cake

Rich Whole Wheat Coffee Cake

This deliciously moist cake is easy to prepare and keeps well. Good buttered or plain for breakfast.

¾ cup unbleached white flour
¾ cup whole wheat flour
1 cup brown sugar
2 teaspoons baking powder
½ teaspoon baking soda

¼ teaspoon salt
1 cup plain yogurt
2 eggs
½ cup each, raisins and walnuts, optional

Topping:
2 tablespoons wheat germ
2 tablespoons butter

2 tablespoons sugar
½ teaspoon cinnamon

1. Preheat the oven to 350 degrees.
2. Mix white and whole wheat flours, sugar, baking powder, soda, and salt.
3. Beat yogurt and eggs, add optional raisins and nuts, and combine with flour mixture. Pour into buttered 9x9-inch pan.
4. Crumble together the topping mixture; sprinkle over the batter and bake 20 minutes.

YIELD: one 9x9-inch cake

Cinnamon Coffee Cake

½ cup butter, softened
1 cup sugar
2 eggs
2 cups sifted cake flour

1½ teaspoons baking powder
½ teaspoon baking soda
1 cup plain yogurt
1 teaspoon vanilla

Topping:
½ cup sugar
½ cup chopped walnuts

2 teaspoons cinnamon

1. Preheat the oven to 350 degrees.
2. Cream together butter, sugar, and eggs.

268

3. Stir together flour, baking powder, and soda. Add to butter mixture alternately with the yogurt, ending with the dry ingredients.

4. Blend in the vanilla and pour into a greased and floured 9x9-inch pan.

5. Combine sugar, walnuts, and cinnamon for topping. Sprinkle over cake. Place in the oven and bake 35-40 minutes.

YIELD: one 9x9-inch cake

Super Rich Chocolate Cake

1¾ cups sifted cake flour
½ teaspoon baking soda
1 teaspoon salt
1¼ cups sugar
½ cup shortening
2 egg yolks

2 squares unsweetened chocolate, melted
1 cup plain yogurt
1 teaspoon vanilla extract
2 egg whites

1. Preheat the oven to 350 degrees.

2. Grease and flour the bottoms of two 8-inch layer pans. Sift flour with soda and salt.

3. Add sugar gradually to shortening. Cream with an electric mixer at high speed until light and fluffy.

4. At medium speed add egg yolks, beating well. Add melted chocolate.

5. At low speed blend in sifted dry ingredients, alternately with yogurt and vanilla extract, beginning and ending with dry ingredients.

6. Beat egg whites until stiff and fold gently into batter. Pour into pans and bake 30-35 minutes or until springy. Cool before removing from pans. Frost with your favorite frosting.

YIELD: one 8-inch layer cake

Chocolate Cake and Glaze

3 squares (1 oz. each) unsweetened chocolate
½ cup water
1 cup plain yogurt
½ cup (1 stick) butter
1 cup sugar

½ cup firmly packed light brown sugar
3 eggs
1 teaspoon vanilla
2 cups sifted cake flour
1 teaspoon baking soda
1 teaspoon salt

Chocolate Glaze:

1 package (6 oz.) semi-sweet   ½ cup plain yogurt
  chocolate pieces

1. Preheat the oven to 350 degrees.

2. Generously butter bottom of baking pan (13x9x2-inch); dust with flour. In a 1-quart saucepan over low heat, melt chocolate in water stirring constantly. Cool. Stir in yogurt; set aside.

3. In a mixing bowl cream butter; gradually add sugars and beat until light and fluffy. Beat in eggs one at a time. Add vanilla.

4. Sift together flour, soda, and salt. Add to creamed mixture alternately with yogurt mixture, beginning and ending with dry ingredients. Turn into pan; bake 35-40 minutes.

To Prepare Glaze:

In a 1-quart saucepan over low heat, stirring constantly, melt chocolate pieces. Remove from heat; stir in yogurt. Cool. Spread on top of cake. Note: To make two 9-inch round layers; bake 30-35 minutes.

YIELD: one 9x13-inch cake

Chocolate Cake

½ cup shortening	¾ teaspoon baking soda
1½ cups sugar	1½ teaspoons baking powder
3 eggs, separated	1 teaspoon salt
1 teaspoon vanilla	½ cup cocoa
¾ cup plain yogurt	½ cup boiling water
2¼ cups flour	

1. Preheat the oven to 350 degrees.

2. Cream shortening and sugar; add egg yolks, vanilla, and yogurt. Sift together flour, soda, baking powder, and salt. Add to shortening mixture.

3. Mix the cocoa in ½ cup of boiling water and allow to cool; add to batter and stir until well blended.

4. Beat egg whites till stiff and fold in last. Bake in two layer-cake pans about 30-40 minutes.

YIELD: one 8-inch layer cake

Yogurt Casserole Cake

Grated rind of one orange
¼ cup butter or margarine
1 pound confectioners' sugar
3 eggs

1 cup plain yogurt
3 cups sifted all-purpose flour
1 tablespoon baking powder
¼ teaspoon salt

Sauce:

2 cups plain yogurt

1 jar (12 oz.) apricot preserves

1. Preheat the oven to 350 degrees.

2. In a bowl, mix orange rind and butter until light and fluffy. Stir in confectioners' sugar. Beat in eggs, one at a time, beating well after each addition.

3. Stir in yogurt. Beat in flour mixed with baking powder and salt.

4. Spread batter evenly into a greased and floured 11-inch square casserole, 2 inches deep.

5. Bake 45-50 minutes. Cool cake in pan; cut into squares.

To Prepare Sauce:

Combine yogurt and preserves. Beat until smooth. Spoon sauce over squares of cake.

YIELD: one 11-inch square cake

Baked Strawberry Pudding Cake

1 pint (2 cups) strawberries, hulled
¼ cup sugar
6 tablespoons (¾ stick) butter
½ cup sugar
1 egg
1¾ cups sifted regular all-purpose flour

1 teaspoon baking soda
½ teaspoon salt
¼ teaspoon mace
¼ cup milk
½ cup plain yogurt
Sweetened whipped cream

1. If strawberries are extra large, cut in half. Cover strawberries with ¼ cup sugar and allow to stand at room temperature for 1 hour to form juice.

2. Preheat the oven to 350 degrees.

3. In a small mixing bowl cream butter; gradually add ½ cup sugar and beat until light and fluffy. Beat in egg.

(cont'd)

4. Sift together flour, soda, salt, and mace; add to creamed mixture alternately with milk; then yogurt, beginning and ending with dry ingredients .

5. Turn into buttered square cake pan (8-inch). Spoon berries and juice over top and bake 30-40 minutes. Serve warm with sweetened whipped cream or ice cream.

YIELD: 8-9 servings

Strawberry Shortcake

1½ cups regular all-purpose flour	¼ cup (½ stick) butter
2 tablespoons sugar	¾ cup plain yogurt
2 teaspoons baking powder	1 quart strawberries, sliced and sweetened
¼ teaspoon baking soda	Sweetened whipped cream
¼ teaspoon salt	

1. Preheat the oven to 450 degrees.

2. In a bowl sift together flour, sugar, baking powder, soda, and salt. Cut in butter until mixture resembles coarse meal.

3. Add yogurt all at once; stir just until dough clings together. On lightly floured surface knead lightly. Pat or roll about ½-inch thick.

4. Cut out biscuits with floured 3-inch biscuit cutter. Place on buttered baking sheet; brush tops with water and bake 10-15 minutes.

5. To serve: split shortcakes. Spoon strawberries in middle and on top. Spoon on whipped cream.

YIELD: 6 servings

VARIATION: Drop Biscuits—Increase yogurt to 1 cup. Omit kneading and drop by heaping tablespoonfuls onto baking sheet, dividing into six portions. Bake and serve as above.

Yellow Cake

½ cup (1 stick) butter	1 teaspoon baking soda
1¼ cups sugar	½ teaspoon salt
2 eggs	½ cup milk
1 teaspoon vanilla	½ cup plain yogurt
2 cups sifted cake flour	

1. Preheat the oven to 350 degrees.

2. Generously butter bottoms of two round cake pans (8-inch) and dust with flour.

3. In a mixing bowl cream butter; gradually add sugar and beat until light and fluffy. Beat in eggs one at a time. Add vanilla.

4. Sift together flour, soda and salt; add to creamed mixture alternately with milk; then yogurt, beginning and ending with dry ingredients.

5. Divide evenly into pans. Bake 30-35 minutes. Cool in pans on wire racks 5 minutes. Turn onto racks and cool completely. Fill and frost with Whipped Strawberry Frosting.

YIELD: one 8-inch layer cake

Whipped Strawberry Frosting

½ teaspoon unflavored gelatin
¼ cup cold water
1 cup whipping cream

1 tablespoon confectioners'
   sugar
1 teaspoon vanilla
1 cup strawberry yogurt

1. In a small saucepan sprinkle gelatin over water to soften; heat over low heat, stirring constantly, until gelatin is dissolved. Cool to room temperature.

2. In a chilled bowl with chilled beaters whip cream until soft peaks form, beat in sugar and vanilla.

3. Fold in yogurt; then gradually fold in gelatin mixture. Chill until serving time.

YIELD: sufficient to fill and frost a two-layer 8- or 9-inch round

Lemon Sponge Cake

½ cup (1 stick) butter
1¼ cups sugar
2 eggs
1 teaspoon vanilla
2 cups sifted cake flour
1 teaspoon baking soda

½ teaspoon salt
½ cup milk
½ cup lemon yogurt
1 teaspoon lemon juice
   Whipped cream

1. Preheat oven to 350 degrees. Butter and flour two 8-inch round cake pans.

(cont'd)

2. In a mixing bowl cream butter, gradually add sugar and beat until fluffy. Beat in eggs one at a time. Add vanilla.

3. Sift together flour, soda, and salt. Add to creamed mixture alternately with milk, then yogurt combined with the lemon juice, beginning and ending with the dry ingredients.

4. Divide evenly into pans. Bake 30-35 minutes. Turn into racks and cool. Fill and frost with whipped cream or whipped topping.

YIELD: one 8-inch layer cake

Orange Cake

1 cup white flour	1 cup plain yogurt
1 cup whole wheat flour	2 eggs
3 teaspoons baking soda	1 cup raisins
½ teaspoon salt	1 large orange, for juice and
½ cup butter	rind
1 cup brown sugar	

1. Preheat the oven to 375 degrees.

2. Sift together the flours, soda, and salt.

3. Cream butter and sugar together. Add the yogurt, slightly beaten eggs, and raisins.

4. Squeeze the juice of 1 orange and add to mixture together with the grated orange rind. Gradually add dry ingredients. Mix well.

5. Pour into large springform pan. Bake 55 minutes.

YIELD: 1 cake

Yogurt Spice Cake

2¼ cups sifted all-purpose flour	½ cup butter or margarine,
1 teaspoon baking soda	softened
1 teaspoon ground cinnamon	1 cup light brown sugar, firmly
1 teaspoon ground allspice	packed
½ teaspoon ground cloves	½ cup honey
¼ teapoon salt	2 eggs
	1 cup plain yogurt

1. Preheat the oven to 350 degrees.

2. Sift together flour, baking soda, cinnamon, allspice, cloves, and salt.

3. Cream butter, brown sugar, and honey with electric mixer at high speed until light and fluffy. Add eggs, one at a time, beating well after each addition.

4. Using low speed of mixer, add flour mixture alternately with yogurt, beating well after each addition until smooth. Pour batter into greased 9x9-inch cake pan and bake 40-45 minutes or until center of cake springs back when lightly pressed with fingertips.

5. Cool cake in pan 5 minutes, then remove and cool completely on rack.

YIELD: one 9x9-inch cake

Mr. and Mrs. Foster's Yogurt Pie

Pearl Byrd Foster, guiding light of one of New York's truly distinctive restaurants (four stars from The New York Times*), developed this recipe. On a menu noted for its original, delectable desserts, this pie has won high praise.*

1 *Graham Cracker Crumb Shell*, recipe below
1 tablespoon unflavored gelatin (if a softer filling is desired, use less gelatin)
¼ cup cold water
2 egg yolks, slightly beaten
¼ cup milk
8 ounces Neufchatel cheese, room temperature (if Neuf-chatel is not available, you may substitute an additional 8 ounces cream cheese)
8 ounces cream cheese, room temperature
1 teaspoon vanilla
1 teaspoon molasses
1 tablespoon clover honey
2 cups plain yogurt
½ cup graham cracker crumbs

1. Soften gelatin in cold water and dissolve over hot water.

2. Add milk to the slightly beaten egg yolks and cook with the gelatin over gently boiling water until it coats a silver spoon. Set aside to cool.

3. Cream the cheese, vanilla, molasses, and honey together (if mixing machine used, cream on low speed only); add 1 cup of yogurt and continue to cream until smooth.

4. Pour the cold gelatin mixture slowly over the cheese, stirring constantly. Add the second cup of yogurt. Mix well.

5. Pour into baked graham cracker crumb shell and chill until firm. When ready to serve, sprinkle top with graham cracker crumbs.

(cont'd)

Graham Cracker Crumb Shell:

24 graham crackers, finely
  rolled (about 2 cups)

¼ cup softened butter or
  margarine
¼ cup sugar

1. Preheat the oven to 375 degrees.
2. Blend together crumbs, softened butter, and sugar. Set aside half the crumbs to garnish top of pie.
3. Press firmly against bottom and sides of greased 10-inch pie plate. Bake 8-10 minutes. Cool.

YIELD: one 10-inch pie

Yogurt Pie

1 8-inch pie shell
  Fresh fruit
1 cup plain yogurt

½ pound small-curd cottage
  cheese, not creamed
1 tablespoon honey
1 teaspoon vanilla

1. Bake an 8-inch pie shell. Line bottom of pie with fresh strawberries, raspberries, blackberries, or sliced bananas. Sprinkle with small amount of sugar.
2. Whip together yogurt, cottage cheese, honey, and vanilla. Fill the pie with the yogurt mixture. Refrigerate for several hours before serving. Serve with whipped cream if desired. May be prepared without fruit filling.

YIELD: one 8-inch pie

Yogurt Cheese Pie

½ cup rolled oats
½ cup pitted dates
2 tablespoons safflower oil
8 ounces soft cream cheese

⅔ cup plain yogurt
1 teaspoon vanilla
2 tablespoons honey
6 dates, cut up

1. Put the oats and pitted dates through the fine blade of a food grinder. Mix with the oil and press into an 8-inch pie plate to make a pie shell.
2. Beat together the cream cheese, yogurt, vanilla, and honey until very smooth. Stir in the cut-up dates and pour into the pie shell. Refrigerate several hours or overnight before serving.

YIELD: 6 servings

Yogurt Cheese Pie DeLuxe

1 cup plain yogurt
½ pound cream cheese
1 tablespoon honey

Dash of vanilla
½ cup well-drained crushed
pineapple

Cream together yogurt, cream cheese, honey, and vanilla; add pineapple last. Fill in baked pie crust. Chill before serving. If desired, top with cracker crumbs.

YIELD: 6-8 servings

Coconut Chocolate Pie

2½ cups flaked coconut
¼ cup butter or margarine,
melted
1 package (3¾ oz.) chocolate
flavor pudding and pie filling
mix

1½ cups milk
1 cup plain yogurt
Whipped cream, optional
Chocolate curls, optional

1. Preheat the oven to 350 degrees.
2. Combine coconut and melted butter; mix well. Press onto bottom and sides of a 9-inch pie pan. Bake 15-20 minutes or until lightly browned. Cool.
3. In saucepan, combine pudding mix and milk. Bring to a boil over medium heat, stirring constantly. Boil 1 minute. Remove from heat and gently stir in yogurt. Pour into cooled crust. Chill until firm. Garnish with whipped cream and chocolate curls if desired.

YIELD: 6-8 servings

Lemon Cream Pie

¾ cup boiling water
1 package (3 oz.) lemon
gelatin
1 teaspoon grated lemon peel
1 tablespoon lemon juice

2 cups plain yogurt
1 9-inch graham cracker crust
1 container (4½ oz.) frozen
whipped topping, thawed
6–8 thin lemon slices, optional

1. In medium-size mixing bowl combine boiling water and gelatin. Stir to dissolve gelatin. Place bowl containing gelatin in a larger bowl of ice water. Stir gelatin occasionally until slightly thickened. Remove from water.

(cont'd)

2. Add lemon peel, lemon juice, and yogurt. Beat with wire whisk or rotary beater until smooth. Turn into graham cracker crust. Refrigerate 4 hours or until firm. Garnish with whipped topping and lemon slices.

YIELD: 6-8 servings

Pineapple Yogurt Pie

1¼ cups graham cracker crumbs
¼ cup sugar
¼ cup melted butter
¼ cup apricot-pineapple preserves
2 cups plain yogurt

2 packages (3¾ oz. each) instant vanilla pudding mix
1 cup (8-oz. can) crushed pineapple
Whipped topping

1. Preheat the oven to 350 degrees.
2. Mix crumbs, sugar, and butter in medium bowl. Press into 9-inch pie plate. Bake for 6-8 minutes. Cool completely.
3. Combine preserves, yogurt, and pudding mix in large mixer bowl. Beat at low speed 2 minutes. Spread pudding mixture over bottom of pie crust. Spoon pineapple over mixture.
4. Cover with plastic wrap; refrigerate 4 hours. Spread whipped topping over pie before serving. Garnish with pineapple chunks or fresh strawberries, if desired.

YIELD: one 9-inch pie

Coconut Cream Pie

⅔ cup plain yogurt
1 cup yogurt cream cheese
2 tablespoons honey

1 teaspoon vanilla
1¼ cups shredded coconut
1 9-inch baked pie shell

Blend together yogurt and yogurt cream cheese. Add honey and vanilla. Fold in coconut, reserving 1 tablespoon for topping. Pour into pie shell; top with remaining coconut and chill until set.

YIELD: 6-8 servings

Orange Chiffon Pie

Crumb Crust:

1⅓ cups vanilla wafer crumbs (about 35 vanilla wafers)

¼ cup (½ stick) butter, melted

278

Filling:

2 tablespoons (2 envelopes) unflavored gelatin
½ cup sugar
1 cup water
2 cups plain yogurt

1 can (6 oz.) frozen concentrated orange juice, thawed
2 egg whites
2 tablespoons sugar
Toasted coconut

To Prepare Crust:

Combine crumbs and butter. Press mixture firmly and evenly against bottom and sides of pie plate building up around rim. Chill.

To Prepare Filling:

1. In a 1-quart saucepan combine gelatin and ½ cup sugar; add water. Heat over low heat, stir occasionally, until gelatin is dissolved. In a bowl gradually add orange juice to yogurt; stir in gelatin mixture. Chill until partially set.

2. Beat egg whites until frothy; gradually add 2 tablespoons sugar and beat until stiff. Fold into orange mixture. Chill until mixture mounds; turn into crust. Chill until firm. Garnish with toasted coconut.

YIELD: one 9-inch pie

Lime Pie

Crust:

1⅓ cups graham cracker crumbs (16 squares)

2 tablespoons sugar
¼ cup (½ stick) butter, melted

Filling:

1 package (3 oz.) lime flavor gelatin
1 cup boiling water

1 package (8 oz.) cream cheese
1 cup plain yogurt
Grated semi-sweet chocolate

To Prepare Crust:

In a small bowl combine crumbs and sugar; stir in butter. Press mixture firmly and evenly on bottom and sides of pie plate, building up slightly around rim. Chill.

To Prepare Filling:

1. In a small bowl pour boiling water over gelatin; stir until dissolved. In a small mixing bowl beat cheese until fluffy; gradually add dissolved gelatin. Chill until partially set.

(cont'd)

2. Fold in yogurt. Pour into crust and chill until firm. Garnish with grated chocolate.

YIELD: one 9-inch pie

Peachy Yogurt Pie

Crust:

1 cup rolled oats (quick or old-fashioned uncooked)
½ cup slivered almonds
½ cup firmly packed brown sugar
⅓ cup butter or margarine

Filling:

2 packages (3 oz.) lemon gelatin
2 cups boiling water
½ cup cold water
1 cup plain yogurt
1½ cups chopped canned peaches, well drained

1. Preheat the oven to 350 degrees.
2. Combine all *Crust* ingredients; mix well. Reserve ¼ cup. Press remaining mixture onto bottom of 8-inch square pan. Bake for 10 minutes or until golden brown. Let cool and chill.
2. For *Filling*, dissolve gelatin in boiling water. Stir in cold water; cool to lukewarm. Blend in yogurt. Chill until mixture mounds; fold in peaches. Spoon over crust, sprinkle with reserved oat mixture. Chill, uncovered, several hours or until firm.

YIELD: one 8-inch square pie

Skinny Strawberry Cheese Pie

1 9-inch unbaked pie crust
1½ cups plain yogurt
1½ cups low-fat cottage cheese
4 large eggs
¼ teaspoon salt
1 teaspoon vanilla
¾ cup sugar
3 tablespoons flour
Fresh strawberries or fruit glaze topping

1. Preheat the oven to 350 degrees.
2. Blend yogurt and cottage cheese in electric blender.
3. Beat together eggs, salt, vanilla, sugar, and flour. Stir in yogurt mixture.

4. Pour into pie crust and bake about 50 minutes or until custard is set. Cool, then refrigerate until thoroughly chilled. Garnish with fresh strawberries and/or fruit glaze.

Yield: 8 servings

Egg and Yogurt Pie (Bulgaria)

This pie, made without a pastry crust, is a Bulgarian specialty that can be cut in cake wedges and eaten hot or cold.

½ cup oil
5 cups plain yogurt
6 eggs
  Salt to taste
  Freshly ground black pepper
2 teaspoons chopped parsley

4 level tablespoons finely sifted bread crumbs
½ pound Gruyere cheese (strong, dry), coarsely grated
2 cups milk

1. Preheat the oven to 350 degrees. Grease a deep round pie pan.
2. Put the yogurt into a mixing bowl. Beat in the eggs one by one. Add salt, pepper, and the chopped parsley.
3. Mix in the bread crumbs and the cheese. Pour this mixture into the baking pan, cover with milk, and bake for 25 minutes.

Yield: 6 servings

Light and Luscious Pie

  Chocolate Crumb Crust, recipe below
1 envelope unflavored gelatin
⅔ cup sugar
2 eggs, separated

⅔ cup milk
1 cup apricot yogurt
1–2 tablespoons apricot-flavored brandy, optional

1. In medium saucepan, mix gelatin and ⅓ cup sugar; blend in egg yolks beaten with milk. Stir over low heat until gelatin dissolves, about 5 minutes.
2. With wire whisk or rotary beater, blend in yogurt and brandy; chill, stirring occasionally, until mixture mounds slightly when dropped from spoon.
3. In medium bowl, beat egg whites until soft peaks form; gradually add remaining ⅓ cup sugar and beat until stiff. Fold in gelatin

(cont'd)

mixture; turn into Chocolate Crumb Crust and chill, until firm, about 3 hours. Garnish, if desired, with additional chocolate wafer crumbs.

Chocolate Crumb Crust:

In small bowl, combine 1¼ cups chocolate wafer crumbs with ¼ cup melted butter or margarine. Press into 9-inch pan; chill.

YIELD: approximately 8 servings

VARIATIONS: peach yogurt with peach flavored brandy; coffee yogurt with coffee liqueur; cherry yogurt with cherry liqueur

Chocolate Chip Cream Cookies

½ cup (1 stick) butter	1 teaspon baking soda
1½ cups firmly packed light brown sugar	½ teaspoon baking powder
	½ teaspoon salt
2 eggs	1 cup plain yogurt
1 teaspoon vanilla	1 package (12 oz.) semi-sweet chocolate pieces
2½ cups sifted regular all-purpose flour	1 cup chopped nuts

1. Preheat the oven to 375 degrees.
2. In a mixing bowl cream butter; gradually add sugar and beat until light and fluffy. Beat in eggs and vanilla.
3. Sift together flour, soda, baking powder, and salt; add to creamed mixture alternately with yogurt, beginning and ending with dry ingredients.
4. Stir in chocolate pieces and nuts. Drop by rounded teaspoonfuls onto buttered baking sheets. Bake 10-12 minutes. Remove immediately to wire rack to cool.

YIELD: 7-8 dozen

Yogurt Marble Brownies

½ cup margarine	½ cup plain yogurt
4½ tablespoons cocoa	1¾ cups flour
4 eggs	Pinch of salt
1¾ cups sugar	½ cup chopped walnuts
½ teaspoon vanilla	½ cup semi-sweet chocolate bits

1. Preheat the oven to 350 degrees.

282

2. Melt margarine and cocoa together in a saucepan and set aside. Mix together eggs, sugar, vanilla, and yogurt. Add sifted flour and salt; mix thoroughly. Remove ⅓ of white batter. Add cocoa mixture to remaining ⅔ batter. Add chocolate bits to white batter; stir in gently.

3. Grease a 9x13-inch pan. Drop spoonfuls of chocolate and white batter, checkerboard-style, into pan; marble lightly with knife. Sprinkle chopped nuts on top. Bake 35-45 minutes. Cool and slice.

YIELD: one 9x13-inch pan

Beverages

Lassi

½ cup plain yogurt   Ice
2 cups cold water

Place yogurt in a blender and blend for 10 seconds. Add water, ice, and flavoring (if desired). Blend briskly for 1 minute. Serve in a tall glass.

YIELD: two 10-ounce servings

VARIATIONS: For salty lassi add salt and pepper to taste. For sweet lassi add 3 drops of rose water and sugar to taste. For masala lassi add ¼ teaspoon of cumin powder and two leaves of coriander. Salt to taste.

Fruit 'n' Yogurt Drink

1 cup plain yogurt   ½ package frozen fruit

Mix 1 cup plain yogurt with a half package of frozen fruit in an electric blender (not necessary to defrost the fruit beforehand). Drink while still foamy.

YIELD: 2 servings

Pineapple-Orange Shake

2 eggs   1 cup milk
2 cups pineapple-orange
   yogurt

Combine eggs, yogurt, and milk in a blender and whirl at top speed until smooth. Serve in tall glasses poured over crushed ice.

YIELD: 4 servings

Pineapple-Orange Thick Shake

2 eggs
1 cup crushed pineapple
1 cup instant nonfat dry milk
2 cups plain yogurt
1 can (6 oz.) frozen concentrated orange juice
2 tablespoons sugar

Combine eggs, pineapple, dry milk, yogurt, orange juice, and sugar in a blender. Whirl at top speed until smooth. Serve in tall glasses poured over crushed ice.

YIELD: 8 servings

Top Banana

1 cup plain yogurt
1 banana, sliced
2 tablespoons honey
3 ice cubes
Wheat germ (for topping)

Combine yogurt, banana, honey, and ice cubes in blender; whip. Pour into a glass and sprinkle with wheat germ.

YIELD: 2 servings

Raspberry Cooler

1 cup raspberry yogurt
½ cup canned pineapple juice
¼ cup canned cream of coconut
3 ice cubes
Shredded coconut for garnish

In blender, whip yogurt, pineapple juice, cream of coconut, and ice cubes. Pour into glass and garnish with shredded coconut.

YIELD: 2 servings

Citrus Delight

1 cup lemon yogurt
¼ cup frozen orange juice
   concentrate

1 fresh peach, sliced, or 1 large
   canned peach
3 ice cubes
   Orange slice for garnish

Combine lemon yogurt, orange juice concentrate, peach, and ice cubes in blender; whip. Pour into glass and garnish with orange slice.

YIELD: 3 servings

Tahn

1 cup plain yogurt

3 cups ice water
   Ice cubes

Combine yogurt and water in an electric blender and blend 1 minute. Pour over ice cubes.

YIELD: 4 servings

Dahi

4 cups plain yogurt
   Juice of 12 limes

½–1 cup raw sugar or honey,
   approximately
   Spring water

1. Place yogurt, lime juice, and sugar to taste in an electric blender and blend until sugar has dissolved.
2. Pour into a gallon jug or container and fill with ice-cold spring water.

YIELD: 16 servings

Borani

This could be called a Pakistani cocktail. Made with yogurt and highly seasoned with black pepper, it is surprisingly refreshing.

2 cups yogurt
   Salt and freshly ground black
   pepper to taste
1 quart water

8 strips lemon peel
⅛ teaspoon chili powder
½ teaspoon fresh chopped mint
   or ¼ teaspoon dried mint

1. Combine yogurt, salt, pepper, water, lemon peel, chili powder, and mint in a cocktail shaker or in a mixing bowl. Shake well or beat with a wire whisk until well blended.

2. Adjust the seasonings according to taste. Refrigerate until ready to use in well-chilled cocktail glasses.

YIELD: approximately 8 servings

Raspberry Yogurt

1–2 cups fruit juice   1 cup plain yogurt

Use canned raspberry juice or juice drained from canned berries. Chill thoroughly and blend with yogurt. Serve as beverage; vary by using orange, grape, pineapple, or other sweetened juices.

YIELD: approximately 3 servings

Orange Yogurt Shake

1 cup orange juice   1 cup vanilla ice cream
1 cup plain yogurt

Combine orange juice, yogurt, and ice cream in blender. Blend until smooth. Serve in chilled glasses.

YIELD: 3 cups

Banana Cooler

1 tablespoon honey   1 cup plain yogurt
1 medium banana

Place honey, banana, and yogurt in blender. Mix on medium speed until smooth.

YIELD: 1 serving

Strawberry Yogurt Shake

1 cup plain yogurt   1 cup whole sweetened straw-
1 cup milk   berries (or 1 ripe banana)

Combine yogurt, milk, strawberries (or banana) in blender. Blend until smooth.

YIELD: 3 cups

Berry Blend

1 package (10 oz.) frozen
  sliced strawberries or raspberries, partially thawed

2 cups plain yogurt

In blender container, combine berries and yogurt. Blend at high speed 30 seconds. Stir. Blend an additional 30 seconds or until thick and frosty. Pour into glasses.

YIELD: four 6-ounce servings

Breakfast Brightener

1 cup plain yogurt
1 banana, sliced
⅓ cup milk
2 tablespoons honey

2 tablespoons frozen orange
  juice concentrate
2 ice cubes, crushed

Combine yogurt, banana, milk, honey, orange juice, and ice cubes in blender container. Blend at high speed for 30 seconds or until smooth.

YIELD: four 4-ounce servings

Banana Booster Shake

1 cup plain yogurt
1 egg
1 banana

2 teaspoons honey
¼ teaspoon nutmeg
  Protein powder (optional)

Whip yogurt, egg, banana, honey, nutmeg, and protein powder in blender. Chill.

YIELD: approximately 2 servings

Spreads

Tuna Spread

1 cup creamed cottage cheese
1 cup canned tuna, packed in water, drained
6 slices crisply fried bacon, crumbled
¼ cup finely chopped celery
¼ cup sweet pickle relish
⅓ cup plain yogurt
1 teaspoon celery seeds
¼ teaspoon seasoned salt
½ loaf white bread

Combine cottage cheese, tuna, bacon, celery, relish, yogurt, celery seeds, and salt. Trim the crusts from the bread and quarter. Spread the tuna mixture over each square of bread. Place on a baking sheet and broil lightly.

YIELD: 2¾ cups spread

Crabmeat Spread

1 can (7½ oz.) king crabmeat, drained and flaked
1 teaspoon prepared horse-radish
½ teaspoon seasoned salt
½ cup plain yogurt

In a small bowl combine crabmeat, horseradish, and seasoned salt; fold in yogurt. Cover and chill. Use as a spread for crackers or sandwiches.

YIELD: approximately 1¼ cups

Molded Shrimp Spread

1 tablespoon (1 envelope)
unflavored gelatin
¼ cup cold water
½ cup milk
½ cup cottage cheese
1 cup plain yogurt
¾ cup (4½-oz. can) small
deveined shrimp, drained

¼ cup finely chopped celery
1 tablespoon grated onion
⅛ teaspoon hot pepper sauce
¼ teaspoon seasoned salt
¼ teaspoon salt
Pimiento strips
Fresh parsley

1. Soften gelatin in water in medium saucepan. Add milk to gelatin. Cook over medium heat, stirring constantly, until gelatin is dissolved.

2. Combine cottage cheese and yogurt in blender. Blend until smooth. Stir yogurt mixture into gelatin. Chill yogurt-gelatin mixture until the consistency of unbeaten egg whites.

3. Stir shrimp, celery, onion, hot pepper sauce, seasoned salt, and salt into the mixture. Blend well. Pour into 2½-cup mold. Chill 4 hours. Unmold and garnish with pimiento strips and fresh parsley. Serve with crackers.

YIELD: 2½ cups

Cheese and Ham Spread

4 cups (1 lb.) shredded
Cheddar cheese
1 can (2¼ oz.) deviled ham

½ cup plain yogurt
1 tablespoon grated onion
¼ teaspoon seasoned salt

In a large mixing bowl beat together cheese and ham until smooth. Add yogurt, onion, and salt; continue beating until creamy. If refrigerated allow to come to room temperature before serving. Use as a spread for crackers or sandwiches.

YIELD: approximately 3¼ cups

Ham and Yogurt Spread

½ Bermuda onion, minced
1 can (2½ oz.) deviled ham
2 tablespoons plain yogurt
¼ teaspoon dried dill

Pinch of tarragon
Pinch of salt
4 slices pumpernickel, toasted
½ Bermuda onion, sliced thin

290

Combine minced onion, deviled ham, yogurt, dill, tarragon, and salt; mix to a smooth paste. Cut pumpernickel into strips and spread with the mixture. Top with rings of Bermuda onion.

YIELD: 4 servings

Yogurt-Chicken Spread

4 teaspoons butter	8 slices chicken or turkey
4 slices pumpernickel	1 cup cooked broccoli tops
⅔ cup plain yogurt	Salt and pepper to taste

1. Preheat the oven to 350 degrees.
2. Butter each slice of bread. Cut in half. Spread each half with yogurt, using up only half the yogurt.
3. Place a slice of chicken or turkey on each. Top with broccoli and a dab of yogurt, finishing it up. Sprinkle salt and pepper over each serving.
4. Place the individual bread spreads on a baking tin. Toast for 5 minutes in oven. Serve hot as a first course, alone or with cold tomato juice. Makes a great lunch.

YIELD: 4 servings

Yogurt-Egg Spread

4 hard-cooked eggs	Salt and pepper to taste
½ cup plain yogurt	4 slices pumpernickel
¼ cup minced scallions	

Mash eggs in a bowl. Add yogurt a little at a time until it is well blended into the eggs (an electric blender would help). Add the scallions, salt, and pepper. Serve as a spread with small squares of pumpernickel.

YIELD: approximately 1 cup

Gouda Spread

1 8-oz. Baby Gouda cheese	1 tablespoon finely chopped
½ cup plain yogurt	chives or 1 teaspoon grated
2 tablespoons minced pimiento	onion
1 tablespoon minced green	½ teaspoon seasoned salt
pepper	⅛ teaspoon garlic salt

1. Allow cheese to come to room temperature. With cookie cutter cut wax from top of cheese; scoop out cheese leaving shell intact. In a small mixing bowl beat cheese and 1 tablespoon yogurt until smooth.

2. Add remaining yogurt, then pimiento, green pepper, onion, seasoned and garlic salts. Spoon enough mixture into the reserved shell to fill and mound on top.

3. If refrigerated allow to come to room temperature before serving. Cover and chill remaining mixture until needed. Serve as a spread for assorted crackers.

YIELD: approximately 1⅔ cups

Dips

Yogurt Dip

1 cup plain yogurt
½ cup small-curd creamed
cottage cheese
1 scallion, thinly sliced

½ teaspoon salt
⅛ teaspoon garlic salt
Dash of pepper

Combine yogurt, cottage cheese, scallion, salt, garlic salt, and pepper in blender container and blend at high speed for 30 seconds or until smooth. Serve with raw vegetables.

YIELD: 1½ cups

Raw Vegetable Dip

2 cups plain yogurt
½ teaspoon onion powder
½ teaspoon garlic powder
½ teaspoon Tabasco sauce
½ teaspoon prepared horseradish

1 tablespoon minced parsley
1 tablespoon Worcestershire
sauce
1 teaspoon sugar

1. Blend yogurt, onion powder, garlic powder, Tabasco sauce, horseradish, parsley, Worcestershire sauce, and sugar until smooth. Chill thoroughly.

2. Serve as a dip with bite-size pieces of raw turnip, carrots, fennel, cabbage, green beans, celery, green pepper, cauliflower, broccoli, yellow squash, zucchini, cucumber, scallions, radishes, mushrooms, and whole cherry tomatoes. Arrange attractively on a platter.

YIELD: approximately 2 cups

Yogurt and Tomato Dip

1 cup plain yogurt
1 cup tomato sauce (not tomato
  paste)
1 small onion, minced

1 teaspoon dried dill
  Salt and pepper to taste
2 teaspoons capers

Combine yogurt, tomato sauce, onion, dill, salt, and pepper in a bowl. Add 1 teaspoon of the capers. Scatter remaining capers on top of the dip and chill. Serve with squares of toasted pumpernickel.

YIELD: 2 cups

Avocado-Yogurt Dip

1 medium-size ripe avocado,
  peeled and cut up
½ cup plain yogurt

½ teaspoon salt
1 teaspoon Worcestershire
  sauce

Place avocado, yogurt, salt, and Worcestershire sauce in blender. Blend 1 minute to puree. Serve with crackers or vegetables.

YIELD: 1 cup

Onion-Yogurt Dip

2 cups plain yogurt

1 envelope (1 oz.) dry onion-
  mushroom soup mix

Combine yogurt and soup mix in small mixing bowl. Stir gently to mix. Chill, covered, 1-2 hours before serving. Serve with chips, crackers, or raw vegetables.

YIELD: 2 cups

Indian Curry Dip

2 cups plain yogurt
4 tablespoons minced fresh
  parsley
2 tablespoons lemon juice

1 teaspoon seasoned salt
2 teaspoons sugar
2 heaping teaspoons curry
  powder

294

Combine yogurt, parsley, lemon juice, salt, sugar, and curry powder until well mixed. Chill thoroughly before serving. Serve with cold cooked shrimp or raw vegetables.

YIELD: approximately 2 cups

Yogurt-Paprika Dip

½ cup plain yogurt
2–4 tablespoons lemon juice
1 finely chopped green onion
  or 1 grated onion

½ teaspoon kelp
½–1 teaspoon paprika
1 minced clove garlic

Combine yogurt, lemon juice, onion, kelp, paprika, and garlic; beat slightly.

YIELD: ¾ cup

Chili Dip

½ cup cottage cheese
¼ cup chili sauce
1 tablespoon chili seasoning
  mix

1 teaspoon prepared horseradish
½ teaspoon salt
½ cup plain yogurt

In a small mixing bowl beat together cottage cheese and chili sauce until fairly smooth. Add seasoning mix, horseradish, and salt. Fold in yogurt. Cover and chill.

YIELD: approximately 1¼ cups

Mexican Chili Dip

½ cup plain yogurt
¼ cup chili sauce
Dash of Tabasco

1 teaspoon grated onion
Dash of salt
2 tablespoons lemon juice

Combine yogurt, chili sauce, Tabasco, onion, salt, and lemon juice. Serve with taco chips.

YIELD: ¾ cup

Holiday Caviar Dip

½ cup plain yogurt
1 jar (2 oz.) red caviar
1 teaspoon minced parsley
1 tablespoon grated onion
¼ teaspoon prepared mustard

Combine yogurt, caviar, parsley, onion, and mustard. Serve with small rounds of melba toast.

YIELD: ¾ cup

Sherry Dip

2 cups plain yogurt
½ cup chopped chives or 3 scallions, chopped fine
1 tablespoon dry sherry
⅛ teaspoon salt
Pinch of white pepper

Combine yogurt, chives or scallions, sherry, salt, and pepper in a bowl. Chill. Serve with squares of toasted protein bread.

YIELD: 2½ cups

Cottage Cheese and Yogurt Dip

½ cup cottage cheese, small curd
1 cup plain yogurt
1 teaspoon horseradish
1 tablespoon grated onion
½ teaspoon salt
Pinch of white pepper

Combine cottage cheese, yogurt, horseradish, onion, salt, and pepper in a bowl. Mix thoroughly. An electric blender is recommended for a smooth dip. Serve with crisp, small crackers.

YIELD: 1½ cups

Spring Garden Dip

½ cup cottage cheese
1 tablespoon finely grated carrot
2 teaspoons finely grated onion
1 teaspoon finely grated green pepper
½ teaspoon salt
⅛ teaspoon garlic salt
Dash of white pepper
1 cup plain yogurt

In a small mixing bowl beat cottage cheese, blend in carrot, onion, green pepper, salt, garlic salt, and pepper. Beat until fairly smooth. Fold in yogurt. Cover and chill. Use as a dip for chips or raw vegetables.

YIELD: approximately 1½ cups

Nippy Dip

2 packages (3 oz. each) cream cheese, softened
¼ cup crumbled blue cheese
½ cup plain yogurt

1 teaspoon lemon juice
¼ teaspoon salt
3 tablespoons chopped pistachio nuts

In a small mixing bowl beat together cream and blue cheeses until fairly smooth. Stir in yogurt, lemon juice, and salt. Fold in nuts. Cover and chill.

YIELD: approximately 1½ cups

Yogurt-Seafood Dip

1⅓ cups finely chopped peeled cucumber
1 cup plain yogurt

2 teaspoons salt
1 teaspoon sugar

Combine cucumber, yogurt, salt, and sugar. Chill. Serve with shrimp or medallions of rock lobster.

YIELD: 2 cups

Clam Dip

1 cup plain yogurt
1 cup minced clams, drained
½ cup cottage cheese, whipped in blender

1 teaspoon onion powder
½ teaspoon salt
¼ teaspoon pepper
1 tablespoon lemon juice

Mix yogurt, clams, cottage cheese, onion powder, salt, pepper, and lemon juice well. Chill.

YIELD: 2 cups

Yogurt-Garlic Dip

1 tablespoon cornstarch
2 cups plain yogurt

1 envelope garlic salad dressing mix

1. Place cornstarch into a small saucepan. Gradually stir in yogurt. Stir over low heat constantly until mixture bubbles and thickens. Remove from heat and cool.

2. Stir in garlic salad dressing mix. Chill until ready to serve. Use with raw vegetables, potato chips, or crackers.

YIELD: 2 cups

Walnut Dip

6 walnut halves
1 clove garlic
1 tablespoon olive oil
1 cup plain yogurt

¼ cup very firm cucumber, peeled and diced
½ teaspoon lemon juice

Place walnuts, garlic, and oil in blender and blend to a paste. Stir into the yogurt with cucumber and lemon juice. Chill and serve with whole-grain crackers.

YIELD: 1½ cups

Bacon and Horseradish Dip

½ cup cooked and crumbled bacon or imitation bacon bits
1 tablespoon horseradish
1 cup plain yogurt

1 slice medium onion, minced
1 tablespoon minced parsley
6 ounces cream cheese

Place bacon, horseradish, yogurt, onion, parsley, and cream cheese in a bowl and cream together with a fork until smooth. Chill to thicken.

YIELD: 2 cups

Guacamole Dip

2 medium or 3 small ripe avocados
1 tablespoon minced onion
1 clove garlic, minced, or ¼ teaspoon garlic powder
¼ teaspoon chili powder

¼ teaspoon salt
Dash of pepper
1 cup plain yogurt
4 slices fried, crumbled bacon or 2 tablespoons imitation bacon bits

298

1. Peel avocados, remove seeds, and mash finely with a potato masher or fork until smooth. Add onion, garlic, chili powder, salt, pepper, yogurt, and half of the crumbled bacon.

2. Mix well and place in plastic storage container. Top with remainder of crumbled bacon. Cover and refrigerate; serve with taco chips.

YIELD: approximately 2 cups

Skinny Dip

1 package dry onion soup mix	2 cups plain yogurt

Mix onion soup and yogurt. Chill. Serve with crackers or raw vegetables.

YIELD: 2 cups

Frozen Yogurt

Basic Vanilla Frozen Yogurt

½ cup evaporated milk
½ cup sugar
1 envelope unflavored gelatin, softened in ¼ cup water

Dash of salt
2½ cups plain yogurt
2 teaspoons vanilla

1. Scald evaporated milk over low heat, stirring occasionally to avoid the "skin" formation over the top of the milk.
2. Add sugar, softened gelatin, and salt. Stir until thoroughly dissolved and mixture is completely smooth. Cool.
3. Add yogurt and vanilla. Mix well.
4. Chill thoroughly in refrigerator for 2 hours or longer. Pour into freezer can and prepare according to manufacturer's directions.

YIELD: approximately 3 cups

Plain Low-Calorie Frozen Yogurt

Frozen yogurt is a variation of ice milk or sherbet in which most or all of the milk has been replaced by cultured yogurt, which lends a characteristic "tangy" flavor. The use of the low-fat variety of yogurt makes true low-calorie frozen desserts possible.

4½ cups plain yogurt

1½ teaspoons flavoring extract, optional

Spoon yogurt directly into cream can and prepare according to manufacturer's instructions. Add vanilla or other flavoring if desired.

YIELD: approximately 4½ cups

Fruit Frozen Yogurt

4 cups plain yogurt
1 cup sugar

1 cup fresh, frozen, or canned fruit of your choice

Spoon yogurt directly into cream can. Puree sugar and fruit together in blender. Add sugar and fruit mixture to yogurt and prepare according to manufacturer's instructions.

YIELD: 5 cups

Frozen Banana Daiquiri Yogurt

1 envelope unflavored gelatin
¼ cup cold water
½ cup sugar
¼ teaspoon salt
1 cup mashed ripe bananas (3 medium)

½ teaspoon grated lime rind
3 teaspoons lime juice
2 tablespoons rum
1 cup plain yogurt
2 egg whites, unbeaten

1. In small saucepan mix gelatin and ¼ cup cold water; let stand 1 minute. Stir over medium heat until gelatin dissolves, about 1 minute. Add sugar and salt, stir until sugar dissolves.

2. Remove from heat; stir in bananas, lime rind and juice, and rum. Stir in yogurt.

3. Pour into freezer tray or 9x5x3-inch loaf pan; freeze until firm.

4. Turn mixture into a large bowl; add egg whites. Beat at high speed with an electric mixer until smooth and fluffy, about 10 minutes.

5. Return to tray; freeze until firm.

YIELD: approximately 5½ cups

Frozen Banana Yogurt

1 envelope unflavored gelatin
¼ cup cold water
½ cup sugar
¼ teaspoon salt

1 cup mashed ripe bananas (3 medium)
1 tablespoon lemon juice
1 cup plain yogurt
2 egg whites, unbeaten

1. In small saucepan over low heat, sprinkle gelatin over ¼ cup cold water; stir constantly until gelatin dissolves, about 3 minutes. Add sugar and salt; stir until sugar dissolves.

2. Remove from heat; stir in bananas and lemon juice. Cool slightly; mix in yogurt.

3. Pour into a freezer tray or a 9x5x3-inch loaf pan. Freeze until firm.

4. Turn mixture into a bowl; add egg whites. With an electric mixer, beat at high speed until fluffy, about 10 minutes.

5. Return to freezer tray; freeze until firm.

YIELD: approximately 5½ cups

Frozen Banana-Raspberry Yogurt

1 envelope unflavored gelatin	1 tablespoon lemon juice
¼ cup cold water	1 cup plain yogurt
½ cup sugar	2 egg whites, unbeaten
¼ teaspoon salt	1 package frozen raspberries,
1 cup mashed ripe bananas	thawed, pureed, and strained
(3 medium)	2 tablespoons light corn syrup

1. In small saucepan, mix gelatin and ¼ cup cold water. Stir over medium heat until gelatin dissolves, about 1 minute. Add sugar and salt; stir until sugar dissolves.

2. Remove from heat; stir in bananas and lemon juice. Mix in yogurt.

3. Pour into a freezer tray or a 9x5x3-inch loaf pan; freeze until firm.

4. Turn banana mixture into large bowl; add egg whites. Beat at high speed with an electric mixer until smooth and fluffy, about 10 minutes.

5. In small bowl, combine berries with corn syrup. Alternate spoonfuls of banana-yogurt mixture with raspberries in freezer tray or loaf pan; freeze until firm.

YIELD: approximately 5½ cups

Frozen Fruit Yogurt

¼ cup fruit juice or cold water	¼ teaspoon salt
1 envelope unflavored gelatin	2 cups fruit yogurt
½ cup sugar	2 egg whites, unbeaten

1. Sprinkle gelatin over cold water or fruit juice in a small saucepan over low heat; stir until gelatin dissolves, about 3 minutes.

2. Add sugar and salt; stir until sugar dissolves. Remove from heat. Cool slightly. Stir in yogurt

3. Pour into a freezer tray or a 9x5x3-inch loaf pan. Freeze until set.

4. Turn into large bowl; add egg whites. With an electric mixer, beat at high speed until smooth and fluffy, about 10 minutes.

5. Return to freezer tray; freeze until firm. Note: If pineapple juice is used, it should be canned, not frozen.

YIELD: approximately 5½ cups

Cherry Berry Frozen Yogurt

½ cup evaporated milk
½ cup sugar
1 envelope unflavored gelatin, softened in ¼ cup water

Dash of salt
2½ cups plain yogurt
½ cup pitted cherries without syrup or juice

1. Scald evaporated milk over low heat, stirring occasionally to avoid the "skin" formation over the top of the milk.

2. Add sugar, softened gelatin, and salt. Stir until thoroughly dissolved and mixture is completely smooth. Cool.

3. Add yogurt and cherries. Mix well.

4. Chill thoroughly in refrigerator for 2 hours or longer. Pour into freezer can and prepare according to manufacturer's directions.

YIELD: approximately 4-5 cups

Apricot Frozen Yogurt

½ cup evaporated milk
½ cup sugar
1 envelope unflavored gelatin, softened in ¼ cup water

Dash of salt
2½ cups plain yogurt
½ cup pureed apricots without juice or syrup

1. Scald evaporated milk over low heat, stirring occasionally to avoid the "skin" formation over the top of the milk.

2. Add sugar, softened gelatin, and salt. Stir until thoroughly dissolved and mixture is completely smooth. Cool.

3. Add yogurt and apricots. Mix well.

(cont'd)

4. Chill thoroughly in refrigerator for 2 hours or longer. Pour into freezer can and prepare according to manufacturer's directions.

Yɪᴇʟᴅ: approximately 4-5 cups

Lemon Frozen Yogurt

½ cup evaporated milk
½ cup sugar
1 envelope unflavored gelatin, softened in ¼ cup water
Dash of salt

2½ cups plain yogurt
4 tablespoons Minute Maid 100% pure lemon juice full strength or the juice of 2 medium-size lemons

1. Scald evaporated milk over low heat, stirring occasionally to avoid the "skin" formation over the top of the milk.
2. Add sugar, softened gelatin, and salt. Stir until thoroughly dissolved and mixture is completely smooth. Cool.
3. Add yogurt and lemon juice. Mix well.
4. Chill thoroughly in refrigerator for 2 hours or longer. Pour into freezer can and prepare according to manufacturer's directions.

Yɪᴇʟᴅ: approximately 4-5 cups

Honey-Vanilla Frozen Yogurt

½ cup evaporated milk
½ cup sugar
1 envelope unflavored gelatin, softened in ¼ cup water

Dash of salt
2½ cups plain yogurt
2 tablespoons honey
1 teaspoon vanilla

1. Scald evaporated milk over low heat, stirring occasionally to avoid the "skin" formation over the top of the milk.
2. Add sugar, softened gelatin, and salt. Stir until thoroughly dissolved and mixture is completely smooth. Cool.
3. Add yogurt, honey, and vanilla. Mix well.
4. Chill thoroughly in refrigerator 2 hours or longer. Pour into freezer can and prepare according to manufacturer's directions.

Yɪᴇʟᴅ: approximately 4-5 cups

Honey-Egg Vanilla Frozen Yogurt

4 cups plain yogurt
½ cup honey

1 egg, beaten
1 teaspoon vanilla

Combine yogurt, honey, egg, and vanilla in a blender or food processor, or mix with an eggbeater until smooth. Pour into freezer can and prepare according to manufacturer's directions.

YIELD: approximately 4 cups

Peaches 'n' Cream Frozen Yogurt

½ cup evaporated milk
½ cup sugar
1 envelope unflavored gelatin, softened in ¼ cup water

Dash of salt
2½ cups plain yogurt
⅓ cup pureed or diced peaches, without juice or syrup

1. Scald evaporated milk over low heat, stirring occasionally to avoid the "skin" formation over the top of the milk.
2. Add sugar, softened gelatin, and salt. Stir until thoroughly dissolved and mixture is completely smooth. Cool.
3. Add yogurt and peaches. Mix well.
4. Chill thoroughly in refrigerator for 2 hours or longer. Pour into freezer can and prepare according to manufacturer's directions.

YIELD: approximately 4-5 cups

Pineapple Frozen Yogurt

½ cup evaporated milk
½ cup sugar
1 envelope unflavored gelatin, softened in ¼ cup water

Dash of salt
2½ cups plain yogurt
½ cup crushed pineapple, without juice or syrup

1. Scald evaporated milk over low heat, stirring occasionally to avoid the "skin" formation over the top of the milk.
2. Add sugar, softened gelatin, and salt. Stir until thoroughly dissolved and mixture is completely smooth. Cool.

(cont'd)

3. Add yogurt and pineapple. Mix well.

4. Chill thoroughly in refrigerator for 2 hours or longer. Pour into freezer can and prepare according to manufacturer's directions.

YIELD: approximately 4-5 cups

Pineapple-Yogurt Dessert

1 can (8 oz.) juice-packed crushed pineapple
1 envelope unflavored gelatin
4 tablespoons sugar

Sugar substitute equivalent to 12 teaspoons sugar
1 cup cold skim milk
1 cup vanilla yogurt
¼ teaspoon salt

1. Drain the juice from the crushed pineapple into a saucepan. Add gelatin and sugar.

2. Wait 1 minute, then heat over very low heat until gelatin and sugar are melted. Remove from heat.

3. Add sugar substitute. Stir in pineapple, milk, yogurt, and salt. Pour into cream can. Chill mixture until ready to process.

YIELD: approximately 4-5 cups

Blueberry Frozen Yogurt

½ cup evaporated milk
½ cup sugar
1 envelope unflavored gelatin, softened in ¼ cup water
Dash of salt

2½ cups plain yogurt
½ cup fresh or frozen blueberries, without juice or syrup

1. Scald evaporated milk over low heat, stirring occasionally to avoid the "skin" formation over the top of the milk.

2. Add sugar, softened gelatin, and salt. Stir until thoroughly dissolved and mixture is completely smooth. Cool.

3. Add yogurt and blueberries. Mix well.

4. Chill thoroughly in refrigerator for 2 hours or longer. Pour into freezer can and prepare according to manufacturer's directions.

YIELD: approximately 4-5 cups

Frozen Strawberry Yogurt I

1 envelope unflavored gelatin
1 cup pureed strawberries, divided
1 cup sugar
¼ teaspoon salt
1 tablespoon lemon juice
3 cups strawberry yogurt

1. In medium saucepan sprinkle gelatin over ½ cup strawberry puree. Place over low heat and stir constantly until gelatin dissolves, about 3 minutes.

2. Stir in sugar and salt; stir until sugar dissolves. Remove from heat.

3. Stir in remaining puree and lemon juice. Cool slightly. Stir in yogurt.

4. Turn into can of 2- or 4-quart ice cream maker. Insert dasher, cover, and freeze according to manufacturer's directions.

5. Turn into container, cover, and ripen about 2 hours in freezer.

YIELD: approximately 2 quarts

Strawberry Frozen Yogurt II

½ cup evaporated milk
½ cup sugar
1 envelope unflavored gelatin, softened in ¼ cup water
Dash of salt
2½ cups plain yogurt
½ cup fresh or frozen straw-berries without syrup or juice

1. Scald evaporated milk over low heat, stirring occasionally to avoid the "skin" formation over the top of the milk.

2. Add sugar, softened gelatin, and salt. Stir until thoroughly dissolved and mixture is completely smooth. Cool.

3. Add yogurt and strawberries. Mix well.

4. Chill thoroughly in refrigerator for 2 hours or longer. Pour into freezer can and prepare according to manufacturer's directions.

YIELD: approximately 4-5 cups

Strawberry Frozen Yogurt III

4 cups (2 pt.) washed, hulled fresh strawberries
4 cups plain yogurt
1½ cups sugar
1 tablespoon vanilla
¼ teaspoon salt

1. Puree strawberries in blender until smooth (makes about 3 cups puree).

2. Combine yogurt, sugar, vanilla, and salt in large bowl. Stir in pureed strawberries. Pour into 1-gallon freezer. Cover.

3. Freeze with ice-salt mixture in proportions recommended for freezer. When yogurt is frozen, pour off brine. Remove cover. Scrape frozen yogurt from dasher.

4. Replace cover; pack with recommended proportion of ice and salt. Let stand 1½-2 hours to ripen.

YIELD: approximately 8½ cups

Easy Mocha Frozen Yogurt

2 cups plain yogurt	1 tablespoon instant coffee
¼ cup honey	1 tablespoon chocolate sauce

Combine yogurt, honey, coffee, and chocolate sauce in blender or food processor, or mix with an eggbeater until smooth. Pour into freezer can and prepare according to manufacturer's directions.

YIELD: approximately 2½ cups

Mocha Frozen Yogurt

½ cup evaporated milk	Dash of salt
½ cup sugar	1 tablespoon instant coffee
1 envelope unflavored gelatin, softened in ¼ cup water	1 tablespoon chocolate syrup
	2½ cups plain yogurt

1. Scald evaporated milk over low heat, stirring occasionally to avoid the "skin" formation over the top of the milk.

2. Add sugar, softened gelatin, and salt. Stir until thoroughly dissolved and mixture is smooth.

3. Add coffee and chocolate syrup. Mix thoroughly. Cool.

4. Add yogurt. Mix well.

5. Chill thoroughly in refrigerator for 2 hours or longer. Pour into freezer can and prepare according to manufacturer's directions.

YIELD: 3-4 cups

Soft-Serve Yogurt Sundae

2 scoops vanilla soft frozen
  yogurt
½ cup sliced peaches, fresh or
  canned

1 teaspoon honey
¼ cup melon balls and grapes
¼ cup coconut and walnuts

Spoon two generous scoops of vanilla soft frozen yogurt on top of a layer of peaches. Drizzle honey on top of yogurt, then add melon balls and grapes. Sprinkle shredded coconut and finely chopped walnuts over all. Serve with two chocolate chip cookies.

Honey-Almond Frozen Yogurt

2 cups plain yogurt
¼ cup honey

⅛ teaspoon almond extract
½ cup almonds, chopped

Combine yogurt, honey, almond extract, and almonds in a blender or food processor, or mix with eggbeater until smooth. Pour into freezer can and prepare according to manufacturer's directions.

Yield: approximately 2½ cups

Maple Walnut Frozen Yogurt

½ cup evaporated milk
¼ cup maple syrup

2 cups plain yogurt
½ cup walnuts, chopped

1. Scald evaporated milk over low heat, stirring occasionally to avoid "skin" from forming on the top. Add maple syrup and allow to cool.

2. Combine milk and syrup mixture with yogurt and nuts in blender or food processor, or mix with egg beater until smooth. Pour into freezer can and prepare according to manufacturer's directions.

Yield: approximately 2½ cups

Frozen Banana Velvet

This is an elegant frozen dessert. Velvety smooth and rich in banana flavor. It will not become icy. Keeps well.

2 cups mashed ripe bananas
1½ cups vanilla yogurt
1 cup Domino Brownulated sugar

1 container (9 oz.) frozen whipped dessert topping (Cool Whip), thawed

1. Thoroughly mix bananas, yogurt, and sugar (if desired, use blender). Pour into 9x5x3-inch bread pan and freeze until mushy.
2. Fold in whipped topping, cover with plastic wrap, and freeze without stirring until ice cream consistency.

YIELD: approximately 1¾ quarts

Bonbon Yogies

1 package (3 oz.) flavored gelatin of your choice
1 cup boiling water
1 cup plain yogurt

8 squares (1 oz. each) semisweet chocolate (for coating 16 Bonbon Yogies)

1. Make these in advance as plain Bonbon Yogies take a few hours to set and the chocolate-covered variety must be frozen overnight.
2. Pour contents of gelatin package into a small bowl. Add boiling water; stir until gelatin dissolves. Cool until lukewarm.
3. Using a whisk or fork, stir in yogurt until well blended. Pour mixture into molded plastic ice cube tray and freeze for 4 hours.
4. Remove from freezer; let sit for 5 minutes. Using a small spatula or the tip of a knife, remove yogurt cubes from tray.
5. Cut each cube in half, place on a plate or cookie sheet, and return to freezer until serving time.

YIELD: makes 32 Bonbon Yogies

Chocolate-Covered Yogies:

Let 16 Bonbon Yogies harden in freezer overnight so they won't melt when dipped in warm chocolate. Melt chocolate in top of double boiler. Let cool till a drop of chocolate feels cool to the wrist. Using

310

two forks, dip cubes, one at a time, into chocolate. Work quickly so the bonbons don't melt. Freeze until hard.

YIELD: 16 chocolate-covered Yogies

Orange-Yogurt Ice Cream

1 cup plain yogurt
½ cup frozen concentrated
　orange juice
1 teaspoon lemon juice
1 cup heavy cream

½ cup sugar
Few grains of salt
1½ teaspoons unflavored gelatin,
　softened in ¼ cup water

1. In a bowl mix the yogurt, orange juice, and lemon juice. Put aside.

2. Scald ¼ cup of cream in a small saucepan over low heat. Add sugar, salt, and softened gelatin, stirring until dissolved. Cool.

3. Add remaining cream and yogurt-orange mixture. Mix well.

4. Chill thoroughly in refrigerator for 2 or more hours. Pour into freezer can and prepare according to manufacturer's directions.

YIELD: 3-4 cups

Cherry Preserve Yogurt Ice Milk

½ cup cherry preserves
1½ cups plain yogurt
½ cup evaporated milk

1½ teaspoons unflavored gelatin,
　softened in ¼ cup water
½ cup sugar
⅛ teaspoon almond extract

1. In a small bowl, blend the cherry preserves and yogurt. Put aside.

2. Scald evaporated milk in a saucepan over low heat. Add softened gelatin and sugar, stirring until dissolved. Cool.

3. Add yogurt-cherry mixture and almond extract. Mix well.

4. Chill thoroughly in refrigerator for 2 hours or longer. Pour into freezer can and prepare according to manufacturer's directions.

YIELD: 3-4 cups

Fruit Sherbet

2 cups plain yogurt
1 small can frozen concentrated
   fruit juice

2 teaspoons vanilla

Combine yogurt, fruit juice, and vanilla. Mix well and place in freezer tray to freeze. Fruit juices may be grape juice, orange juice, or any of the concentrated fruit juices.

YIELD: 2-3 cups

Orange-Yogurt Sherbet

2 cups orange juice
1 envelope unflavored gelatin
1 cup sugar
¼ teaspoon salt

2 teaspoons grated orange rind
½ cup flaked coconut
2 cups plain yogurt

1. Sprinkle gelatin over ½ cup of the orange juice in a medium saucepan over low heat; stir constantly until gelatin dissolves, about 3 minutes.

2. Add sugar and salt; stir until sugar dissolves. Remove from heat; stir in remaining orange juice, orange rind, and coconut. Cool slightly; mix in yogurt.

3. Freeze yogurt mixture in a 2- or 4-quart ice cream maker (hand-turned or electric) according to manufacturer's directions.

4. Turn into a container, cover, and ripen about 2 hours in freezer.

YIELD: approximately 2 quarts (8 cups)

Fruit Fantasy

4 cups any fruit yogurt

1 cup frozen or canned fruit of
   your choice, optional

Stir yogurt thoroughly before spooning directly into cream can. Puree fruit in a blender. Add to yogurt if additional flavoring is desired.

YIELD: 4-5 cups

312

Lemon Delight

4 cups lemon yogurt

5 tablespoons frozen orange
juice concentrate

Spoon yogurt directly into cream can. Add orange juice concentrate. Freeze according to manufacturer's directions.

YIELD: 4-5 cups

Honey Freeze

4 cups plain yogurt
½ cup honey

1 egg, beaten
1 teaspoon vanilla

Beat together the yogurt, honey, egg, and vanilla. Place in cream can and freeze according to manufacturer's directions.

YIELD: 5-6 cups

Honey and Lemon Frozen Yogurt

2 cups plain yogurt
¼ cup honey
¼ cup brown sugar

Juice of 2 large lemons or
about ½ cup

Combine yogurt, honey, sugar, and lemon juice in blender or food processor, or mix with an eggbeater until smooth. Since this makes a very tart and tangy concoction, taste and adjust sweetener and lemon juice as desired. Pour into freezer can and prepare according to manufacturer's directions.

YIELD: approximately 2½ cups

Cantaloupe Frozen Yogurt

2 cups plain yogurt
1 small cantaloupe, with fruit
cut into wedges

¼ cup honey

Combine yogurt, cantaloupe, and honey in a blender or food processor. Or, chop cantaloupe finely and mix ingredients until blended. Pour into freezer can and prepare according to manufacturer's directions.

YIELD: approximately 2½ cups

The Big Freeze

1 package (10½ oz.) frozen
  pound cake
1 cup heavy cream
¼ cup confectioners' sugar

1 teaspoon vanilla
1 cup strawberry yogurt
Fresh strawberries for
  garnish

1. While pound cake is partially frozen, cut it horizontally into three layers. In a medium-size bowl, whip cream, confectioners' sugar, and vanilla until stiff. Fold in the yogurt.

2. Stack cake layers, spreading yogurt frosting in between. Set aside about ¾ cup of the yogurt frosting to make a decorative piped border around the cake. Use remainder to frost top and sides of cake.

3. For piping: fit pastry bag with a small star tube. Fill bag with frosting. Pipe on all edges, including bottom. Refrigerate or freeze cake. (If frozen, cake must be thawed for 15 minutes before serving.)

4. Garnish with strawberries if you like. For variety, make The Big Freeze with other yogurt flavors and garnishes.

YIELD: 8 servings

Soft Frozen Raspberry Yogurt

1 envelope unflavored gelatin,
  about 1 tablespoon
¼ cup cold water

1 package (10 oz.) frozen
  raspberries, thawed
3 cups plain yogurt

1. Place water into small heatproof bowl or custard cup. Sprinkle gelatin over water. Let stand 5 minutes to soften. Meanwhile puree raspberries through sieve. Discard seeds.

2. Place bowl containing gelatin into simmering water. Stir gelatin until completely dissolved.

3. Pour gelatin into a mixing bowl and add yogurt 1 cup at a time, mixing well after each addition. Stir in pureed raspberries.

4. Place bowl into freezer and freeze 3 hours, stirring well every 30 minutes.

5. After 3 hours, with electric mixer beat yogurt at medium speed until smooth. Freeze an additional 30 minutes before serving.

YIELD: 4 cups

Frozen Peppermint Yogurt

1 envelope unflavored gelatin, about 1 tablespoon
½ cup milk
2 eggs
2 tablespoons sugar
2 tablespoons light corn syrup
2 cups plain yogurt
¾ cup finely crushed peppermint candies
1 teaspoon lemon juice
½ cup whipping cream, whipped

1. In 1-quart saucepan combine gelatin and milk; let stand 3 minutes. Cook over low heat, stirring constantly until gelatin dissolves. Remove from heat and cool slightly.

2. In large mixing bowl beat eggs with electric mixer at medium speed until thick and lemon colored. Gradually add sugar and corn syrup. Add gelatin mixture, yogurt, peppermint candy, and lemon juice. Beat until smooth. Gently fold in whipped cream.

3. Place bowl into freezer and freeze until mixture forms a ½-inch frozen ring around side of bowl, about 2 hours. Remove from freezer, scrape side of bowl and beat with mixer at medium speed until smooth, about 1-2 minutes. Return to freezer and repeat above process when mixture forms a ½-inch frozen layer. Serve immediately or transfer to freezer storage container and freeze.

YIELD: 4 cups

Frosty Yogurt Pops I

3 packages (3 oz. each) flavored gelatins (3 different fruit flavors)
3 cups boiling water
6 tablespoons honey
1 tablespoon vanilla extract
3 cups plain yogurt
8 paper cups (6 oz. each)
8 lollipop sticks

1. Dissolve gelatin flavors separately, using 1 cup boiling water for each. Stir 2 tablespoons honey and 1 teaspoon vanilla into each. Put in refrigerator to cool about 10-15 minutes.

2. Stir 1 cup of yogurt into each gelatin flavor. Pour ¼ cup of one yogurt-gelatin flavor into each of 8 paper cups. Place cups in freezer 15-20 minutes or until firm on top. Set remaining two yogurt-gelatins aside at room temperature.

3. Gently spoon ¼ cup of second yogurt-gelatin flavor into each of the 8 cups. Place in freezer 15-20 minutes or until firm on top.

(cont'd)

4. Insert a lollipop stick into each of the cups. Gently spoon ¼ cup of remaining yogurt-gelatin flavor into each of the 8 cups. Freeze 3-4 hours until firm. Peel off paper cups before serving.

YIELD: 8 yogurt pops, about 215 calories each

Frozen Yogurt Pops II

1 cup fresh strawberries, mashed, or 1 package (10 oz.) frozen sliced strawberries, thawed and drained

2 cups plain yogurt
¼ cup honey
6 waxed paper cups (4-oz.)
6 wooden sticks

1. In mixing bowl combine strawberries, yogurt, and honey; mix well.

2. Spoon mixture evenly into waxed paper cups. Freeze 20 minutes and insert wooden stick into center of each cup. Freeze until hard. Remove from paper cups for serving.

YIELD: 6 yogurt pops

General Index

318

cholesterol and, 115–18
constipation and, 118
diarrhea in infants and, 118–19
fever blisters and canker sores and,
121–22
plain yogurt and bananas for babies,
120
sunburn and freckles, 125–27
Metchnikoff, Dr. Ilya, 23, 24
Metzger, Juan, 5, 6, 26
Milk, 11, 128–31
acidophilus, 114
canned and dry, 130
certified, 107
cows and, 129
digestion and, 20
grades, 129
quick guide to dairy foods, 130–31
types of, homemade yogurt and, 44
See also Goat's milk

Natural food, yogurt as, 32–33
Nittler, Dr. Alan, 123
Niv, Dr. Molly, 118

Pasteurization, 36
Plain yogurt, flavoring, 41–42, 120
Premo, Barbara, 17n
Preserves as flavoring, 39
sugar and, 40
Proctor-Silex, Deluxe Electric, Ice
Cream Maker, 95
Products made from yogurt, 132–33
face and body powder, 133
face cream concentrate, 132, 133
tablets, 133
Powder, yogurt, for face and body, 133
Puree as flavoring, 39

Quackenbush, Dr. G. G., 8, 36

RCW Frost King Five-Quart Electric
Ice Cream Freezer, 98–100
Rosell, Dr. José-Maria, 7
Rosell Institute, 7–8

Salton Family Size Yogurt Maker,
54–55
Salton Frozen Dessert Maker, 91
Salton Thermostatically Controlled
Yogurt Maker, 52–53

Salton Yo-Cheese Maker, 55–56
Sourdough starter, yogurt as, 74–75
Soy milk, 11n
Spoerry, Anne, 116
Starter, for homemade yogurt, 44–45
Stillman, Dr. Irwin, 16
Sugar, preserves and, 40
Sunburn, yogurt and, 125–27

Tablets, yogurt, 133
Taste, mild or strong, of homemade
yogurt, 45–46
Temperature, homemade yogurt and, 46
Tenderizer, meat, yogurt as, 73
Thin vs. thick yogurt, 30–31
Tille, Richard, 7
Toupin, Prof. Gustave, 7

United States, yogurt in, 5–6
U.S. Department of Agriculture, 10

Vavra, Dr. James, 123

Wagner, Mrs. William, 109–10
Waring Ice Cream Parlor, 92–93
Weekes, Dr. Don J., 121
Weight gain, reasons for, 15
West Bend Electric Yogurt Maker,
68–70
Whey, 10
White, Dr. Ruth, 33n
White Mountain Electric Four-Quart
Freezer, 97–98

Yami, 112
Yogurt (general), 9–13
acidophilus, 111–14
attitudes toward, 36–37
and babies, 120–21
calories and, 14–18
in Canada, 7–8
children and, 119
foreign names for, 4–5
future of, 8
goat's milk, 108–10
history of, 3–8
longevity and, 23–25
as sourdough starter, 74–75
as substitute for other foods, 17–18,
72–73
as tenderizer, 73

Recipe Index

Marinade, 36
Meatballs, 167, 168
Meats, 164–85
  salad, 233
  See also Beef; Lamb, *etc.*
Mocha
  cake, 77
  frozen yogurt, 308
Moussakas, 175, 176
Mousses, 253, 263
Muffins, 249
Mushrooms, 150, 215
Mussels, 154

Nectarine mold, 255
Nut bread, 249

Omelets, 205–206
Onion(s), 213
  appetizers, 148, 151
  dips, 294, 299
  salad, 223
Orange
  beverages, 284, 285, 287
  desserts, 256
  frozen yogurts, 311, 312
  pie and cakes, 274, 278
Oysters, 198

Pancakes, 246–47
  sourdough, 80
Parfaits, 59, 252
Pea and cauliflower appetizer, 148
Peach
  dessert, 253
  frozen yogurt, 305
  pie, 280
  salad, 230
Peanut salad dressing, 244
Pear dessert, 257
Pecan salad dressing, 244
Peppermint frozen yogurt, 315
Pies, 60, 275–81
Pineapple
  desserts, 255–56
  frozen yogurts, 305, 306
  pie, 278
  sandwich, filling, 59
  shakes, 284, 285
Popsicles, frozen yogurt, 315–16
Pork dishes, 164–65

Potatoes, 175, 212–14
  appetizer, 149
  salads, 220–22
Poultry. *See* Chicken; Turkey
Pound cake, frozen yogurt, 314
Pudding, 263
  cake, 271
Pumpkin, 212

Quiche, 184

Raitas, 148–49, 150
Raspberry
  beverages, 285, 287, 288
  dessert, 254
  frozen yogurts, 302, 314
Rhubarb dessert, 253
Rices, 209–11
Rolls, 77, 78

Salad dressings, 235–44
Salads, 106, 219–34
Salmon, 200
  salad, 228
Sandwich fillings, 58–59
Sauces, 245
Seafood appetizers, 148, 153
Shakes, 106, 284, 285, 287, 288
Sherbet, 255
Sherry dip, 296
Shortcakes, 272
Shrimp, 196–97, 202, 227
  spread, 290
Sole, 197–98
Soups, 155–63
Sourdough bread, 76
  starter for, 75–80
Spice cake, 274
Spinach, 216–17
  appetizer, 150
  salad, 223
Sponge cake, 273
Spreads, 57, 58, 289–92
Stews, 181, 193
Strawberry
  beverages, 287, 288
  cakes, 271, 272
  desserts, 254
  frosting, 273
  frozen yogurts, 95, 307
  parfait, 59
  pie, 280